CHAUCER STUDIES XIII

CHAUCER'S NARRATORS

CHAUCER STUDIES

ISSN 0261-9822

CHAUCER'S NARRATORS

DAVID LAWTON

D. S. BREWER

First published 1985 by D. S. Brewer
240 Hills Road, Cambridge
an imprint of Boydell & Brewer Ltd
PO Box 9, Woodbridge, Suffolk IP12 3DF and
51 Washington Street, Dover, New Hampshire 03820, USA

British Library Cataloguing in Publication Data

Lawton, David
   Chaucer's narrators.—(Chaucer studies,
   ISSN 0261-9822; v. 13)
   1. Chaucer, Geoffrey—Criticism and interpretation
   2. Persona (Literature)
   I. Title   II. Series
   821'.1   PR1927

   ISBN 0-85991-217-5

Library of Congress Cataloguing in Publication Data

Lawton, David A., 1948–
   Chaucer's narrators.

   (Chaucer studies, ISSN 0261-9822; 13)
   Bibliography: p.
   Includes Index.
   1. Chaucer, Geoffrey, d. 1400—Technique.
   2. Chaucer, Geoffrey, d. 1400—Characters.
   3. Narration (Rhetoric) 4. First person narrative.
   5. Persona (Literature) I. Title. II. Series.
   PR1933.N27L3 1985   821'.1   85-12728
   ISBN 0-85991-217-5

Photoset in Great Britain by
Rowland Phototypesetting Ltd, Bury St Edmunds, Suffolk
and printed by St Edmundsbury Press,
Bury St Edmunds, Suffolk

For Derek Pearsall
and
Leslie Rogers

Contents

'The Pilgrims do not exist for the sake of the stories, but *vice versa.* Structurally regarded, the stories are merely long speeches expressing, directly or indirectly, the characters of the several persons.'
—G. L. Kittredge, *Chaucer and His Poetry*
(Cambridge, Mass., 1915), p. 155.

'The "dramatic principle" in the *Canterbury Tales* has been much overworked.'
—Derek Pearsall, *Old English and Middle English Poetry*
(London, 1977), p. 207.

'Chaucer's poetry is in some ways like medieval polyphony—music in which a number of different voices are singing the same words to different melodic lines. Except that Chaucer's poetic line, until the mind is alerted, may seem deceptively simple, and the careless reader may notice only one of the voices.'
—Derek Brewer, *An Introduction to Chaucer*
(London, 1984), p. 171.

A Modern Preface

In short, I am full of doubts. I really don't know why I have decided to
pluck up my courage and present, as if it were authentic, the manuscript
of Adso of Melk. Let us say it is an act of love. Or, if you like, a way of
ridding myself of numerous, persistent obsessions.

I transcribe my text with no concern for timeliness. In the years when I
discovered the Abbé Vallet volume, there was a widespread conviction
that one should write only out of a commitment to the present, in order to
change the world. Now, after ten years or more, the man of letters
(restored to his loftiest dignity) can happily write out of pure love of
writing. And so I now feel free to tell, for sheer narrative pleasure, the
story of Adso of Melk, and I am comforted and consoled in finding it
immeasurably remote in time . . . , gloriously lacking in any relevance
for our day, atemporally alien to our hopes and our certainties.

For it is a tale of books, not of everyday worries . . .

Umberto Eco, The Name of the Rose

Umberto Eco prefaces his novel, *The Name of the Rose*, with a brilliant display
of narratorial self-consciousness. He pretends that the narrative he introduces
is an act of translation made possible by antiquarian good luck, the discovery of
a volume by the Abbe Vallet which has led to the reconstruction of 'the story of
Adso of Melk': 'On sober reflection, I find few reasons for publishing my
Italian version of an obscure, neo-Gothic French version of a seventeenth-
century Latin edition of a work written in Latin by a German monk toward the
end of the fourteenth century' (p. 4). The book is therefore 'gloriously lacking
in any relevance for our day', being concerned only with itself, other books and
'pure love of writing'. Its writer is not an anxious polemicist or a worried reader
but 'the man of letters'. This, at once claim and disclaimer, is sweeping. It is
also disingenuous, both in fact and in posture—the latter, at least, for those
readers who find *The Name of the Rose* a fascinating and lucidly intelligible
gloss on Eco's own theory of semiotics. It is unstably ironic; that is, it achieves
something quite different from what it says, without being quite the opposite
of what it purports.[2] It is implicitly an address to the reader of *The Name of the*

Rose ('*our* hopes'), though no use of the deictic 'you' appears in the passage ('if you like' passing as a well-timed cliché), and it seeks to establish a basis for their response in the puzzle it presents. Its irony alerts its readers to the *fictional* nature of the book, and it validates that fiction by an appeal to 'sheer narrative pleasure' untroubled by 'concern for timeliness'. In one way, it is an honest clue to the plot of the book, which is 'immeasurably remote in time'; in another, it challenges the sense of significance with which we read, grounded in 'our hopes and our certainties', and these we are urged to abandon as if it were simply a matter of turning the page. Do we read a *persona* here, Umberto Eco's fictional recension of Umberto Eco, or something less, a tone? In either case, he or it intrudes heavily and promptly vanishes, giving place to the book. The narratorial voice becomes a narrative voice. The narrative gains its authority from the very grounds on which it has irrevocably lost it. It is the work of a narrator who, however 'restored to his loftiest dignity', is yet 'full of doubts', leaving behind 'everyday worries' in order to rid himself of 'numerous persistent obsessions'. He is a liar—a writer of fiction; presenting his book '*as if* it were authentic', and in the next breath reverting to the stance of a humble transcriber. He is a liar because he and his book are the same fiction; and thus, whatever he may say, he is an honest liar.

Eco's preface is a bravura example of exactly the kind of narratorial display that I shall be concerned with describing throughout this book. It also raises a question of anachronism: is there a failure of 'commitment to the present' of modern criticism, not of course in taking a subject from 'the end of the fourteenth century' but rather in the theme of narratorial voice?

The last writer to publish a theoretical book on 'the literary persona' thought so. In his preface Robert C. Elliott contrasts the 'I' of his criticism with that of structuralist and post-structuralist criticism, which

> attempts to abolish the notion of the self as a conscious subject altogether. To write about an author's 'I' as though it had some kind of substantial existence is to write about an illusion: the self is a construct, constituted actively by a variety of social and linguistic codes of which it is a mere function. Man in this view has been displaced as a center or source of creativity . . . Thus although some of the writers of this newest New Criticism and I may have a subject in common—the writer's 'I'—there is no true engagement of ideas: the two discourses do not meet.[3]

'The two discourses do not meet': this is categorical yet unconvincing, of the order of Eco's proclamation that his book has nothing to give to the present. It draws attention to a theoretical limitation in Elliott's highly perceptive book, which is firmly rooted in the 'New' Criticism. Different orders of narratorial activity are gathered together under the term '*persona*'. This is inevitable given the New Critical premise of a work's organic unity. If the 'I' of a work is an extratextual sign, primarily referring to a person outside the work, then the work would cease to be self-sufficient; since the work is self-sufficient, the 'I' must be a *persona*. This unstated position forces Elliott forever to turn aside to respond to another, equally extreme view that recanonises the value of sincerity. This is a choice between person and *persona*, and binary oppositions —to adapt a comment of Dorothy Parker's—run the whole gamut of human experience from A to B. It is the rest of the alphabet, the numerous other options that are in fact inherent in the range from person to *persona*, which are the subject of this book.[4] In the main, like Elliott, I do not engage directly with structuralist and post-structuralist discourse; but the two discourses meet. What Elliott might usefully have observed in modern criticism is a dialectic about the status of the fictive 'I'. Its most common sign is the systematic hesitation between *persona* and voice.

Since I believe that such hesitation is entirely proper, some brief documentation is relevant. The hesitation is seen clearly in Roland Barthes's late work (1975), *Roland Barthes by Roland Barthes*, where the status of the 'I' subject is naturally of particular concern. Mindful perhaps of Maurice Blanchot's dictum that 'the novelist is a person who refuses to say "I" but delegates that power to other people',[5] Barthes generally, but inconsistently, refers to himself in the third person and insists: 'All this must be considered as if spoken by a character in a novel'.[6] This appears as the book's epigraph, and also in the entry *le Livre du Moi*, where it is at once qualified (pp. 119–20):

All this must be considered as if spoken by a character in a novel—or rather by several characters. For the image-repertoire, fatal substance of the novel, and the labyrinth of levels in which anyone who speaks about himself gets lost—the image-repertoire is taken over by several masks (*personae*), distributed according to the depth of the stage (and yet *no one*—*personne*, as we say in French—is behind them).

The self here is a series in a multiple theatrical performance, *persona* or *personae*; yet a *persona* is a nobody. This is a thoroughgoing decentering of the self, justifying Elliott's apprehension that it is 'constituted entirely by a variety of social and linguistic codes' called by Barthes the image-repertoire. This is in line with Barthes's earlier work, with its view that the self affirms itself only in the art of utterance; when it is written, it is alienated, displaced, granted the status of 'voice' only by metaphorical transference on the part of a kindly reader (and by the critic's sleight of hand, Barthes's determined retention of the language of speech):

'Who speaks here?' asks Barthes, when we are told that 'Zambinella, *as if* terror-stricken . . .' It is not an omniscient narrator. 'What is heard here is the *displaced* voice which the reader grants, by proxy, to the narrative . . . it is specifically the voice of reading.'[7]

In *Roland Barthes by Roland Barthes*, however, the question is not so expeditiously put to rest. This 'I' must be turned into a 'he'—'as if'; it is an altogether more forceful proposition. When characterising *Sa Voix*, Barthes begins, parenthetically: '(No-one's in particular. Yes, in particular! It is always someone's voice)' (p. 67). Barthes is here writing of the physiological voice that articulates speech-acts; but the formulation leaves no room for the abstract 'voice of reading' that characterises the transposed speech-act, writing, and is specifically 'no one's in particular'. To deny that the 'I' of narration is 'someone's voice' would seem here to be an act of '*hypocrisie*?':

Speaking of a text, he credits its author with not manipulating the reader. But he found this compliment by discovering that he himself does all he can to manipulate the reader, and that in fact he will never renounce an art of *effects*.   (p. 102)

'I', 'he', 'as if': all belong to the same art, or play, of effects. In this strange text deixis is renounced; but its effect is foregrounded by its obtrusive absence. Even when self-effacement is carried to its extreme, when the 'I' is rigorously suppressed, the writing subject reasserts itself. Here is the beginning of Barthes's entry for *Moi, je*, heavily marked by its return to the first-person pronoun of narration:

> An American (or positivist, or disputatious: I cannot disentangle) student identifies, as if it were self-evident, *subjectivity* and *narcissism*; no doubt he thinks that subjectivity consists in talking about oneself, and in speaking well of oneself. This is because he is a victim of the old couple, the old paradigm; *subjectivity/objectivity*. Yet today the subject apprehends himself *elsewhere*, "subjectivity" can return at another place on the spiral: deconstructed, taken apart, shifted, without anchorage: why should I not speak of 'myself' since this 'my' is no longer 'the self'?   (p. 168)

The paradox is well-presented: the 'I' of writing is here not a *persona*, a nobody, but 'someone's voice'; yet it does not conform to the person of the writing 'outside' the writing. In writing himself the author is transfigured: that is, he becomes figurative. The self is elsewhere, a function of writing, yet still 'myself'. After the subject is deconstructed, reading remains obdurately intersubjective. The register shifts from one occurrence to the next, as Blanchot realised: 'In the interval of the tale, the voice of the narrator can be heard with more or less appropriateness, sometimes fictive, sometimes without any mask'.[8] Such a narrator's voice, reviewed in terms of 'appropriateness', is in essence a serial figure. Sometimes it is a *persona* (fictive), sometimes not (unmasked): never a person, always a voice.

The voice interacts with other voices of the text—both other characters within the text and other features of style and register—in a process best described as dialogic. The term is M. M. Bakhtin's, to whose work modern theorists, including Barthes, are much indebted. As Bakhtin also saw, the narrator's voice has a special role in initiating a further dialogue between text and context; for the utterance of a narrator is always in effect an address, whether marked or not, to a reader/auditor, and so presupposes a context or contexts of reception which may well be at odds with any given actual context, over which the writer has no control. The dialogue, already polyphonic, expands to incorporate both text and context: the author's address becomes a quotation in his own work, and the narrator's voice is the voice of the other. To this process of dialogic interaction Bakhtin's translators give the name 'heteroglossia'.[9] Etymologically ('other-tonguedness'), and theoretically, 'heteroglossia' is a close linguistic relation of allegory ('other-speaking').

The relation is not fortuitous for the narratorial 'I' is a rhetorical trope, mobile in the field between deixis and evaluation. In Greek rhetoric it might have been listed under *ethopoeia* ('speech conferred on concealed persons') or *prosopopoeia* ('the introduction of a person not present'—the writing of a person). The alternatives provided by Barthes ('someone's voice'; 'the voice of reading') could have been grouped together by a medieval student of the *Rhetorica ad Herennium* under the two heads of *confirmatio*, personification[10]: impersonation by a speaker (or writer) of an absent person ('someone's voice': 'myself'); and attribution of speech, form, appropriate actions to mute or inanimate things ('the voice of reading', the book—and so, by extension, the reader). The narratorial 'I', sometimes *persona*, always voice, is a personification of the text or, since all these tropes are related to allegory, it is an allegory of the author's presence in the text. Both presence and author are thereby allegorised, signified by unstable, because shifting, abstractions. Modern insights are in agreement with classical and medieval rhetoric.

The rhetorical 'I' is often addressed to an equally rhetorical 'you' that is no less a personification. Paul de Man, writing on 'impersonality in Blanchot', offers the following gloss on the act of reading:

> The two subjectivities involved, that of the author and that of the reader, co-operate in making each other forget their distinctive identity and destroy each other as subjects. Both move beyond their respective particularity towards a common ground that contains both of them . . .[11]

When a rhetorical 'I' addresses a rhetorical 'you' in a written context, we might adapt de Man's argument to postulate that the process often involves something more than a performative sincerity, the poet's depiction of an imaginary audience, or the straightforward urging of a particular response. For what happens here in a written context, where the 'I' and 'you' are (and remain) strangers, is radically different from an oral one, where there is an 'I' co-present with a 'you'. I would suggest that in the written context these are troping pronouns, collaborating to 'destroy each other as subjects'. The imaginary audience apparently postulated in the work is frequently an impossible audience, meant to be wholly *other* than the audience that is in fact (or in probability and in all foresight) addressed. For one thing, it is not a collective audience at all, but a single reader; Chaucer commonly and pointedly addresses both in the course of a single work, thus rendering void either as a point of reference. Alternatively, the single reader (or auditor), who cannot be prevented by authorial *fiat* from being male and middle-class, may still suddenly be addressed as an assembly of noble ladies. As Jonathan Culler writes: 'Apostrophe is not the representation of an event; if it works, it produces a fictive, discursive event.'[12] The reader is propelled from his or her own time (or self) to 'the time of the apostrophic *now*' which is itself the whole or a part of the discourse. There is no reason to believe the 'I' any less alienated than the 'you' to which it corresponds, for it too partakes in, and is, a discursive event belonging to the work's time—a time other than the author's. This sort of 'I' is therefore a vanishing-point, all but signifying the author's absence. It is a means, as Blanchot maintains, 'to rid [the work] of the presence of the author'[13] by establishing a fictive time in which his presence is logically impossible. Fiction cannot exist without, and only remains fiction within, fictive time. Thus, where first-person narratorial intervention is frequent, it may well serve (as Blanchot observes of Thomas Mann) to represent 'the intervention of the narrator challenging the very possibility of narration'.[14] The success of narration in face of such narratorial intervention inspires admiration. Both reader and writer are subsumed by fiction: they become a part, an act, of literature. This is a product, and distinctive feature, of a 'voice' marked by a desire to be written and read.

No English poetry more manifests this desire, and the process of realising it (Eco's 'pure love of writing') than Chaucer's. No reader of Chaucer can avoid the issue of narratorial *persona* or voice. Chaucer's narratorial voice moves with increasing confidence in an ostensibly 'oral' and self-consciously written medium. In the process, it loses authority and presence: the Chaucerian 'I' is more self-effacement than self-projection. Its interaction, especially in narratorial interjections, foregrounds the poet; but it also fictionalises him by embedding his voice in an avowedly fictional discourse. In deconstructionist parlance, it loses meaning and gains supplementarity. The narrator defers to writing so that the authorial 'I' becomes a synecdoche of the book. The transferred 'I', given to overtly fictional narrators as in *The Canterbury Tales*, is doubly supplementary: a further indirect self-effacement, and the introduction of a new construct, or 'character'. Such a narratorial proxy is not at all psychologically conceived, but one of what Todorov calls narrative-men: 'a character is a potential story . . . Every new character signifies a new plot'.[15] In both cases, speech asserts and loses itself as literature.

A study of Chaucer's narratorial voices can therefore profit, as I hope this one has, from structuralist and post-structuralist criticism. None the less, I have as far as possible in this study refrained from overt engagement in modern debate, or at least from using the language in which it is cast. This is partly a rhetorical strategy. The use of a certain critical terminology imposes an immediate theoretical constraint on the reader and if, as Barthes suggests, writers do all they can to manipulate readers they may as well be subtle about it: *The Name of the Rose* is a more persuasive semiotic textbook than *A Theory of Semiotics*. Another reason for reticence is that the study undertaken here requires a survey of influences, an activity (wrongly, in my view) frowned upon by most recent theorists. However, there is a more substantial defence. The theories which form the premises of structuralist and post-structuralist terminology have been devised for the most part in study of canons of literature, language and period radically different from Chaucer and the English fourteenth century. If our theoretical debates had been structured primarily from study of medieval literature, let alone Middle English poetry, their terms would be somewhat different again. The body of this study has theoretical implications, but they must be made to measure.

Nor is this book preoccupied with a search for ingenious new interpretations. It is an essay in literary understanding, in Chaucerian poetics. It seeks to trace the provenance of an effect in Chaucer's poetry, and then to read some of the shifting registers of that effect. The effect discloses the invention of a textual rhetoric from a spoken one, the first full-hearted assent by an English poet to the proposition that poetry expresses the intricate interrelations between writing and speech, audience and reader. It is the moment when English poetry, however 'full of doubts', however chattily defensive in its antiquarian pretensions and its claim to do no more than 'transcribe', accepts the role of 'the man of letters'. A written voice claims its privilege, audibly.

CHAPTER 1

Apocryphal Voices

Critical Contexts

Modern critics over the last thirty years or so have tended to approach medieval narrators with tools imported from, and better suited to, the traditional novel. The notorious example is that of *Canterbury Tales* criticism, in which the portrait of an individual pilgrim given in the General Prologue has often been read as the key to the narratorial voice of the tale ascribed to that pilgrim as narrator: hardly any teller has been immune from a psychological reading based on portrait and tale together, and the tale has therefore been treated as an ingeniously ironic extension of the portrait. Detailed examples of such critical approaches occur throughout this book. I shall argue that this is an erroneous way of reading the *Canterbury Tales*: what applies to Moll Flanders will not necessarily apply to the Wife of Bath, still less to the Second Nun. The model is inappropriate generically. Even if it were not, it would be unsuitable because different historical circumstances, of literary production and publication as well as worldview, have a great impact on authors' sense of their audience and therefore on their handling of narratorial voice and *persona*.

Middle English poetry, whether or not it was composed for actual public recitation, sees itself essentially as a performance. If only for the private reader, the conditions of public performance are enacted in the poem. In very little Middle English poetry is there any strong sense that the poet is unsure of the public he expects (or desires). Just such an uncertainty, however, is at the root of the traditional novel, which is addressed to a mass and amorphous reading public. Narratorial essays by, for example, Fielding and Thackeray form one sort of attempt not so much to define that public as to train it. Such overt discourses are one of the closest points of connection between the novel and medieval poetry, if only because they are self-conscious rhetorical addresses. The most common basic strategy of the traditional novelist, however, is to insist that the unknown readers must accept the differences between their world and values and those of the novel. For many novelists, an 'I' narrator, especially a highly characterised one like Moll Flanders or David Copperfield, is a detailed way of authenticating the book. The anonymous reader is to approach the narrator not as one approaches something shared—like a performance or received truth—but as one approaches another human being, an authentic stranger. For the reader it is like sneaking a look at someone's diary, or surreptitiously scanning his correspondence: journals and letters are the (exclusively written) forms from which the traditional novel developed. With Chaucer, by contrast, the model is conversation. To be sure, the reader is at a severe disadvantage in the conversation, for Chaucer alone is allowed, as it were, privileged reference to his notes. Nevertheless, the relation between reader and writer occupies a space that is oral as well as textual; and this should make a radical difference to our response.

This is not to say that study of the novel is irrelevant to a modern reading of Chaucer's narratorial voices; but for it to become relevant, one would need a revised understanding of the novel very different from that which informs modern novelistic Chaucer criticism. Such a revision is available in the work of M. M. Bakhtin, and it is all the more interesting that Bakhtin's discussion of 'heteroglossia' would lead an unprejudiced reader to see Chaucer as a novelist, not a poet.

For Bakhtin, all language is conducive to heteroglossia: 'As a living, socio-ideological concrete thing, as heteroglot opinion, language, for the individual consciousness, lies on the borderline between oneself and the other. The word in language is half someone else's'.[1] Bakhtin sees poetry as the form that resists this, working against the odds and in a state of tension to create the illusion of a language unique to the one utterance of a single unitary voice. The novel, on the contrary, is that form or set of forms—and because of his definition of poetry Bakhtin calls them 'prose' forms—that accepts and extends heteroglossia, 'the notion that all transcription systems—including the speaking voice in a living utterance—are inadequate to the multiplicity of meanings they seek to convey', while other 'less repeatable features' of a text 'are in the power of the particular context in which the utterance is made; this context can retract, add to, or in some cases even subtract from the amount and kind of meaning the utterance may be said to have when it is conceived only as a systematic manifestation independent of context'.[2] Heteroglossia is thus the counterpoint, the dialogue, between text and context. This is not an easy idea, however, especially since Bakhtin would argue for an interpenetration of text and context, the different sorts of languages used in it; the style of the text is already in part a series of possible contexts, some of them incompatible. Such work is marked by the avoidance of 'pure and unmediated authorial discourse' (p. 375). Authorial speech itself becomes merely another manifestation of heteroglossia:

> Authorial speech, the speeches of narrators, inserted genres, the speech of characters are merely those fundamental compositional unities with whose help heteroglossia can enter the novel; each of them permits a multiplicity of social voices and a wide variety of their links and interrelationships (always more or less dialogised). (p. 263)

Even when we exclude character speech and inserted genres, authorial language itself still remains a stylistic system of languages: large portions of this speech will take their style (directly, parodically or ironically) from the languages of others, and this stylistic system is sprinkled with others' words, words not enclosed in quotation marks, *formally* belonging to authorial speech but clearly distanced from the mouth of the author by ironic, parodic, polemical or some other pre-existing 'qualified' intonation . . . An authorial emphasis is present, of course, in all these orchestrating and distanced elements of language, and in the final analysis all these elements are determined by the author's artistic will—they are totally the author's artistic responsibility—but they do not belong to the author's *language*, nor do they occupy the same plane. (pp. 415–16)

The style of the novel is thus an interaction of languages, a multiplicity of voices, marked and unmarked.

An example may make Bakhtin's point more comprehensible. This is his commentary on a passage from *Little Dorrit*; it is worth quoting at some length, for there is no Chaucer criticism that moves so comfortably between *persona* (the notion of masking and unmasking) and extended close analysis of style:

> 'It was a dinner to provoke an appetite, though he had not had one. The rarest dishes, sumptuously cooked and sumptuously served, the choicest fruits, the most exquisite wines; marvels of workmanship in gold and silver, china and glass; innumerable things delicious to the senses of taste, smell and sight, were insinuated into its composition. *O, what a wonderful man this Merdle, what a great man, what a master man, how blessedly and enviably endowed*—in one word, what a rich man! [book 2, ch. 12]'
> The beginning is a parodic stylisation of high epic style. What follows is an enthusiastic glorification of Merdle, a chorus of his admirers in the form of the concealed speech of another (the italicised portion). The whole point here is to expose the real basis for such glorification, which is to unmask the chorus' hypocrisy: 'wonderful', 'great', 'master', 'endowed' can all be replaced by the single word 'rich'. This act of authorial unmasking, which is openly accomplished within the boundaries of a single simple sentence, merges with the unmasking of another's speech. The ceremonial emphasis on glorification is complicated by a second emphasis that is indignant, ironic, and this is the one that ultimately predominates in the final unmasking words of the sentence.
> We have before us a typical double-accented, double-styled *hybrid construction*.
> What we are calling a hybrid construction is an utterance that belongs, by its grammatical (syntactic) and compositional markers, to a single speaker, but that actually contains mixed within it two utterances, two speech manners, two styles, two 'languages', two semantic and axiological belief systems. We repeat, there is no formal—compositional and syntactic—boundary between these utterances, styles, languages, belief systems; the division of voices and languages takes place within the limits of a single syntactic whole, often within the limits of a simple sentence. (pp. 304–5)

3

This sort of volatile and unmarked shift from one's discourse to another's can be paralleled again and again in Chaucer. One example would be the narratorial comment in the Merchant's Tale after January's preposterous speech about marriage: 'Thus seyde this olde knyght, that was so wys.'[3] This is what Wayne Booth would call stable irony; its effect on the reader is to make one believe the opposite about the aged January's 'wisdom.'[4] But there is also the implication that somebody takes it seriously. This is somebody's opinion: whose? January's own? Were it not for the tense of the verb, 'was', which puts the comment into *oratio obliqua*, one would be tempted to supply inverted commas. The brief comment would probably be classified by modern linguists as Free Indirect Discourse; but that might be to lose sight of its kinship with other narratorial comments such as that on Dorigen's grief at Arveragus's absence in the Franklin's Tale:

> For his absence wepeth she and siketh,
> As doon thise noble wyves whan hem liketh.
>
> (V (F) 817–18)

This has a similar quality of intrusive tonal shock in spite of the slight difference in grammatical form. Booth would classify it as unstable irony, since the statement, while undercutting, does not reverse itself. Again, however, who says it? The narrator? Certainly, but is this the Franklin? To reflect on the ostensible narrator of the particular tale is again to miss its tonal kinship with the previous example, which has a different ostensible narrator, and with many other examples that could be cited from many other tales. It would be foolish to deny that the various ostensible narrators speak linguistically 'in character': they do, sometimes, generally in their prologues or in the first or last few lines of their tales. It may just be that only the Franklin would malapropise 'Marcus Tullius Scithero' and make Mount Parnassus rhyme with him.[5] To acknowledge this, however, is by no means to admit the application of speech-act theory to the entire narrative ascribed to the Franklin. If all the ostensible narrators are different, then they all spend most of their time quoting Chaucer. The Chaucer they quote is no more susceptible to speech-act theory than they are. This is what heteroglossia does: Chaucer's voice, whichever one it may be, has been reduced to parity with the other voices, the other languages of the text. This example may help demonstrate what heteroglossia means. We are left not with a speaker but with a tone.

Yet this tone is not single or unitary. It is a complex and multiple play of voices. All of these voices are equally alienated from their ostensible, presumed or possible source. They are apocryphal voices.

I prefer this term to heteroglossia. Not only have I foresworn new-fangled terms; it also seems a pity to work so hard to establish multiple phenomena and then lump them together, or have one's translator lump them together, under a singular noun. Heteroglossia is a useful term in Bakhtin's argument because he aspires to tell a chronological story: the stages of the development of the 'novel' as he has redefined it. I see no need to follow him in this, partly because most critical systems offering a narrative of chronological development are covert allegory and partly because heteroglossia, under the chronological pressure, has to be a sliding scale. Bakhtin's one frontal definition of heteroglossia brings together two definitions that deserve to be separated:

Heteroglossia, once incorporated into the novel (whatever the forms for its incorporation), is *another's speech in another's language*, serving to express authorial intentions but in a refracted way. Such speech constitutes a special type of *double-voiced discourse*. It serves two speakers at the same time and expresses simultaneously two different intentions: the direct intention of the character who is speaking, and the refracted intention of the author. In such discourse there are two voices, two meanings and two expressions.   (p. 324)

One might ask why only two different voices are envisaged here when in practice Bakhtin's analysis is far more gregarious. Taking two to mean two or more, however, I find the idea of 'double-voiced discourse' entirely relevant to Chaucer's poetry, and not at all the same thing as 'another's speech in another's language'—unless another is the other—which seems to lead right back, when applied to narrators, to the highly characterised first-person *personae* of some nineteenth-century novels and stories.

Those idiosyncratic nineteenth-century narrators underlie much Chaucer criticism, by critics who approach their task with far less subtlety in their thinking about the novel than Bakhtin. A title like 'The Unlikely Narrator of the *Troilus*'[6] speaks for itself. Only one very extreme point of Bakhtin's sliding scale is even entertained: the narrator is conceived not as a voice or as a stylistic device but as a character in the tradition of A. C. Bradley.

The most famous example is also by far the best: E. T. Donaldson's classic essay on the *Troilus*-narrator. What Donaldson proposes is literally a 'double-voiced discourse', but of the order of that between Frankenstein and the monster:

> At some of the moments when his narrator is striving most laboriously to palliate Criseide's behaviour, Chaucer, standing behind him, jogs his elbow, causing him to fall into verbal imprecision, or into anticlimax, or making his rhetoric deficient, or making it redundant—generally doing these things in such a way that the reader will be encouraged almost insensibly to see Criseide in a light quite different from the one that the narrator is so earnestly trying to place her in.[7]

So unsettled is the narrator by this authorial victimisation, and so perturbed by his discovery during the course of Books IV and V that Criseyde really does abandon Troilus, that he eventually succumbs to 'a kind of nervous breakdown in poetry' (p. 91). In little less trouble, the reader is left to plot a course between the schizoid narrator and the elbow-jogging Chaucer, in despair of attaining the critical maturity to determine whose rhetoric is whose. Donaldson's position could hardly be more extreme. Not only does he try to assign the rhetoric of the discourse to a narrator-*persona*, which is highly problematic, but, for all that the model is Wayne Booth's *The Rhetoric of Fiction*, he also assumes a degree of fictionalisation that falls somewhat outside the mainstream of the traditional novel. Donaldson's *Troilus*-narrator does not belong with Fielding or the Thackeray of *Vanity Fair*, whose own self-portrait as narrator —as a middle-aged man of sentiment, portly and diffident—indeed has resemblances to 'Chaucer'. It belongs rather with Charles Kinbote, the narrator of Nabokov's *Pale Fire*, whose ostensible narrative is merely the pretext for his increasingly demented self-revelation of his own role, identity and attitudes. The focus is on the teller here, and the tale takes a subsidiary part in, and is dislocated by, his internal drama.

I have discussed Donaldson's essay on the *Troilus*-narrator elsewhere, in an essay on Skelton arguing for a distinction between 'closed' and 'open' *persona*.[8] The distinction is needed to account for those narratorial *personae* that are highly fictionalised and generally named, like the dreamer in medieval dream poetry or Skelton's Parrot or Colin Clout, yet stand as a means of bringing the text, rather than themselves, into moral or rhetorical focus. Charles Kinbote is a closed *persona*: the first-person narration of *Pale Fire* is his psychological history, a madman's untrustworthy confession. Thackeray in *Vanity Fair*, however, like most medieval dreamers or Parrot or Colin Clout, is an open *persona*, making an occasional cameo appearance in the foreground but there mainly, offstage, to mediate the dialogue between the text and its readers. *Pale Fire* is about Charles Kinbote, whereas *Speak Parrot* is not about Parrot, *Colin Clout* is not about Colin Clout, and—I shall argue—the Pardoner's Tale is not about the Pardoner nor the Squire's Tale about the Squire. In the essay on Skelton I gave the *Troilus*-narrator as an example of an open *persona*, and quoted against Donaldson's view the argument of Dieter Mehl about Chaucer's creating an imaginary or ideal audience:

> To be one of his audience does not mean just to listen to what he tells us, but to encounter a fictional reality that is full of questions and provocative blanks and to be in mental contact with an author who makes us aware of the truly sociable character of narrative poetry . . . It is not our business as readers and critics to discover what Chaucer 'really meant', how he himself judges his characters or what he thought about courtly love, but to respond to his appeal and participate in the dialogue his poetry wants to provoke.[9]

I then added:

> The *persona* of *Troilus and Criseyde* is what I would call an 'open' *persona*, which looks outwards in order to challenge an audience's responses, rather than a 'closed' *persona*, which turns inwards, hermetically seals the artefact, and requires independent solution. Since the *persona* of *Troilus and Criseyde* is by no means completely fictionalised, it operates on the level of response and relationship; it is conceived not as a kind of drama but as a rhetorical extension of the poem's narrative. (p. 11)

Self-quotation here is not meant to exemplify narratorial solipsism; it is used because the distinction is important for the present book and because, while I remain sure of the point, I am less sure of the example. The examples from Skelton are stronger than the *Troilus*. Mehl sought to avoid any *persona* of any kind, and may well have been right. The *Troilus*-narrator is not named, though we assume that it is a sometimes fictionalised rendering of 'Chaucer'; the narrator is given a temporary *persona*, like that of the Ovidian *servus amatorius*, for local effects, but by and large it is no more fictionalised within the poem than the imaginary audience. It is a mask, of course, or rather a series of masks, but tonal instabilities and complexities always are: this is in the nature of

6

apocryphal voices. It is probably better to reserve the term *persona* for cases in which there is a clearly named and identified ostensible narrator as in the *Canterbury Tales*, or narrator-participant as in dream-poems. I shall argue that when these occupy the role of narratorial voices in Chaucer's work they are generally open, not closed, *personae*. A *persona* may be open as narrator of the tale yet closed in the frame around the tale, like the Pardoner. As for *Troilus*, I shall look at the narrator in detail in Chapter Four; it is best seen as a narratorial voice, or series of such voices, that only fitfully becomes an open *persona* at all, and the tonal complexity and apparent inconsistencies that set off Donaldson's quest of a closed *persona* are best seen as just that, not to be reduced to a singular resolution.

The concept of *persona* was probably salutary when it first appeared in Chaucer criticism, for it helped correct an unliterary emphasis on 'what Chaucer thought'. It has long since ceased to be so, for if it makes two where before there was one, it is none the less doggedly singular and univocal in its approach to each. Once more, the criticism would have to be that multiple phenomena are lumped together; and while with 'heteroglossia' they are at least made to add up to a sum dealing on one level with language and styles, the real demerit of *persona*-oriented criticism is that it diverts attention from language and styles into a reckoning that is dramatic and psychological. Questions about tone are therefore referred in the wrong direction. Yet questions about tone, not questions about *persona*, are the most interesting questions of Chaucer criticism. The same would hold true of Dickens, in whose protean use of apocryphal voices we have found common ground with Chaucer. If a model from the traditional novel has to be supplied, let it be a Dickensian model. If it is, sensibly handled, it will not engage with closed narratorial *personae*; and it will return us to something approaching a valid critical context for Chaucer's narratorial voices. For Dickens is unique among traditional novelists in his active appreciation of the potential of oral performance, and catering for a dual reception of his work in both written and oral models of publication. He is the closest thing to an English prose Chaucerian.

There are welcome signs that Chaucer criticism has begun to move away from *persona* to tone, and will try to accommodate the 'telling difference' in a conceptual framework informed by language and style rather than the dramatic fallacy.[10] This book is an attempt to accelerate this movement. At the least, it seeks to rid Chaucer's poetry of the shadow of the closed *persona*.

What will replace it? Since there is no point substituting one singular term for another, the answer must be not one device but a scale, a register, of different ones, ranging from a highly fictionalised open *persona* to the shifting tones that are unmarked, sometimes barely implied, apocryphal voices. To redefine terms: 'narrator' here means any linguistic and stylistic device appearing on the scale; 'open *persona*' means a clearly marked narrator who is nevertheless a dramatically neutral voice, as opposed to a 'closed *persona*'; 'narratorial voice' means something less than this, an unmarked narrator; and 'character' is used in the normal way, for a character may be both highly fictionalised and linguistically characterised yet be, as narrator, a dramatically neutral voice, a rhetorical extension of the poem's narrative. The resources for this account are critical reading and literary history. Chapters Two and Five argue the case in detail about individual *Canterbury Tales*; Chapters Three and Four try to trace the provenance of this register in Chaucer's poetry and assess its use, arguing that his interest in it moves through a definite *persona* at an early stage to multiple use of the less definite 'narratorial voice' in his later career, even though that was crowned by the *Canterbury Tales*.

One principle needs to be stated here. No argument for a dramatically conceived narrator would restrict itself to passages of explicit first-person narratorial activity, but it is logical to suppose that no such argument could possibly be acceptable if it failed to account for all such passages. I have therefore in large measure restricted myself to them, not to caricature dramatic readings but because these are their stress-points. A further caution is required. What follows may seem to incline at times towards the writer's voice rather than the character's. This is for polemical purposes of correction only. The voice of the writer is the voice of writing, already other. The premise is Chaucer's 'dialogic imagination'. I do seek to show, however, how it is that a babel of apocryphal voices is enacted, stylistically and rhetorically, with enormous consistency.

Middle English Contexts

The first task is still an introductory one, to provide some contexts for Chaucer in the treatment of narratorial voice in Middle English poetry generally.

The plausibility, the authority of a narrative, whether realistic or not, is experiential. The more literary the narrative, the more something in it must arbitrate between the reader's experience and that described. The exception in Middle English lies in much romance, where the fantastic conventions, and their reception in a folkloric mode, may demand little experiential verification to satisfy the reader's (or auditor's) structural expectations. Romance is a dialogue in which the reader/auditor stays silent. Most other narrative modes, however, require a more active response; and here the need for arbitration comes in. Its realisation may take a range of forms, from minor stylistic devices through tonal discordance and direct address, to a fully developed narratorial *persona*. I shall characterise the entire range by the term 'narrator': not every narrator is a *persona*, and not every *persona* really amounts to more than a narratorial voice. The impression of a *persona* is extremely common, if only because the task of arbitration is conveniently and persuasively assumed in the grammatical first person. Again, not all first-person narratorial interventions signal a narratorial *persona*; indeed, 'interventions' is a misnomer, for narratorial voice is an already existing feature of a text and we are in no position to judge what the text would look like without it. The term narrator is therefore elastic; so too is a narrator's function. At the least, it is to convince us to endorse events or emotions recounted, however unlikely, as possible in the world of the work, and at the most it is to direct our sympathies and help shape (or frustrate) our expectations.

I have placed the emphasis on narratorial voice rather than narratorial *persona* because it seems to me that in medieval poetry most narrators are part of, rather than subsume, the rhetoric of a work. They are elements in a larger strategy. Sometimes a narrator is no more than a product of rhetorical imperatives, the decorum either of the style or the set of structural conventions adopted.[11] Readers of Richard Rolle's devotional composition may be forever unsure whether an almost boisterous exuberance characterises his spirituality or his alliteration. Chaucer's realisation of the effect of style on narratorial voice is expectedly acute: the juxtaposition of an overripe tail-rhyme in *Sir Thopas* with a sober expository prose in *Melibeus* creates two different 'Chaucers'.

Subject-matter can have an equally determining effect:

> Wanne ich þenche þinges þre
> ne mai (ich) neure bliþe be:
> þe on is ich sal awe,
> þe oþer is ich ne wot wilk day.
> Þat þridde is mi meste kare,
> i ne woth nevre wuder i sal fare.[12]

These lines are merely a rendering of a Latin aphorism and 'the intention is not to arouse emotion but to enumerate three points to be memorised'.[13] Any dramatic promise is resolutely unfulfilled, and a reaction of sympathy or concern for the poem's speaker would be inappropriate. The first-person narrator is there not to concentrate attention but to generalise it, to establish a basis for the poem's unpleasant truths in human perception, and the voice it offers is meant to be wholly interchangeable with that of the reader/auditor. If this is a *persona*, it is none the less so open as to be thoroughly transparent, a rhetorical means to a meditative end. Similarly, the 'I' of a *chanson d'avanture* exists to ride out 'this ender daye', not (except in formally circumscribed fashion) to tell us about himself. The same applies to other sort of quasi-dramatic *personae*. In a debate, bodies will be bodies and souls will be souls, the more predictably the better. We are not invited to look at the personalities, say, of owls and nightingales, but at the dialogue between them dictated by the nature and name of the form, *conflictus*. The *persona* is mainly subsumed by the rhetorical strategy: its name matters less than its voice.

Rhetoric's primary mode is the spoken. Such, at least, is the medieval convention. Also conventionally, the primary mode of literary presentation is oral delivery. In reading Middle English poetry we see the relics of this convention everywhere in the stage business of oral appeals: would the audience kindly shut up, would you please now go back to dinner, and so on. The conventional conception has a striking impact on tone: even medieval poems that were probably intended for private reading often address their readers as if they were auditors.[14] This is not self-evidently justifiable, as it would be with most other rhetorical arts. In the case of a legal address or a sermon, a written text is presumed to memorialise an authentic original performance. With a poem the first performance may be merely an imaginary event embedded in the poem together with an imaginary audience. In legal or homiletic contexts where the speaker and author are one, a direct address to the audience is generally made more or less *in propria persona*, and whatever strangeness may infect the speaking voice will come from the conventions of rhetoric employed. Drama, in which the speaker is always a fully developed *persona*, still resembles such contexts more than poetry in one important respect: the speaker is always physically present in view of the audience. With poetry, however, the position is rarely so straightforward. For one thing, the medieval adumbration of poetic rhetorical theory is a late development and arises out of a naturally written medium, the teaching of grammar.[15] For another, the relation of poet to audience is volatile, liable to vary according to each specific occasion, even where the poem was bespoke. Medieval poets lack copyright over their work with which to guard against rival performances or from private reading, and they may seek to ensure that the voice of the poem is alienable from any particular conditions of reception.

There are various methods. Poets may seek some way of counterfeiting an address *in propria persona* with an address *ostensibly* so: Chaucer in the Prologue to *The Legend of Good Women* and perhaps Langland in *Piers Plowman* offer themselves in spurious actuality. They may speak fitfully *in propria persona* and fitfully not, like Gower in the *Confessio Amantis*. They may seek to abolish most traces of an idiosyncratic narratorial voice, a method favoured in some excellent romances like *Sir Gawain and the Green Knight* or *The Morte Arthure* but rarely in other genres except lyric.[16] Or they may decide to ascribe the poem to a wholly fictionalised narrator, as for example in *Pearl*. The permutations are many, and the rest of this book does no more than illustrate some of them.

In England, questions of narratorial voice and *persona* become pressing and difficult quite suddenly towards the end of the fourteenth century, at a time of the general revival of English vernacular poetry and at a time, crucially, when poets are with reason much aware of the bifurcation of oral and written frameworks. Poets are conscious that they need to write for two radically different kinds of reception, the heard and the privately read, that their work may be either misread or mismetred, 'red . . . or elles songe'. Chaucer's interest in these dual possibilities culminates of course in *The Canterbury Tales*, where a work which at the least caters for private reading, daring us to turn over the leaf, is given a frame in which the tales are orally delivered to a fictitious audience; but the interest is clear too in his early work. *The Book of the Duchess* is self-consciously lucid in its evaluation of poetry that is written and read like Ovid's *Metamorphoses*, or comes complete with 'text and glose' like the *Roman de la Rose* on the narrator's bedroom wall, against poetry that is spoken or even sometimes extemporised by the Black Knight. The fluctuation between writing and speaking is reflected in the structure of *The House of Fame*, where a mainly written tradition of Fame is depicted in terms of sound and acoustic interference.

There is no need to labour this point. The situation in which English poets of the late fourteenth century found themselves, and the dual type of reception for which their poetry had to cater, was formative. It encouraged an increasing bookishness, and a sense of an author's detachment from his matter. Authors who could allude to their own reading of a source felt themselves to be at an advantage. Many a sober author used source-tags ('as the boke sais', 'as the geeste tellis') shamelessly to cover a small bloom of his own fancy. In Chaucer such disingenuousness becomes a positive deceit when the *Troilus*-narrator defers (and refers his audience) to the authority of a non-existent source, Lollius. Such devices foreground the writer in his study, not the poet in front of his audience. We do not know often Middle English poets did in fact find themselves in front of an audience; but we can be sure that this was only one of several possible contexts, public or private, in which their work could receive a performance. We may take it that in most later medieval performances the speaker (or reader) was not the writer. This gap between reader and poet marks an important stage in the development of narrators. Intonation becomes a feature of writing. If the writer is not physically engaged in the performance of his work, he is denied access to a large repertory of means—tone of voice as well as non-verbal resources such as gesture—by which he may control the responses of his audience. He must employ other, more literary, techniques. He must try to ensure in effect that another speaker or a private reader operates as his proxy. This is where a narrator comes into its own: the proxy is inscribed in the poem, to relate to an imagined audience.

The 'I' narrator is most likely to become complex in extended narrative. Most treatises present few problems: there is little narrative, and a didactic voice is generally self-effacing despite the seriousness of what it has to say. Middle English lyrics, while not devoid of narrative content or implication, take pains to restrict it frugally within a relatively brief compass and the relatively simple scope of their immediate, intended and generally declared effect. Typically, a couple of quasi-naturalistic details quickly give place to a representative or transparent narrator:

> Wynter wakeneþ al my care,
>   nou þis leves waxeþ bare;
> ofte y sike & mourne sare
>   when hit comeþ in my þoht
> Of þis worldes ioie hou hit geþ al to noht.[17]

We may compare the case of the four religious lyrics among the prose *exempla* of BL MS Harley 2316. These are inserted in a narrative framework, but this framework proves on examination to be worse than redundant. Miss Woolf's judgement on one, that 'the narrative context here constricts the feeling of the poem' (p. 316), is applicable to all. In three of the lyrics, the *persona* is a transparent or representative one: and in the fourth, entitled by Carleton Brown 'The Sinner's Lament', we have a short dramatic monologue, explicitly signalled and monochrome in nature, of the bitter type familiar to Middle English lyricists from the Latin elegies of Maximian.[18] The *persona* in this is not transparent, but it is certainly not problematic.

Rarely, and in general fortuitously, do the lyrics present problems in their narrator. In the following thirteenth-century example, one verse survives of what, since the rest of the leaf is lost, may have been a longer poem:

> Mirie it is while sumer ilast
> wið fugheles song,
> oc nu necheð windes blast
> and weder strong.
> Ei! ei! what þis nicht is long,
> and ich wið wel michel wrong
> soregh and murne and fast.[19]

The problem here is really one of rhetorical conventions, but it means that we are unable to disencode the first person. From what is extant it is not possible to know whether the 'sumer', 'windes blast / and weder strong', and 'nicht' of this poem are intended literally, metaphorically or allegorically; moreover, we cannot be sure whether the 'michel wrong' suffered by the narrator is disease, scorned love or Christian guilt. We cannot now tell therefore whether this is a religious lyric or a secular one, or whether the narrator is again an open *persona*, or, say, a conventional lover of courtly love poetry. Because the narrative implied by the lyric is left by accident or design incomplete, at its end there are outstanding narrative alternatives which the first person has done nothing to resolve.[20] What creates the problem with the narrator here is this failure to foreclose multiple narrative possibilities.

Yet the problem with a narrator in extended narrative is never that of narrative alone. Nor is a narratorial voice inevitable. Many romances, whose concern is narrative pure and simple, get away virtually without one: one of the many running jokes in *Sir Thopas* is the incongruity of a poet working on a romance in tail-rhyme who draws attention to his narratorial *persona*. A narrator is activated by a poet's affective or intellectual designs upon his narrative: it is an invitation to the reader to look beneath the surface structure of the narrative, its 'text', to some sort of underlying truth, its 'glose'. The technique, and the understanding of it, has much in common with allegory and must have owed a lot to it. A narrator cannot be detached from the whole meaning of the work it inhabits. Its presence is a riddle, and the solution to it carries us well beyond consideration of a literary device. For this reason a study of narrators cannot stop where, in theory, it should. It must also engage with the larger strategy in which the narrator plays a part.

Literature cannot but be open to influence from the society and culture in which it is produced. In the later fourteenth century, when serious vernacular authors were unconfident of the worth and status of their activity, the influence was strong. I have noted the willingness to benefit from allegorical exegesis, though this was already a highly developed literary model. The narratorial voice is similarly shaped by the fact that an ecclesiastical model was ready to hand. Whatever the true historical circumstances of literary performance in their period, English poets of the later fourteenth century showed no desire to abandon the guise of a public speaking voice. In the famous *Troilus* frontispiece of Corpus Christi College, Cambridge MS 61, we find this guise translated into iconography. The illustration is highly enigmatic, not least because there may be some sort of serial narrative progression from the picture's top to its bottom. Modern scepticism of its significance is a necessary reaction against Ford Madox Brown's several paintings of Chaucer reading to the court of Edward III. The fact remains that in the frontispiece someone (presumably Chaucer) is reciting something (presumably, from the context of the illustration, *Troilus*) to a royal court. It is probably not a portrayal of any specific occasion but an idealised image, a manifesto for what English poets should more often be asked to do. Recent research has demonstrated, however, that the iconography is not drawn from a pictorial tradition depicting poets' command performances but from a more familiar and accessible model: preaching.[21] The serious vernacular poet is therefore cast in the role of preacher-manqué. There is ample evidence that many Middle English poets were happy to accept such a model: the narratorial *persona* of Langland or Gower, for instance, is greatly indebted to a homiletic voice. The irony of the *Troilus* frontispiece is that its iconography is less suited to Chaucer in this respect than it would have been to any of his major contemporaries. Indeed, one could distinguish two key patterns of narratorial voice in the poetry of the later fourteenth century: the non-Chaucerian, and Chaucer's.

The first and older type of narratorial voice addresses itself '"as if" to the entire community': Anne Middleton has described it as 'the idea of public poetry'.[22] This retains the social activism, the militant readiness to rebuke high and low on issues of public policy or spiritual welfare, that we associate with late medieval preaching and teaching, and it is derived in large part from what we would now see as non-literary origins, the penitential tradition. This sort of narrator, when a full *persona*, is always open, intrinsic to the work's purposes as a register of content and a means of moral and rhetorical focus, and its structural role is important and widely ranging. Its great advantage is that it softens what would otherwise be—in vernacular poetry—an inappropriately authoritative voice, and in doing so it fulfils a major penitential function, forcing the audience of the poem to experience rather than observe moral conflict and spiritual quest. It is a means by which theology is transformed into literature, with some loss of authority and a substantial, compensatory gain in immediacy.

The second type of explicit narratorial activity is that developed by Chaucer, literary in its origin and generally more secular in its purposes: its greatest debt is to the dreamer *persona* in the *Roman de la Rose*, but Chaucer's use of it in his later poetry extends well beyond dream vision into other, generically still more unstable forms. Insofar as it is a narratorial *persona*, it too is almost always an open one. Some of its characteristics may be described as extrinsic to any particular poem, as the poet's means of mediating between himself and a specific, socially powerful audience, and as a prolonged humility-*topos* for vernacular poetry of a highly literary flavour. Its main task, however, is to mediate the interplay of the particular poem and all its possible audiences, with an increasing number of possible reading conditions to take into account. It ensures that the poem, whatever the form of any one reading, is always read as a performance, and in the *Canterbury Tales* one level of performance, the frame, is incorporated in the poem. One of its major devices, then, is direct address, and the focus is generally rhetorical rather than moral. Its great advantage is to highlight the deliberately problematic authority of the poem in performance as a work of fiction; and the narratorial *persona* developed in dream poetry, with an explicit time-lapse between the writer as poet and the writer as dreamer, is a powerful instrument to facilitate the tonal range that comes from fluctuating distance and a number of temporal perspectives. Especially when the context is not a dream, the concept of *persona* is subordinate to the tonal range and rhetorical focus; I shall argue that we are left with a narratorial voice that is less than a *persona*. Accordingly, when the narratorial *personae* are multiple, as in the *Canterbury Tales*, the fictional nature of the performance is ever more forcefully stressed, but the narratorial voice remains fairly constant, subject to rhetorical, not dramatic or phychological, decisions.

By being tied to the fictional enactment of the work's performance, this sort of narratorial voice inevitably surrenders the public voice and activist stance of poetry that employs a penitentially conceived *persona*. There is a narrowing, a self-selection of audience. There is also a shift in idealism: the vision of poetic value is located less in the New Jerusalem and more in 'bokes olde' and, implicitly, new. One might say that poetic value becomes culturally élitist. But it does not thereby become authoritarian, despite claims to the contrary by some Marxists. Chaucer's poems form a prototype for works of high culture in the extraordinary confidence they repose in the reader, whose responses are as far as is conceivable from being over-determined.[23]

I have called the voices of this chapter 'apocryphal' because the multiple meanings of the modern adjective cover the permutations of narratorial voice, *persona* and literary strategy with which I deal. The first use of 'apocryphal' recorded in the *Oxford English Dictionary* dates from 1590; in all occurrences cited the word covers a fairly constant but broad semantic field, defined thus: 'of doubtful authenticity; spurious, fictitious, false; fabulous, mythical'. The Dictionary then gives three fields of use: originally, of any 'writing, statement or story': specifically of 'uncanonical literature': generally, 'unreal, counterfeit, sham' or—here, unusually, the Dictionary itself resorts to inverted commas—"imitation". Only one of these is of doubtful relevance: the rigorous scrutiny of uncanonical literature belongs of course to the Protestant Reformation. There was no medieval Hooker to say: 'We hold not the apocrypha for sacred'.[24] The medievals were little concerned with the scholarly pedigree of what they held sacred, and this is important. Penitential manuals, for example, were probably regarded by their authors as honest uncanonical extensions of canonical truth to do with human conduct in mundane situations; at least, they are undeniably digests of canon law. Much Middle English poetry seems to me to experiment with the same end, to test the power of poetry to be trustworthily apocryphal. The other senses of 'apocryphal' need no defence against anachronism or irrelevance: the Dictionary entries all but epitomise Chaucer. A narrator of a work of fiction is by nature fictitious—hence the difficulty in trying to be trustworthy. In its relation to its author, to the world outside the poem and sometimes to that within it, it is 'of doubtful authenticity'. Its use raises questions both about the nature of fiction (the questions perhaps wisely begged by inverted commas around 'imitation'), and the degree of fictionalisation: when does an 'unreal' narrator truly become 'fabulous' or 'counterfeit'? Narrators are always concealments, bookish secrets: apocrypha.

It is not in a punning spirit, then, that I refer in this chapter to different kinds of apocrypha and apocryphal voice. I have in mind several facets or phases of Middle English writing that may so be described: on the one hand, the attempt to create a trustworthy vernacular apocrypha in the scriptural sense, a series of texts which, while not canonical, serve and partake of an inherited authority; a bolder, a more literary attempt such as Langland's to embellish that *apocrypha*, to render truth into English poetry, which involves narrative fiction, the unfolding of *archana verba* and the creation of apocryphal speaking characters, *personae*; and on the other hand, what will occupy the rest of this book—Chaucer's use of such apocryphal voices in a rather contrary direction, the voluntarily apocryphal manipulation of authority to license his 'imitation'. These different phenomena are held together not by semantic good luck but by the conditions of the period in which they all occur. Chaucer's achievement changes the course of its literary history.

The period of Chaucer and his immediate successors is the crucial one in the growth—or invention—of an English literary tradition, and it is also the only period in which the study of narratorial voice and *persona* may be restricted to poetry without reference to prose. During its course the narrator moves on the whole from a moral to a literary, and even a material, basis; and it moves, whether the narrator is named or not, from a kind of moral anonymity to poetic individuality. Chaucer's impact here is crucial. The movement is that from penitent to poet.

J. A. Burrow has recently stressed the importance of the petitionary mode in the growth of poetic individuality. Poets name themselves in order to win favour: 'They are discovered, as it were, upon their knees; and they speak of themselves most often, not in the pride of the poet, but in the humility of the petitioner. Their usual tone is one of complaint and of entreaty.'[25] Burrow then cites several examples, ranging in date from Cynewulf in Old English to Dunbar. What I find interesting in these examples is that, with one exception, they move chronologically from the request for spiritual grace to that for money. The exception is Nicholas of Guildford in *The Owl and the Nightingale*, and there, as Burrow says, 'his plea is conducted obliquely' (p. 40), without direct address by the poet to an audience or patron. Cynewulf, and Laȝamon, ask to be remembered in the prayers of others for the salvation of their souls; in Gower and Langland, the act of poetic naming is penitential rather than material. The religious note by no means thoroughly fades from later petitions —Burrow cites the *explicit* of the *Canterbury Tales* and that of Caxton's Malory—but the more common later request is financial. Dunbar begs for a benefice, and Hoccleve, taking his cue from Chaucer's *Complaint to his Purse*, frequently directs laments for his financial indigence to those like Lord Fournevall in a position to put it right. In *La Male Règle de T. Hoccleve*, as Burrow puts it, 'a moral confession slides into a complaint for an empty purse' (p. 42). Moreover, Hoccleve's *persona*, tied as it is to his personal finances, becomes for the first time in English poetry directly autobiographical. The 'Chaucer' *persona* of the *House of Fame* or the *Canterbury Tales* is a fiction, a true *persona*; the Hoccleve of *La Male Règle*, who writes of going home through London to the Privy Seal, is, however, comically presented, Hoccleve himself. There is a change here in the use of *persona*; and, most important, there is a substantial shift in the value located in it. After Chaucer, the English poet is no longer necessarily a gifted variant of everyman, a public microcosm; he has the potential to be a special person.

That moral and didactic works make up such a preponderance of extant Middle English poetic texts before Chaucer is not necessarily a sign that the English were unremittingly pious in their tastes. It is an index of the status of the English language, which was usually regarded at least until the last decades of the fourteenth century as suitable for the 'lewed' folk but not for their Francophone social superiors; and it is an index too of an attitude to the 'lewed' that stressed instruction more than entertainment. It is a clerkly attitude, and it may also be a sign of strong ecclesiastical influence on the modes of literary production as late as the fourteenth century. Much is yet unknown about possible commercial production of manuscripts in fourteenth-century England, but it is probably not a coincidence that Chaucer and Hoccleve both worked as civil servants in London, Hoccleve as a scribe. It may not be vulgar Marxism to suggest a correlation between the development of a more secularised yet serious vernacular poetry and the development of a thriving commercial book trade. In France and Italy these two happened early. In Paris, as in Bologna, a metropolis and a university existed together from the twelfth century; in London they did not, and the book-trade in thirteenth-century Oxford was mainly oriented to the academic courses on which it depended. By the fourteenth century in France and Italy, access to a commercial book trade had stimulated a market for vernacular and secular literature, humanism, and a lay interest in classical scholarship. In England, these developments may not have occurred on any scale until late in the fourteenth century, and then perhaps haphazardly, with Chancery scribes like Hoccleve making an important contribution—as they did too to the fixing of a standard dialect that happened to be Chaucer's.[26]

Some such shift is the *sine qua non* of a literary tradition. Literature has to have or take for itself a place of its own, protected to some extent from any other demands that may be made on writing by social or moral concerns. Literature does not cease to show these concerns, or to have affective designs on the reader, but these are no longer inbuilt in the social basis of textual production. Literature, so to speak, has a separate economic base and demands payment for its labours; it is more open to the desire to write it, and freer to be as those who write it are. Chaucer, Spenser's Tityrus and Hoccleve's 'dere mayster', created the English literary tradition. This is the true perspective for understanding his use of narratorial voices, and its significance. Writing becomes an end in itself.

Chaucer's poetry is the very act of its becoming. For Chaucer's position —given the temper of his work, his genius and his dialect—is uniquely fortunate: being at the mainspring of the English literary tradition, he is unconstrained by it. Once writing has become an end in itself, there are always problems—practically as well as philosophically—of compatibility with speech; to these Chaucer is oblivious. He spans two modes of textual production, reception and expression—the oral and the written—and enjoys his mastery of both impartially. The rest of this book celebrates narratorial ambidexterity.

CHAPTER 2

The Pardoner: Morality in its Context

I

Chaucer's Pardoner is not at first sight a subtle creation. The General Prologue presents us with a portrait of memorable abnormality and extreme villainy. The Pardoner's Prologue confirms our worst suspicions and—just in case we are still in doubt—Chaucer has the Host reject the Pardoner after his tale with an excremental vehemence which, we might think, perfectly places the Pardoner in a context of filth:

> 'Lat be,' quod he, 'it shal nat be, so theech!
> Thou woldest make me kisse thyn olde breech,
> And swere it were a relyk of a seint,
> Though it were with thy fundement depeint!
> But, by the croys which that Seint Eleyne fond,
> I wolde I hadde thy coillons in myn hond
> In stide of relikes or of seintuarie.
> Lat kutte hem of, I wol thee helpe hem carie;
> They shul be shryned in an hogges toord!'   (947–55)

Even here, in the Host's rejoinder as in the initial portrait of the Pardoner, there is ample room for critical disagreement about the nuances of tone and meaning. But what makes the Pardoner the subject of a bewildering diversity of conflicting critical speculations is the fact that Chaucer gives to so corrupt a character so potent and sombre a tale. The Pardoner's Tale is by any standards one of the most impressive and serious of the *Canterbury Tales*; the subtleties of Chaucer's design are in the juxtaposition of this tale with this pardoner. For critics the juxtaposition has proved irresistible. As. G. G. Sedgewick wrote in 1940:

> If subtleties really exist, they are not 'solved' by waving them aside. And
> . . . Chaucer's design in this whole affair is very subtly complicated: it
> extorts 'interpretation', however much one may shrink from the
> process.[2]

The results of frequent 'interpretation' are such that, in the opinion of a recent and optimistic critic, 'critical diversity can go no further'.[3]

The juxtaposition of tale and teller has led almost all critics in one of two directions: towards rationalising the Pardoner, in psychological or spiritual terms, or towards rationalising his tale, by seeing in it a moral commentary on the teller. The two approaches are not mutually exclusive, and we have reason to be grateful for both. Psychological exploration of the Pardoner began with G. L. Kittredge's fine reading of 1893 in which he concluded that the Pardoner is a 'lost soul', and it has yielded a variety of glosses on his physiognomy, his frauds and his actions.[4] Such criticism, entertaining as it is, is exposed to two crucial objections. Firstly it asks questions about the Pardoner's motives—for his presence on the pilgrimage, for his self-revelation, for his final bizarre essay in salesmanship—to which Chaucer provides no answers. It is dangerously close to treating the Pardoner in the past tense, as historical personage or dramatic incarnation to whom there is more than the deft caricature which Chaucer supplies. Secondly, in the words of David V. Harrington, 'Chaucer's interest in psychological consistency is apparently rather limited'; and, after summing up the occasional psychological insights into the Pardoner that Chaucer allows, Harrington adds:

> . . . all of these are immediately apparent psychological effects. There are no ponderable subtleties. One can catch the ironies in each case without slackening the pace of his reading.[5]

Whatever psychological depth of characterisation we may feel, it proves to be illusory on close examination. This is of course true of all characterisation in fiction, but it must be emphasised, I think, that there is a difference in kind between Chaucer's treatment of character and that in a Shakespeare play (even when we have laid Bradleyan hypothesis aside) or a nineteenth-century novel; and critics' attempts to compare the Pardoner to Edmund in *King Lear* or Fyodor Karamazov[6] cannot fail to remind us of that difference. The point at which the psychologically-minded critic may be accused of sentimentality comes remarkably early in Chaucer studies. For Chaucer does not try hard for verisimilitude, and he does not invite a willing suspension of disbelief. If we keep in mind the portrait of the Pardoner in the General Prologue, we should have to compare him with one of those improbable, overblown and foul-minded fops of Restoration comedy. The two-dimensional type, not the three-dimensional individual, predominates.

For critics who have felt the quality of Chaucer's Pardoner as a type, the second approach has seemed more fruitful—that is, the rationalisation of the Pardoner's Tale by seeing in it the true analysis of the spiritual condition which the Pardoner embodies. So R. F. Miller applied Curry's account of the Pardoner as eunuch to his internal state and found in it the key to the Tale. The Pardoner, as an unholy eunuch, perverting the letter of Christian doctrine and ignoring its spirit, reflects his own sin and despair not only in the three 'riotoures' but also, and most significantly, in the Old Man; for the Old Man, like the Pardoner himself, is the *vetus homo*, the Old Adam, earthbound and perennially unregenerate.[7] This interpretation has been modified by Lee W. Patterson, who would see the Pardoner as a more common exegetical type —the tree that bears no fruit—but would agree with Miller's idea of the Tale as mirror of the Pardoner's true sin, and would supplement the parallel between the Pardoner and his old man with the tree of the Tale whose fruit is money and death. For Patterson, the Tale 'read spiritually . . . is a moral allegory about the Pardoner himself, and it figures not avarice but despair'.[8] On this reading the old man embodies failed penance, in the private hell of his and the Pardoner's despair. I confess that I am not quite convinced by precise attempts to link the Pardoner with any of the characters of his Tale: particularly to equate the old man with the Pardoner seems to me an effort to resolve one set of ambiguities by courting another.

In a less precise sense, the Tale unquestionably tells us something about the Pardoner. It tells us what Chaucer has already had him tell us throughout his Prologue, that he has marked its moral but has no intention of inwardly digesting it. It is a sign of the richness and symbolic (or archetypical) allusiveness of the Tale that almost any element may be extrapolated from it—or projected into it—and the product plausibly offered as a 'key'. On the other hand, the weakness of such readings is that—by seeing the Tale as a tidy epitome of its narrator—they trivialise its moralistic, still more its poetic, grandeur. So much of that richness and allusiveness is not accounted for. This is a key of sorts, but it does not open much more than the broom cupboard.

Yet I do not seek to add to the 'critical diversity'; what I propose will be consistent with, and is indebted to, several extant interpretations.[9] What I propose is a restructuring of the terms and framework of the debate. Many studies of the Pardoner implicitly treat Chaucer as a novelist—they move in an orderly manner through the General Prologue, the Pardoner's interruption of the Wife of Bath, his Tale, and his social destruction by the Host. R. M. Lumiansky, for instance, would see a developing characterisation of the Pardoner: he has been trying to sell his relics all along, and fumbles his opportunity at the last moment. Most, if not all, studies consider the Pardoner's Prologue and Tale in a block, as a consistent and unified performance. This may lead to some superb criticism—such as Donald R. Howard's recent discussion of the Pardoner as actor[10]—but it would not seem to be the only way of looking at the Pardoner; and it is a viewpoint from which we may easily lose sight of Chaucer as shaping artist. Moreover, it does not give full play to the obvious structural division into Prologue and Tale. I intend to explore this division. For if the central critical challenge of the Pardoner is Chaucer's juxtaposition of teller and tale, this is directly presented as a structural dichotomy—of Tale and Prologue or, more accurately, of Tale and frame. I propose to treat the Tale, in the first place, separately from its frame.

For this purpose I would classify lines 463 to 903 as the Tale proper, and everything else as frame. The frame then includes not only the Pardoner's Prologue and the 'afterthought' (919) which leads to the Host's rejoinder, but also lines 904–18, which are normally regarded as the end of the Tale itself. In these lines, the Pardoner returns to his insistence solely on the sin of avarice, which has been the central feature of his Prologue but has played no overt part in his commentary during the Tale:

> Now, goode men, God foryeve yow youre trespas,
> And ware yow fro the synne of avarice! (906–14)

It includes in the frame his habitual sermon peroration, attempting to sell his pardons to the 'lewed' folk (906–14), and the famous benediction of the pilgrims in which Kittredge saw a 'paroxysm of sincerity':

> And lo, sires, thus I preche.
> And Jhesu Crist, that is oure soules leche,
> So graunte yow his pardoun to receyve,
> For that is best; I wol yow nat deceyve.   (915–18)

It is proper, I think, to treat these fifteen lines as part of the frame, for they return us to the Canterbury pilgrimage and the self-consciously fraudulent Pardoner of the Prologue. I may be thought to prejudge the issue by my use of the word 'frame'. But it is the normal critical term, and it is my case that what I call frame *is* frame: its primary function is to draw attention to the Tale itself. Its secondary function is to mirror the importance of the Pardoner as an uncomfortable reflex of the ingenious artefact that is *The Canterbury Tales*.

II

The Pardoner is a professional preacher, and his Tale resembles a sermon in content and rhetoric;[11] but it is a tale rather than a sermon. This is evident from the end of the Pardoner's Prologue:

> 'For though myself be a ful vicious man,
> A moral tale yet I yow telle kan,
> Which I am wont to preche for to wynne.
> Now hoold youre pees! my tale I wol bigynne.'   (459–62)

The imperative addressed to the pilgrims in line 462—'Now hoold youre pees!'—should not be taken as a sign of his contempt for them, or as stemming from his fear of interruption. It is a formula of oral delivery which Chaucer has drawn from the sort of Middle English romance that he affectionately parodies in *Sir Thopas* ('Now holde youre mouth, par charitee'),[12] and it signals the transition to a narrative. The Pardoner also tells us that he is in the habit of preaching this particular story: the story, then, is a sermon *exemplum*. So was Chaucer's source for the Friar's Tale; and in this context the Pardoner's Tale is not much more of a sermon than the Friar's. Both Tales give an exemplum largely emancipated from its original homiletic context. The difference is that the Friar's Tale is almost exclusively narrative. Only at the end does the Friar remind his audience that he could have embellished his exemplum with homiletic digressions or a sermon frame ('After the text of Crist, Paul, and John / And of oure othere doctours many oon').[13] The Pardoner, however, is concerned with establishing his 'compaigny / Of yonge folk' (463–4) as an epitome of vice. No sooner has the narrative opened than it moves, by means of a catalogue of sins, into the long sermon digression denouncing them (483–659)—a digression which leads so far away from the narrative that a fresh start is necessary in line 660, 'But, sires, now wol I telle forth my tale'.

The denunciation of vices involved in these lines is germane to the purpose of the Tale. It is not quite enough, then, to call it a digression. For the Pardoner is setting the scene of his narrative: the spiritual condition of the three 'riotoures' is essential to an understanding of their actions and their fate. We have already been told that 'eche of hem at otheres synne lough' (476). The narrative, when it occurs, would demand a moral commentary of some kind. Our responses are all the more controlled, and the narrative all the more successful, for our having had it in advance. Nor can the denunciation of gluttony, lechery, gambling and swearing be criticised as irrelevant in a sermon ostensibly condemning avarice. The Tale is not a sermon for all that its moral commentary is extracted from one. The Pardoner's theme in the Tale is a more general one than *Radix malorum est cupiditas*, something more like the moral of the Physician's Tale that precedes his own—'Forsaketh synne, er synne yow forsake' (286). Avarice appears not in the commentary but in the narrative itself, as the immediate motive for murder, as the superbly literal realisation of the doctrine that sin is death. Part of the point of the Pardoner's Tale is the very number of sins that lead to death. For nobody in Chaucer's day would have thought of the Deadly Sins as seven separate compartments. They are overlapping classification of what nowadays we call a lifestyle.

There is good reason, then, for the denunciation of vices to be where we find it: and there is nothing in the denunciation that is unorthodox or unusual in the context of fourteenth-century Christian teaching. Chaucer seems to have been scrupulous in rendering approved sources, one of which, the *De Contemptu Mundi* of Pope Innocent III, he is known to have translated, others of which (Jerome's *Adversus Jovinianum*, Seneca's Epistles) he may have read or merely come across salient lines anthologised in friars' preaching manuals. Diatribes against a host of particular sins were a staple form of medieval preaching, and it is inconceivable that they held much potential for amusement. We have the example of Chaucer's near-contemporary, San Bernardino of Siena:

'The reasons why God hates you,' said Fra Bernardino one day to his congregation in Siena, 'are called vanity, curiosity and self-indulgence', and to this list he added, on another occasion, the sins of avarice, sodomy, blasphemy, vindictiveness, fickleness, factiousness and arrogance . . .[14]

One of San Bernardino's favourite topics was the evil of gambling, preached in language at least as fierce as the Pardoner's and showing a considerably more detailed knowledge of the games than the Pardoner's 'Sevene is my chaunce, and thyn is cynk and treye!' (653). Much of what is most lurid, and most clearly visualised, in the Pardoner's Tale is directly translated from Pope Innocent's treatise, especially in the violent tirade against gluttony: the debt includes Chaucer's translation of Innocent's scholastic wordplay, that cooks 'turnen substaunce into accident' (539). However, intemperate this part of the Padoner's Tale may seem today, it is mild stuff beside Innocent's work: Innocent's title, Contempt for the World, is no understatement. The Pardoner's frenzied apostrophe to the human intestines

> O wombe! O bely! O stynkyng cod,
> Fulfilled of dong and of corrupcioun! (534–5)

is more in tune with the view of most medieval divines than St Paul's advice to 'use a little wine for thy stomach's sake' (1 Timothy v:23).

The high place given to gluttony among the sins is also typical of medieval theology. When Chaucer has the Pardoner attribute to it the Fall (505–12) he is echoing the opinion of St Jerome. That opinion is grounded on two ideas. Firstly, as the Pardoner says, when man eats or drinks he is taking into his body the corruption of the world, and to eat or drink in excess is therefore a sin against the spirit. Secondly, gluttony is seen metaphorically as an enemy of human consciousness (as drunkenness is literally), and thus a denial of the central Christian mystery, the eucharist, in which earthly bread and wine is transubstantiated into the body and blood of Christ. Gluttony is therefore a rejection of one's neighbour (when one man's plenty is another's want) and of Christ. In the same way, 'ydel sweryng', by taking the divine name in vain, denies its reality, and gambling involves a superstitious confidence in luck rather than grace.

It is tempting to go further by seeing, in the denial of Christ which these sins all imply, the Pardoner's own perversion of the letter and disregard of the spirit. There is indeed an undeniable irony in this, but Chaucer does not draw attention to it in these many lines of moralising. Exegetical interpretations of the Pardoner's Tale make some play of the fact that the Pardoner is a false exegete like the Wife of Bath:[15] he quotes out of context, and he sometimes fails to meet the spirit of the context surrounding whatever he quotes. For example, in lines 483–4 the Pardoner refers us to Ephesians 5.18, 'And be not drunk with wine, wherein is excess', but—the argument would run—ignores the rest of the verse, 'but be filled with the Spirit'. Much the same occurs in his use of Philippians iii:18–19, closely translated in lines 528–32:

> The apostle wepyng seith ful pitously,
> 'Ther walken manye of whiche yow tolde have I—
> I seye it now wepyng, with pitous voys—
> That they been enemys of Cristes croys,
> Of whiche the ende is death, wombe is hir god!'

Stephan A. Khinoy (p. 262) considers this 'one of the most brilliant' of the 'ironies' of the Tale: the Pardoner is somehow trivialising Paul's words by using them merely as a text against gluttony. This is all indefensible. If we turn to gluttony in Chaucer's own Parson's Tale, we find that the Parson, like the Pardoner, asserts that gluttony caused the Fall ('This synne corrumped al this world, as is wel shewed in the synne of Adam and Eve') and proceeds immediately to quote exactly the same verses, Philippians iii:18–19, which he introduces by saying: 'Looke eek what seith Seint Paul of Glotonye' (Parson's Tale, 818). If we accuse the Pardoner of false exegesis, we must extend the accusation to the Parson, Pope Innocent III and St Jerome. It hardly seem probable that there are any closely textured 'ironies' of the kind detected by Khinoy in this section of the Tale.

What Khinoy wants is to feel the Pardoner's continuous pressure through-out the Tale: 'our attention is riveted on the Pardoner'. I find it hard to believe that any teacher would agree with this who has attempted 'close reading' of lines 483–659 in front of a class of increasingly restless students. We may expect the Pardoner's presence: but it would seem as if the only way to avoid disappointment is to conjure with untenable ironies. The language in which criticism is conducted may unintentionally foster what, in imitation of

Sedgewick, we may call the 'psychology heresy'. Even in this brief discussion so far, I have not avoided constructions like 'the Pardoner sets out' or 'the Pardoner says'. It would be too clumsy to keep emphasising that Chaucer has the Pardoner set out to say whatever he says. Chaucer has given us the name of a fictitious narrator and there seems no harm in using it. But we should not mistake the name for the thing itself. When I use such shorthand I am not psychoanalysing the Pardoner but evaluating the literary content and effect of certain lines attributed to him.

I see nothing in the Tale to bring to mind the malevolent charisma delineated in the Prologue. There are only a few moments in lines 483–659 when it could be claimed that Chaucer intends us to focus on the narrator's personality. Some are too slight to be material: Atilla sits a little oddly among the exempla, but it is a misreading of the text to claim that the Pardoner believes him to be an Old Testament character;[16] and the fussy Lamuel-Samuel pedantry ('Nat Samuel, but Lamuel, seye I,' 585) is convincingly presented by N. R. Haveley in terms of Chaucer's lack of confidence in his scribes.[17] Most of the rest were singled out by J. Swart, who argued that Chaucer has the Pardoner make certain character-revealing mistakes in this section: he shows too intimate a knowledge of dicing (653), too worldly an interest in wines (562–71), and bad judgement in 'the rather strange use of the name "Sampsoun" to depict the hiccoughs of a drunken man'.[18] Like most critics Swart assumes that the Pardoner is currently preaching a sermon on the theme of avarice, so that incongruities are easily detected: and, like some other critics, Swart assumes, implausibly, that the Pardoner is drunk.

These points have little substance. The one line on dicing appears in one of the four examples of oaths (651–5) which exemplify the vulgar blasphemies of riotous livers. The idea that a self-respecting medieval preacher would have blushed to repeat such oaths is misconceived: it turns a Bromyard or Bernardino into a Mr Slope. Medieval preachers were not afraid of crude examples, especially ones which made their auditors blush at what they normally took for granted. As for 'Sampsoun' and wine, especially the detail of lines 562–72: these serve to characterise, perhaps all too successfully, the befuddlement of a drunkard. Whatever we think of 'Sampsoun' as onomatopoeia, the name has its Biblical appropriateness. Samson as a Nazarite, dedicated to God, was forbidden to touch wine.[19] The drunkard is like Samson after he was shorn and 'the Lord was departed from him' (Judges, xvi:20) —blind and confused. When he thinks he is at home in Cheapside, he is 'in Spaigne, right at the toune of Lepe' (570). He is under the influence of Spanish wine, a captive—eyeless in Lepe. The drunkard thinks that he takes wine; but in reality, the wine takes him. The joke is scarcely uproarious, but there is surely no reason to postulate that its author is therefore drunk. On the contrary, he sounds too sober by half. And we should certainly refuse to keep company with the critic who sees in the apostrophe to a drunkard, 'foul artow to embrace' (552), the Pardoner's own feminoid imaginings.[20] There is far too much strain in these attempts to hear behind a speaker's voice the Pardoner's reedy treble, 'as smal as hath a goot' (A 688).

There is, however, a moment in this attack on drunkenness when I would agree that we are invited to recall the circumstances of the Canterbury pilgrimage. As Bronson noted, at the reference to dishonest commercial practices in the wine-trade of Fish St and Cheapside (562–6), a London-based audience would probably have seen a joke at the expense of the Host, whose Tabard inn stood nearby.[21] However, the subtlety points outwards—at the pilgrims—not inwards, at the Pardoner's character.

I have discussed this moralising section at some length because it is often misread, and more often neglected. Structurally, it is a digression, a loose set of sermon elements within a tale, but—to summarise—it is relevant to the concerns of the Tale, which it articulates fully and clearly; it is entirely orthodox in its theology and penitential technique, and it is not remarkably unconventional in tone of utterance. It is therefore to be taken seriously, and defeats analysis conducted in terms of 'ironies'. It seems reasonable to conclude that the explicit moral commentary does not serve to reflect the character of the Pardoner, although its style and content serve to characterise its narrator as a preacher.

And a good preacher at that. The abstract moral invective has not seemed short (few would wish it longer)—but it has in fact covered an impressive range of apposite offences in an extraordinarily brief compass. Harrington has examined the style of the Pardoner's Tale closely and well in terms of its 'narrative speed': in this section, as throughout the Tale, transitions are mostly quick, abrupt or non-existent (*asyndeton*), and the order of words or ideas is sometimes unnatural (*hyperbaton*): the effect is of a controlled haste. Rather than seeing the Pardoner as inebriated by his own verbiage or his one verifiable cup of beer, we should consider the purpose behind the effect. I would suggest that this section not only succeeds in pre-empting, and taking control over, our moral responses as we read, but also in creating a sense of frenzy, of phantasmagoria, of the lurid unreality of a life of sin that rushes headlong to death.

III

We return to the 'riotoures thre'. We are told almost nothing about them by way of background, and the Tale scarcely individualises them. When 'the yongeste' has gone to town, Chaucer speaks of 'that oon' and 'that other'. It is sobering to be reminded that 'the yongeste', with his ploy of poisoning, is not 'the worste'. What is important, however, is that they all end up the same, dead. In life they share too many vices to have distinct personalities. They function in the Tale as a pattern of action which we see laid over all the sins, one by one, of the preceding commentary. They begin as Pride of Life figures —indeed, their life *is* pride.[22] They set out in boozy mateship to recreate the terms of existence—'Deeth shal be deed, if that they may him hente' (710) —and they perish in murderous cupidity. The implication, had we time to think of it, is that perilously little separates those who through their sins deny Christ from actual homicide; and we accept the moral absolutism of the proposition because we see it happen out of its dark causality. It is the logic of those that 'haunteden folye' (464): it is the logic of folly, and the 'riotoures' are folly incarnate.

As folly they are played off against a setting of wisdom, two very different species of wisdom: the calm of youth, the boy who has already accepted death as a moral imperative (670–84), and the chastened experience of age, the old man who reminds us that there are worse things than to die. In a moral and physical setting so stark as to be open to multifold symbolic associations—the old man and the boy, the tavern, the stile, the 'croked way' (761), the treasure, the tree—the 'riotoures' choose death (768–9). Their actions express not so much sin in the abstract as the cumulative negation that is the sum and consequence of many particular sins. It can only serve to pervert friendship, blood brotherhood, and the spirit of merriment. The first 'riotour' outlines his plan for the death of the youngest by telling the third:

> '. . . Arys as though thou woldest with him *pleye*,
> And I shal ryve hym thurgh the sydes tweye
> Whil that thou strogelest with hym *as in game* . . .'   (287–9)

They proceed to commune with death over the corpse of their fellow:

> 'Now lat us sitte and drynke, and make us merie,
> And afterward we wol his body berie.'   (883–4)

After a brutish life of pleasure, they die in a ghastly parody of play. The terms of the murder agreement return us to the Pardoner's last example of an outrageous oath:

> 'By Goddes armes, if thou falsly *pleye*,
> This daggere shal thurghout thyn herte go!'   (654–5)

We have seen its literal fulfilment; we now know both the 'fruit' and the tree:

> This fruyt cometh of the bicched bones two.   (656)

The Pardoner's Tale is full of bones: the bones out of which cooks extract marrow (541), the bones with which 'hasard' is played, the bones to which one of the 'riotoures' swears ('I make avow to Goddes digne bones', 695), the old man's bones which find no rest (733), and the bones of, in all, four corpses and 'a thousand' (679)—all of them in different ways the agents or forms of death. They have their correlatives outside the Tale, in the bones of the Host's favourite oath, 'for Goddes bones',[23] and the bones which the Pardoner warns the pilgrims they may break (936). Bones—in every respect the frailty of human beings—are the theme of the Pardoner's Tale. The Tale is more than a *memento mori*. It is a literary charnel house.

We should take at least some of the Tale's morality: we should be diffident as critics about extracting the marrow from these bones. I do not mean that published criticism of the Tale is unhelpful. It is useful to have clearly articulated elements which may have played a part in our response to the Tale on a less than conscious level: that the three 'riotoures' are exactly an unholy trinity; that two of them drinking under a tree over the body of the third is symbolically a violent perversion of the mass;[24] that the old man is at once the exact opposite of the three 'riotoures'[25] and the frightful realisation of what they want, life without death.[26] But criticism tends to be tidy, and we are unfortunately vulnerable to that tidiness if we have responded properly to the Tale, allowing it to work on us without seeking precise symbolic equivalences. It does not at first sight seem a great step to agree with Miller that the old man of

the Tale is the Old Man of St Paul; but we should be stopped firmly in our tracks by the ramifications, not least the preposterous notion that the mother of the young boy (684) 'is' the Church.[27] This is one of many explanations of the old man that fail to explain very much. He can, for example, hardly be the figure of Death, since he speaks of Death's spurning him (727); he is an intimate of Death (622), but all old people are—one is reminded of Anatole France's adage that old age is the only means yet devised of living a long life. He could conceivably be the figure of Old Age; but since Old Age is conventionally portrayed as an old man, this scarcely advances us.[28] It takes a wise and learned critic, J. M. Steadman, to sift through conflicting theories and tell us what we should always have known: that the old man is not quite any old man but a typical, or prototypical, or archetypal old man.[29]

The old man, in fact, is a challenge to our imaginations: he is whatever we think—of old age and of death. If we think him sinister, we must face the fact (and it would be an interesting fact) that we are sympathising with the 'riotoures'. If we think him good, we esteem his Christian resignation to suffering (726, 749, 766). If we think him pathetic, we respond to his near-despair (721–38). So it is with the tree and the treasure buried in a field. The Bible offers us a fair number of each, and to choose one would be to limit needlessly the potential for suggestiveness. Both are central Christian images, and more yet: they are archetypes. It is even intrusive to be told which archetypes.[30] One develops a great respect for criticism tactful enough to speak of 'elemental' forces in the Pardoner's Tale.[31]

The Tale has a splendidly understated and unemotive apotheosis—the remaining 'riotoures' drink the poisoned wine: 'For which anon they storven bothe two' (888). Never has summary narrative been used more effectively to postpone a climax. Then, in an abrupt transition of style, Chaucer combines an appeal to authority with the 'overdoing topos' ('their end was as awful as all Avicenna's symptoms put together') in lines 889–94. The end of the narrative inaugurates a brief reprise of the 'moral':

> O cursed synne of alle cursednesse!
> O traytours homycide, O wikkednesse!
> O glotonye, luxurie, and hasardrye!
> Thou blasphemour of Crist with vileynye
> And othes grete, of usage and of pride! (895–9)

This is a final parade of all the sins involved in the Tale, ending with the cornerstone sin of pride (899). With its repeated *exclamatio*, the *adnominatio* of 895, its concentration of abstract Romance nouns (homycide, luxurie, vileynye, usage), it is Chaucer's highest style—the style which his aureate fifteenth-century successors sought assiduously to emulate. The *exclamatio* edges into the *apostrophe* of 900–3, into vocabulary which is less ostentatious, and into one sustained syntactic construction; and the 'Thou' of 898 is specified—it is not a sin, but mankind itself:

> Allas, mankynde, how may it bitide
> That to thy creatour, which that the wroghte,
> And with his precious herte-blood thee boghte,
> Thou art so fals and so unkynde, allas? (900–3)

The 'riotoures thre' of the Tale have yielded place to the sins of which they were the product. The target now is all who indulge in gluttony, lechery, blasphemy and trust in luck rather than grace: mankind, familiarly, even tenderly apostrophised as 'Thou'.

In a moment the voice of the crass Pardoner will break in. We are to move from 'mankynde' to 'goode men' (904), from the anguish of original sin to special pleading against avarice (905). Yet nothing can detract from the spiritual magnificence and passionate intensity of these closing lines. They are the true climax of the Tale: and it is a lamentable consequence of the 'psychology heresy' that they have been undervalued beside the infinitely less effective benediction of lines 916–18. Chaucer, who cared about such matters, never wrote half so stirring a call to repentance. It would take one of the 'riotoures' themselves not to be radically moved. And we, in return, should not diminish the penitential and poetic stature of these lines, simple but totally involving, by reading into them the imprint of the phony Pardoner. Indeed, so far was the glossator of the Ellesmere manuscript from such a trivial misconception that he wrote in the margin beside this passage (as beside some of the earlier moralising commentary) the one firm judgement: *Auctor*.

IV

From the extraordinary power of the Tale we move to the extravagant abnormality of the teller. We move, that is, to the frame. The first thing to be said about the portraits of the Pardoner in the General Prologue (669–714) is that it is remarkably, and comically, overdrawn. There is no need to look further than his relics, which P. E. Beichner rightly considers

> . . . ludicrous . . . a pillowcase which he said was Our Lady's veil, a piece of sail from St. Peter's boat, reliquaries crammed with rags and bones, a shoulder bone of a holy Jew's sheep, and a magic mitten. It seems to me that oftentimes the Pardoner's relics are taken too seriously.

Beichner stigmatises the 'righteous reader' who 'becomes so incensed at the fraud that he cannot laugh at the absurdity of the objects'.[32] Then there is the absurdity of the man; or rather the absurdity of an account that hints at everything and confirms virtually nothing. I do not myself see how the Summoner's 'stif burdoun' can be anything other than a bass accompaniment to the Pardoner's incongruous ditty: but some good philologists have thought otherwise. The context encourages innuendo.

Only nine lines (675–9, 688–91) are devoted to the Pardoner's physiognomy. From them, Curry concluded that the Pardoner's 'secret' is that he is a eunuch; Jill Mann found a stereotype of the liberated homosexual so overt that she wondered how the Pardoner could ever have been said to have a 'secret' at all; and Beryl Rowland, on the basis of medieval beliefs about hares and goats, argued that he is neither eunuch nor exactly homosexual but a 'testicular pseudo-hermaphrodite of the feminine type', whatever that is.[33] Of these accounts Curry's still seems the most reliable. As Donald R. Howard urges, 'the symptoms are unmistakable—after you've read Curry'. The only problem is that the pilgrims have not: for them, the Pardoner is 'a mystery, an enigma—sexually anomalous.'[34] Chaucer does not identify the anomaly. He says only

'I trowe he were a geldyng or a mare'   (691),

and geldings and mares, while far from virile, are erotic universes apart. Chaucer serves up a fine stew—like the Pardoner as he prepares to add a little saffron to pardons 'comen from Rome al hoot' (687). But the ingredients are wonderfully elusive.

We know only that this is no ordinary Pardoner—it is a 'Pardoner / Of Rouncivale' (669–70), that is, for anyone remotely familiar with the financial scandals of the 1380s, a phony Pardoner.[35] This is, for once, straightforward enough; but critics who have argued for vehement anti-clerical satire in this characterisation do not seem to have appreciated it. Since he is immediately identified as a phony, we do not know what we can believe—whether he has come from Rome, as he claims, or even whether he is in holy orders. Pardoners did not need to be, and Chaucer's use of the highly unusual noun 'ecclesiaste' in 708 ('he was in chirche a noble ecclesiaste') is not unambiguous. There is a similar ambiguity in the Pardoner's statement that he stands in the pulpit '*lyk* a clerk' (391). If the Pardoner really comes from Rouncival he would be an Austin canon, and this would add point to the fact that he wears no hood, 'for jolitee' (680). Equally, the fact that he wears no hood could be taken as undermining his pretension to be an Austin canon. It is the same with his interruption of the Wife of Bath: is he interested in the Wife's 'preaching' (see D 165), in hearing about women (D 166), or in confession (D 184–8)? Whatever inquisition we conduct, the Pardoner slips by, a phantasm of possibilities. Chaucer is having a fine game, and we are all its victims.

This is not to say that the Pardoner can be anything other than unpleasant. There have been persuasive and sophisticated readings of the Pardoner as, at heart, a good fellow, pretending to be worse than he is because he is only a humble fund-raiser, or as self-parodying, deciding to give the pilgrims the stereotyped wickedness they imagine.[36] These readings founder, however, on one crucial couplet from the General Prologue describing the Pardoner's successful frauds:

And thus, with feyned flaterye and japes,
He made the person and the peple his apes.   (705–6)

The reference here is to *babwineries*, the marginal animal grotesques of medieval manuscript illumination: it is difficult to assess their function, especially when in religious manuscripts they proliferate on the page and intrude into the pictorial space; but what they represent is clear, human activities carried on by animals—not only baboons, as their name suggests, but also, for example, the famous rabbits of the Luttrell Psalter. Their effect has little in common with Beatrix Potter: they are intentionally disturbing. They ornament the page and they draw attention to the text, but at the same time they represent a distorted, belittling view of human activity. Like the Yahoos they present us with a view of ourselves so reductive that we do not want to entertain it as sane. They can make us laugh, but such laughter may not itself be healthy, any more than the laughter of the 'riotoures' at each other's sins is healthy. Chaucer's Parson speaks of 'the synnes of japeres, that been the develes apes; for they maken folk to laugh at hire japerie as folk doon at the gawdes of an ape' (Parson's Tale, 650). To turn people into apes is to carry them off into an alien half-light. It is no pleasant thing: in modern stereotypes it has more to do with mad scientists than whimsical wizards. The portrait of the Pardoner is grotesque, and his function is to show us the grotesque in ourselves.[37] And the grotesque challenges our selves and our world.

The Pardoner's Prologue is an analysis of the challenge. It is the Pardoner's response to the Host's request for 'som myrthe or japes' (319) and the amended request from 'thise gentils' for 'som moral thyng' and 'som wit' (323–6). The Pardoner seems to interpret 'wit' in its sense of 'strategem' (OED, 6c), and in outlining his scheme of fraud all too literally fulfils his promise of 'som honest thyng' (328). The ingenuities of his technique and his total pride in them require little further close analysis. Generally, it is worth repeating Charles Mitchell's comment: 'The Pardoner is able to fool the sinful because the sinful first fool themselves.'[38] It is also worth remembering that the Pardoner's theme, *Radix malorum est cupiditas*, is taken from St Paul's first epistle to Timothy, and that the whole epistle is written as a warning to the Ephesians against their habit of paying attention to false teachers. The epistle has several points of resemblance to the Pardoner's Tale: the main sin denounced is blasphemy, allied (as in iii:3) to drinking and covetousness; and some stress is laid upon respect for the aged (as in v:1, 'Rebuke not an elder, but intreat him as a father.').

A third general point deserves special emphasis. It is well known that the Pardoner's Prologue is based on the figure of Faux-Semblant in the *Roman de la Rose*.[39] Unfortunately, it is so well known that we mostly take it for granted. In fact, the relation of the Pardoner to Faux-Semblant is so close that he can scarcely be considered, in his Prologue, as an entirely independent creation.

The C-Group of the *Canterbury Tales* seems to have been shaped by Chaucer's reading of the *Roman de la Rose*. In Amant's long colloquy with Reason (4221–7230) we find Reason speaking of poverty and wealth. This involves a denunciation of those who spend their money and talents carousing in taverns, and passes on immediately to an attack on avaricious physicians. This brings to mind the portrait of the Physician in the General Prologue, whose tale opens the C-Group. Reason's next theme is the falsity of avaricious preachers, who, to quote the Middle English translation (fragment B2),

> prechen for to get
> Worshipes, honour and richesse . . .
> And outward shewen holynesse,
> Though they be full of cursidnesse.
> Not liche to the apostles twelve,
> They deceyve other and hemselve. (5746–7, 5755–8)

The resemblances to the Pardoner's Prologue are manifest (see particularly 400–4, 421–2, 447). The next lines are even more striking—they are the programme for the *Roman*'s later character, Faux-Semblant, and for Chaucer's Pardoner:

> For prechyng of a cursed man,
> Though it to other may profite,
> Hymsilf it availeth not a myte;
> For ofte good predicacioun
> Cometh of evel entencioun.
> To hym not vailith his preching,
> All helpe he other with his teching:
> For where they good ensaumple take,
> There is he with veynglorie shake.   (5760–8)

We can only regard these lines as the direct source for some key lines of the Pardoner's Prologue:

> For certes, many a predicacioun
> Cometh ofte tyme of yvel entencioun;
> Som for pleasaunce of folk and flaterye,
> To ben avaunced by ypocrisye,
> And some for veyne glorie, and som for hate.   (407–11)

> But though myself be gilty in that synne,
> Yet kan I maken oother folk to twynne
> From avarice, and soore to repente.
> But that is nat my principal entente . . .   (429–32)

In this section of the *Roman*, Reason's scrupulous honesty leads her to be direct in her language; and in a famous passage Amant objects to her use of the word *coilles*. Reason replies that she alone has the power to name things: she could have called 'coilles' 'relics' and 'relics' 'coilles' (6928–7115). As Khinoy shows,[40] it is inconceivable that Chaucer does not have these lines in mind when he has the Host silence the Pardoner:

> I wolde I hadde thy coillons in myn hond
> In stide of relikes or of seintuarie.   (952–3)

Chaucer's implication (the Host appears oblivious to it) is that the Pardoner's testicles are as phony as his relics. This whole fragment of the *Canterbury Tales*, then, is shaped by Chaucer's reminiscence of the *Roman*.

We have not yet considered Faux-Semblant. Here there is a proximity in language to the C fragment of the English *Romaunt* (as there is to the B2 fragment in the lines already quoted) sufficient to make it probable that Chaucer worked from the translation.[41] This in itself is odd: Chaucer claimed to have translated the *Roman*, and it is improbable that the B2 and C fragments of the *Romaunt* are his work.[42] Since there is no way of dating the B2 and C fragments at all precisely (the only extant manuscript is of the mid-fifteenth century), we cannot even rule out the possibility that a later translator recognised in the Pardoner an imitation of Faux-Semblant and included reminiscences of the Pardoner's Prologue in his translation. However, it is more likely that Chaucer never completed a translation of the whole *Roman*, and used the work of others for his version of Faux-Semblant. Faux-Semblant, the allegorical personification of false seeming, is called upon by the god of love to make a true revelation of his life and practices. At first feigning horror, Faux-Semblant complies: wearing the habit of a friar, he exemplifies the type of the false preacher condemned by Reason. His techniques, as he reveals them, are the pattern and prototype of the Pardoner's Prologue.[43] His motivation,

> To wynnen is alwey myn entente   (6837)

is exactly that of the Pardoner,

> For myn entente is nat but for to wynne.   (403)

He is an apocalyptic force; as he reveals, he is one of Antichrist's men (7009), serving his father Guile, Emperor of the world (7213–4). He concludes with what could almost be the Pardoner's motivation for his final offer of pardons to the Canterbury company:

> But unto you dar I not lye;
> But myght I felen or aspye
> That ye perceyved it no thyng,
> Ye shulde have a stark lesyng
> Right in youre honde, thus, to bigynne;
> I nolde it lette for no synne.   (7287–92)

The response of the court of Love to his truthful 'confession' is laughter, like that of the pilgrims after the final exchange with the Host (961).

The overwhelming implication of the evidence is that Chaucer intends us to recognise in his Pardoner a type of Faux-Semblant, or rather the quintessence of false seeming. His presentation of the Pardoner operates on two levels: the Pardoner is the most abnormal and eccentric 'character' of all the pilgrims; and he is an abstraction, characterised morally not physically (we are not invited during his Prologue to recall the sexual peccadilloes of the General Prologue) and embodying the false seeming in us all. False seeming is our acceptance of our own hypocrisy, our smugness about failing to match ethics with actions, our cultivated internal blindness. False seeming is the opposite of truth. It is the pleasure we derive from double standards and, in the Pardoner's case, from a knowing denial of Christ: 'What is Truth, said jesting Pilate: and would not stay for an answer.'[44]

It is in this light that we should approach the last part of this careful frame (904–68). The Pardoner is the Pardoner, but he is also False Seeming. As the Pardoner, he is the image of Pride as defined by the Parson, and he may have fallen into the last manifestation of pride which the Parson discusses: 'Jang-lynge is when a man speketh to muche biforn folk, and clappeth as a mille, and taketh no keep what he seith' (405). He is the proud man as defined in 1 Timothy vi, five verses above the Pardoner's text, 'Knowing nothing, but doting about questions and strifes of words, whereof cometh envy, strife, railings, evil surmisings.' We could gloss the ending in these terms: the Pardoner, albeit in jest (I cannot believe that he seriously thinks to transact a sale) 'jangles', and is crushed by the 'strife' and 'railings' that are the consequences. He is crushed by the Host's (seemingly unknowing) reference to the one thing that the Pardoner has overlooked and cannot avoid: his own biology. The Host is the Pardoner's target because he keeps a tavern and sells wine, and because he is the leader of the company. He responds as he does because no man likes to be singled out as 'moost envoluped in synne' (942), and because, having been lulled by the Pardoner's confidences into mental complicity, into a sense of superiority over the 'lewed folk', he is alienated by the Pardoner's sudden show of contempt. Some such psychological speculation, at any rate, would do. In his rejoinder the Host himself oversteps the mark, and both Pardoner and Host are brought into line by a perfunctory kiss of peace, 'and ryden forth hire weye' (968).

But there is more to it than this. The Host is leader of the pilgrims, and he presides over a fragile game of story-telling. It is a game of fiction to pass the time on a pilgrimage of earnest Christian intent, and for a more fundamentalist medieval Christian than Chaucer this way of spending the time could have been grounds for unease. St Paul, after all, exhorted Timothy to 'refuse profane and old wives' fables, exercise thyself rather unto godliness' (1 Timothy iv:7). The rules of the game, as the Host interprets them, are antipathetic to preaching. When urging the Clerk to 'telle us som myrie tale' (E 9), the Host explicitly contrasts 'pley' and preaching:

> 'For what man that is entred in a pley,
> He nedes mote unto the pley assente.
> But precheth nat, as freres doon in Lente,
> To make us for oure olde synnes wepe . . .'   (E 10–13)[45]

These are rules which the Clerk observes only 'as fer as resoun axeth' (25), and which the idealised Parson will have nothing to do with at all: 'Thou getest fable noon ytoold for me' (I 31). The Host seeks to prevent the Parson from following the Man of Law on the grounds that 'we schal han a predicacioun' (B 1176), and the Shipman lends support ('heer schal he nat preche' 1179). The Parson must wait his turn until twilight near Canterbury when 'as it semed, it was for to doone, / To enden in som vertuous sentence' (I 62–3); and the Parson gets by with citing Paul's prohibition to Timothy (I 32–4). The purpose of the pilgrimage, then, is penitence—but until this last stage the company will hear nothing of it. When 'thise gentils' ask the Pardoner for 'som moral thyng', they probably have in mind a tastefully sensational saint's life, like the Prioress's or Second Nun's tales, conducive to a certain soporific piety. The Pardoner in this tale offers them instead a rousing call to repentance, a clamorous 'Vigilate!' It is in his Tale not his Prologue that he breaks the rules. The rules of play establish a holiday, a space and context within which the normal moral judgements are inapplicable, *Saturnalia* in which a phony Pardoner is all part of the fun. Such play is easily punctured by truths as uncompromisingly vivid as those of the Pardoner's Tale.

It is probably not over-ingenious, in retrospect, to see the Tale as containing several challenges to the pilgrims. This is the one tale which does not begin, at least, in movement along the road but in stasis, as the Pardoner toys with his cakes and ale. It virulently attacks dicing, which it calls 'pley'. On the level of wordplay there is some room for discomfort. The 'riotoures', like the pilgrims, are 'a compaignye'; like the pilgrims, they contract friendship, and they draw lots like the pilgrims did when 'the cut fil to the knyght' (A 845). The murder-plot of the Tale is a travesty of play. The Tale shows that the friendship of the 'riotoures' is false. The Host's reaction to the Pardoner's last jest suggests much the same about the company. For the Host is as pleased to be reminded of Christian morality as the 'riotoures' were enchanted by the old man. I have noted the possible attack on the Host in the section on wines (562–72), and we may note further that the Pardoner's echo of the Host's malapropistic oath ('By Seint Ronyon' 320, cf. 310) may show that the Pardoner has already marked him out as a target. In the original design of the frame there may have been a further piquancy. The unfinished Cook's Tale shapes up as an attack on the Host. The Cook's Prologue has the Cook warning the Host not to take offence at his tale about 'an hostileer', balancing the Host's 'A man may seye ful sooth in game and pley' (A 4355) with the warning that a true jest is a bad jest (4357).

In small and subtle ways, then, the Pardoner can be seen to have put forward a grotesque, reductive view of the pilgrims and their 'pley.' However, there is no need for ingenious and detailed retrospection for us to accept this proposition. If the 'riotoures thre' of the Pardoner's Tale have expanded to be an image of 'mankynde' in the closing apostrophe, the image can hardly fail to comprehend the Canterbury pilgrims. The life of play is a life of sin. It is not constructed to stand up to a *memento mori* as cheerfully callous as the one which the Pardoner addresses to the company:

> 'Paraventure ther may fallen oon or two
> Doun of his hors, and breke his neeke atwo.
> Looke which a seuretee is it to yow alle
> That I am in youre felaweshipe yfalle,
> That may assoille yow, bothe moore and lasse,
> Whan that the soule shal fro the body passe . . .' (935–40)

These lines engender a violence, in the Host's response and the Pardoner's angry silence, which flattens the concept of game: even the Host says that he will no longer 'pleye' with the Pardoner. The best thing to do is to overlook the challenge and restore the game. The Knight acknowledges this in his request to the Pardoner: 'drawe thee neer, / And, as we diden, lat us laughe and pleye' (966–7). The reconciliation is cursory; and one of the central symbols of the Tale lingers long enough for us to wonder about the 'weye' that the pilgrims 'ryden forth' (968). The Tale, then, is shown to be subersive by its coda.

For the Pardoner is also False Seeming, and false seeming is an abstraction. It is a nasty truth about humanity. Chaucer recognises this by distributing the qualities of Faux-Semblant in the *Roman* among all his ecclesiastical characters in the General Prologue except the killjoy Parson. The Pardoner as false seeming is not the Pardoner as pardoner but a quality of the entire Canterbury company. This is how Faux-Semblant in the *Romaunt* begins to substantiate his claim that he can be *all* men:

> Full wel I can my clothis chaunge,
> Take oon, and make another straunge.
> Now am I knyght, now chastelayn,
> Now prelat, and now chapelayn,

Now prest, now clerk, and now forster;
Now am I maister, now scoler,
Now monk, now chanoun, now baily . . .   (6325–31)

It takes another type of Bailey altogether to make the connection after the Pardoner's closing address; and to respond in the manner that Faux-Semblant predicts when he demurs at the instruction of the god of love to tell the truth. His prediction is so apposite a gloss on the ending of the Pardoner's Tale that I feel justified in quoting it at some length:

For if that I telle you the sothe,
I may have harm and shame bothe.
If that my felowes wisten it,
My talis shulden me be quytt;
For certeyn, they wolde hate me,
If ever I knewe her cruelte.
For they wolde overall holde hem stille
Of trouthe that is ageyne her wille;
Such tales kepen they not heere.
I myghte eft soone bye it full deere,
If I seide of hem ony thing
That ought displesith to her heryng.
For what word that hem prikke or biteth;
In that word noon of hem deliteth,
Al were it gospel, the evangile,
That wolde reprove hem of her gile,
For they are cruel and hauteyn.   (6085–6101)

The Host is certainly 'cruel and hauteyn', and the Pardoner is certainly 'quytt'. The 'trouthe that is ageyne her wille', the 'word that hem prikke or biteth', is his Tale; and it is in the twist he provides to his Tale in his closing address. For the Pardoner's tripartite conclusion (904ff., his habitual exhortation—916ff., his conventional 'minstrel' benediction—919ff., his 'afterthought') can fairly be paraphrased as follows: 'I am a purveyor of phony pardons. I am being honest to you, and in my tale I have stressed the need for true penitence and true pardon from Christ. But I am false seeming, and I know that you are like me: I know that you will always, unto death, prefer the phony to the true. Would anyone like a phony pardon?' It is an extension of that terrible indictment of 'mankynde', and we can hardly feel that the Host has adequately answered it. The Pardoner is fully aware of absolute Christian standards. And he chooses to ignore them. He expresses, he *is*, the truth about the company, which prefers 'pley' to penitence.

The Pardoner mirrors what the pilgrims are; and he therefore mirrors what we are—for we too are 'mankynde.' The frame turns back inwards to the high Christian moral absolutism of the Tale; and it turns outwards on ourselves, as the real rather than the fictitious audience. We shrink from the absolute standards, and intractable logic, of the Tale—so much so that we base most of our criticism on nine lines of quizzical anatomy in the General Prologue. And we remain the victims of Chaucer's game. For Chaucer would have understood our reaction well enough. In its false seeming, in the tension between 'pley' and absolute Christian morality, it is the product of exactly the same mentality that ends the game which is *The Canterbury Tales* with the Retracciouns. The frame of the Pardoner's Tale highlights the potency of the Tale; and the Tale highlights our unwillingness to entertain its judgement of us.

CHAPTER 3

Chaucer's Development of Persona

I The Public Voice and Courtly Aspiration

In the Pardoner's Prologue and Tale, teller and tale, *persona* and theme, are
dramatically at odds. We should not use this disparity to modify the impact of
the tale, or to reduce the tale to a tidily ironic commentary on its teller. It
follows that Chaucer's procedure is paradoxical: by the most self-conscious of
means in the prologue, a dramatic monologue, he sets up a roundly fictionalised *persona* which until the very end of the tale we are then required to
suspend. Even though on the return to the frame the teller is to reclaim, and
abuse, the moral of the tale, the voice of the tale is not that of its ostensible
teller. The *persona* vanishes in the narrative attributed to him by an author who
asserts, then subverts, what sounds like his own voice. But only *sounds like* it:
for the voice of the *persona* effectively complicates talk of the author's 'own'
voice. Chaucer's English exercise in false seeming leaves us with the ancient
questions about rhetoric: how can a disguise do other than conceal truth, and
what is truth that can be disguised?

There is nothing new in a narratorial voice that fluctuates on a scale from
fictionalised *persona* to author: English parallels are evident, for example, in
Gower and in Langland. What is new is the flamboyance with which Chaucer
reminds us of the fluctuations, and the self-consciousness with which he
employs the two extreme points of the scale to occlude each other. On the one
hand, a fully fictionalised *persona* can turn out, in the Pardoner's Tale, to be not
so much open as absent. On the other, we may end up being all too aware that
when the Ellesmere scribe glosses '*Auctor*' beside that Tale's peroration, he is
reponding mainly to his own notions of rhetorical decorum. His is not Chaucer
the man but Chaucer the high style. Even so, we should not rest too
comfortably on modern confidence that writers never offer themselves but
only a kind of fictitious facsimile. For much medieval literature relies upon
creating a different sort of confidence, in the writer as author, as authority,
palpably present in, or presiding over, his work. The use of *persona* by both
Gower and Langland subsists in, the exploits, such a confidence. By contrast,
Chaucer's use of *persona* often serves to fictionalise the writer as much as his
creatures. The author appears as a variant version of an apocryphal voice.

This is no small difference. It points to a radical philosophical and rhetorical difference—in Chaucer's sense of the truth of poetry, and consequently his unstable attitude to 'authority'. Chaucer's work often seems to distinguish between absolute truth and contextual, poetic truth; and it often seems to serve the latter. In this sense, Chaucer is the first great English poet to be a sophist; and he develops a sophist's resources. This entails drastically different literary strategies from those employed by Gower or Langland. The Pardoner's Prologue and Tale reveal the difference. In the first place, the Tale is unusual among Chaucer's works in one very important respect: penance is at the thematic core of the poem. This is not to say that Chaucer has no interest in the value of penance. As a prose writer, he has. Nor is it to ignore his pious and hagiographic poems, the ending of the *Troilus* or his Retracciouns. It is simply to note what the Retracciouns concedes: that by penitential standards most of Chaucer's poems 'sownen into synne'. In the second place, however, the narratorial voice of the Pardoner's Tale is close to the standard voice of 'public poetry' in the last decades of the fourteenth century. This has been characterised in Chapter One. Such a public voice is normally authoritative, as befits its moral concerns. Chaucer's provision of the Pardoner-frame, his appropriation of the figure of False Seeming in this of all moral contexts, alienates the public voice from its authority and immediately produces a new and unstable literary context. It is unstable precisely because it is unauthorised; for Chaucer does not substitute one pre-existent paradigm for another. He makes his own, by *ars combinatoria*, and he makes it new. It challenges precedent, it questions authority, and it is therefore unstable by design.

Chaucer's new kind of English poetry no longer interacts, primarily, with a public value like penance but with courtliness—the 'note' of the *Parliament of Fowls* that 'imaked was in fraunce'. This is not to say that courtliness is 'modern' and penance 'old-fashioned'. Indeed, most of the models by which Chaucer was most deeply influenced belong to the thirteenth century, not the fourteenth. At times in the fourteenth century one is tempted to see courtly values as archaising, several deliberate steps behind contemporary realities. The same is surely true of Malory; but then it is no less true of Chrétien. For courtliness as a literary value is a variant of the Golden Age myth, ever receding as it is glimpsed through the wrong end of a telescope. The pastoral allegory and the Chaucerian archaisms of Spenser's *Shepheardes Calender* testify accurately to this: courtly values are in part a conservative response to change, and they are often ambivalent when circumstances of literary production become courtly in the narrower sense described by R. F. Green, when, that is, poets are within social range of a ruling élite whom they must nevertheless serve.[1] The poetic voice, no longer public, is individualised and addressed to a group of like-minded people: in this sense, 'courtly' is the opposite of 'public'. The courtliness here, in socio-historical terms, is not an accident but a substance: a value in which from writing or 'endityng' is asserted the more exclusive privilege of literature, and a particular public—for perhaps the first time in the English language—transcribes itself in the idealistic image of a 'culture'.

In Chaucer's poetry, instability of content goes hand-in-hand with instability, and unpredictability, of narratorial voice. The third and fourth chapters of this book explore this instability and the essential contribution it makes to a new poetic 'note'. This chapter deals with the development of *persona* in Chaucer's dream poetry, and the next with *Troilus* and the use of a babel of narratorial voices in the *Canterbury Tales*. I try to record both the limited number of literary resources Chaucer calls upon and their extraordinary variation to achieve many effects. There is a historical question to be faced: where did Chaucer learn his techniques of *persona*? There are also two critical tasks. The first is to show how Chaucer's use of *persona* interacts with his larger literary purposes, and becomes a protean narratorial range. The second is to put forward a method of reading Chaucer's narrators as apocryphal voices.

II *Theme and* Persona *in 'The Parliament of Fowls'*

I begin by demonstrating some of the potential of Chaucer's narratorial *persona*: its structural role in forging a new and unstable English literary form, its modes and the pitfalls it can present to modern criticism. Here I follow what is by now almost a tradition of Chaucer criticism of seeing the *Parliament of Fowls* as a kind of complex, 'closed' poetic manifesto. In this poem a public (and penitential) worldview is made to yield place to a courtly value. That value is unnamed, but might be called play or immanent delight. It interconnects the author's act, poetry itself, with the narrator's act, reading, and the concerns of the birds in the narrative, love and the ordering of instinct.

Penance is at least congenial to the 'chapitres sevene' of the *Somnium Scipionis*, with its grandly public perspective of eternal bliss as dependent on the love of 'commune profyt'—the opposite of law-breaking and lechery—and Africanus' teaching

> that oure present worldes lyves space
> Nis but a maner deth, what wey we trace,
> And rightful folk shul gon, after they dye,
> To hevene.   (53–6)[2]

From this vantage point the earth is insignificant,[3] and man should live in hope of hearing heavenly harmony, the music of the nine spheres. The spirit is that of *contemptus mundi*, flatly summarised in Africanus' advice to Scipio:

> Than bad he hym, syn erthe was so lyte,
> And ful of torment and of harde grace,
> That he ne shulde hym in the worlde delyte.   (64–6)

This account of a cosmic hierarchy is so detached from temporal concerns as to parallel Troilus' view from the eighth sphere or the more humorous view of the earth as a mere pinprick afforded to Chaucer as narrator of the *House of Fame* from aboard a talkative eagle. This lofty view is contrasted with the substance of the dream itself, the actual parliament of fowls in which the concern is mundane enough to be centred upon the question of sexual coupling. The contrast is subtle, and its realisation rests with the narrator.

The dreamer of the *Parliament*, like that of the earlier poems and the *Troilus* narrator, is presented as a poet who is anxious about love rather than in love—and anxious too about the role of the poetic imagination caught within an existence that is transitory. The poem therefore commences with a confident display of oxymoronic rhetoric purporting to translate the maxim *Ars longa vita brevis* but referring, ostensibly, to love in place of art:

> The lyf so short, the craft so long to lerne,
> Th'assay so hard, so sharp the conquerynge,
> The dredful joye, alwey that slit so yerne:
> Al this mene I by Love . . .   (1–4)

In this opening Chaucer implies that for him 'art' and 'love' are synonymous. He claims that his knowledge of love, as narrator, is vicarious, and that he, like Pandarus, cannot speak from successful experience. The disclaimer 'For al be that I knowe nat Love in dede' (8) refers to a specific kind of love, that found in European love literature, just as the weight of the first stanza lies in its last line, 'Nat wot I wel wher that I flete or synke' (8)—that is, in the narrator's proud assertion that he works in a state of articulate ignorance. In the third stanza, Chaucer plays on the notion of vicarious experience, that of reading books 'Of usage—what for lust and what for lore' (15), and contrives to lay almost pedantic stress on the fact that he reads books habitually, and recently read a certain book in particular. His enigmatic statement of motive, that he read this book 'a certeyn thyng to lerne' (20), sets the first conundrum of the poem: what is the 'certeyn thyng'? Chaucer supplements his account with a slightly fuller statement at the end of stanza four:

> To rede forth hit gan me so delite,
> That al that day me thoughte but a lyte.   (27–8)

This is the end of the introduction, and it marks a pronounced shift in tone. The keyword is 'delite', and we are prepared for an interaction between the 'certeyn thyng to lerne' and delight which is the dominant theme of the poem.

Delight is just what the 'lore' of the *Somnium Scipionis* fails to provide. The *Somnium*'s message is social, but it is hardly sociable. As light fades, Chaucer lays down his book in a mood—'fulfyld of thought and busy hevynesse' (89)—which is best described as dissatisfied:

> For bothe I hadde thyng which that I nolde,
> And ek I nadde that thyng that I wolde.   (90–1)

The thing he has which he did not want is a set of good abstract spiritual and intellectual reasons, on good authority, to despise the world. The thing he does not have, and what he wants, is a set of equally good reasons to delight in it. As a good student of the *Roman de la Rose*, Chaucer knows where he may find it:

> For suche solace, suche ioy and pley,
> I trowe that neuer man ne sey,
> As was in that place delycious.
> The gardyn was not daungerous
> To herberowe byrdes many one.
> So ryche a yerd was neuer none
> Of byrdes songe, and braunches grene.
> Therein were byrdes mo, I wene,
> Than ben in al the realme of Fraunce.
> Ful blysful was the accordaunce
> Of swete, pytous songe they made,

For all this worlde it ought glade.
And I myselfe so mery ferde
Whan I her blysful songes herde,
That for an hundred pounde nolde I
If that the passage openly
Had be vnto me free,
That I nolde entren for to se
Th'assemble—God kepe it fro care—
Of byrdes whiche therin ware,
That songen, through her mery throtes,
Daunces of loue, and mery notes.

(Romaunt of the Rose, 487–508)[4]

In the *Parliament*-narrator's mood of dissatisfaction, the act of reading,
which had seemed a delight, is now characterised very differently, as a
chore—a 'labour' from which his 'spirit' must take rest (92–4). He goes to
sleep, having, as it were, flung down an intellectual challenge to Africanus; and
Africanus, when he appears to the narrator as he sleeps, takes a rather
defensive attitude to his own advice as recorded in the *Somnium Scipionis*, 'myn
olde bok totorn' (110), accepting that the poet's reading of it is a 'labour' which
deserves repayment (112). There follows a brief invocation to Cytherea, the
benign aspect of Venus, and the dreamer's sudden removal by Africanus to the
gates of a park whose two doors carry inscriptions alluding to the two kinds of
love and, one might add, of art: the one that offers

> the welle of grace,
> There grene and lusty May shal evere endure   (129–30);

and the other that offers 'the mortal strokes of the spere' (135), a state of
sterility which may equally well apply to poetic imagination as to love:

> Ther nevere tre shal fruyt ne leves bere;
> This strem yow ledeth to the sorweful were
> There as the fish in prysoun is al drye.   (137–9)

The dreamer stands astonished; and while he is busy expressing his astonishment in an epic simile, Africanus shoves him through the gates without
ceremony and with a reminder that since Chaucer is not a servant of Love, he
may enter the park as a neutral observer. Again, Africanus gives prominence to
Chaucer's capacity for vicarious experience:

> But natheles, although that thow be dul,
> Yit that thow canst not do, yit mayst thow se.   (162–3)

Africanus associates this with the dreamer's position as a poet (hence my use of
'Chaucer' as the narrator's name, legitimate as long as we remember that such a
'Chaucer' is a self-fictionalisation):

> And if thow haddest connyng for t'endite,
> I shal the shewe mater of to wryte.   (167–8)

40

Again, we see there the interplay of love and art in this poem, an interplay which began when Chaucer in his opening lines twisted the aphorism '*ars longa, vita brevis*' by adding the gloss 'Al this mene I be Love'—knowing as he did so, I think, that the aphorism was too familiar to succumb to such casual rewriting. Love here seems to be the vehicle for a discussion of art, an impression which is confirmed when we see what lies within the garden. In the first of three stanzas (190–6) the song of the birds is compared to that of angels in its harmony, and the second stanza (197–203) adds that God the creator could never have heard more beautiful music. Earthly creation thus answers the colder music of the spheres. The description of the animals in the garden has all the energetic immobility of a medieval tapestry, and the clear statement in the third stanza (204–10) that this world precludes ageing and excludes time confirms that we have entered a world of artifice, a world animated with a more concentrated life than temporal existence because Chaucer's poetry compels it to be so:

> No man may there waxe sek ne old;
> Yit was there joye more a thousandfold
> Than man can telle; ne nevere wolde it nyghte,
> But ay cler day to any manes syghte.   (207–10)

This type of artifice is at once contrasted with false artifice, which is the area around and inside the temple of Venus, and its description opens with a dreary list of allegorical abstractions, some good, some bad, all essentially meaningless not because they inhabit a world of artifice but because they are themselves, as presented, artificial. The timelessness of this world is an effort to maintain and a labour to perform. Of the maidens who dance in front of the temple, we are told 'That was here offyce alwey, yer be yeere' (236); and before the temple door sits 'Dame Pacience . . . / With face pale, upon an hil of sond' (242–3). Her hill of sand emblematises the pressure of time on fake artifice; and as the dreamer catches sight of Venus herself, blatantly artificial and artificially blatant, her loins titillatingly 'kevered' with a see-through kerchief, the timeless nature of bad artifice, already questioned by the hill of sand, is further undermined when an element of time is inserted into her depiction:

> Derk was that place, but afterward lightnesse
> I saw a lyte—unnethe it myghte be lesse—
> And on a bed of gold she lay to reste,
> Til that the hote sonne gan to weste.   (263–6)

It is not quite enough to note that 'the "timeless" nature of park and garden is forgotten here';[5] rather, it is subverted. The Venus here is not the Cytherea to whom Chaucer's brief invocation is addressed; but both are aspects of one goddess, who expresses in herself the two possibilities represented on the gates, the timeless fruition provided by art and a sterile hell. This mythographic reading is perhaps inspired by Boccaccio's own gloss on the passage.[6] The most damning characteristic of the kind of stagnant artifice which the temple of Venus incorporates is that it distorts whatever it depicts, so that it ceases to relate to real human experience at all, and again Chaucer's commentary dissents from this distortion when describing the scenes painted around the temple by stressing with habitual compassion the reality of love and suffering whether in history or in fiction (288–94).

So Chaucer leaves the temple, again in need of 'solace' (297), for he has found nothing in it to delight him. He walks through the park until he comes to the goddess Nature. Whereas the interior of the temple of Venus was dark, Nature is suffused with light; and she is sitting 'upon an hil of floures' (302), as ephemeral as Dame Patience's hill of sand but self-renewing and beautiful. We may naively believe, on first reading, that we are about to encounter a total contrast to the artifice that the temple of Venus represents. There is no such total contrast. For this is *natura naturans*. The picture of Nature and the parliament of fowls over which she presides is at least as contrived as anything we have met previously in the poem. Therefore one needs the distinction between good and bad artifice rather than one between artifice and that which is spontaneous and natural, which, whatever it is, and it may well be love, is certainly never a medieval poem. Despite this almost paradoxical artifice, then, Brewer is surely right to say that 'the complex image of Nature, and the speeches of the birds, contrast with and implicitly correct the wrongful, selfish and barren sensuality of the temple of Venus; Nature complements and crowns the full, positive image of the park; and she supplements the view of life represented by the Dream of Scipio' (p. 21). It seems to me, however, that she 'supplements' it by opposing it with a literally delightful alternative. There is no antithesis between order and Nature. Nature stands for the kind of order we impose and have to impose on the external world, in order to perceive and in order to think.

Yet what happens in the parliament itself appears at first sight to be a singularly pointless kind of ritual. Nature presents on her hand a most excellent and gentle lady formel, and suitably courtly speeches of proposition for the formel are heard from three male tercels. All three speeches and the whole debate are in vain. Notwithstanding Nature's open patronage of the first tercel, the formel steadfastly refuses to make any choice: 'I wol nat serve Venus ne Cupide / Forsothe as yit' (652–3). She is in no hurry to know Love 'in dede'; and she asks for a year's remission to think things over, which Nature reluctantly grants. One could argue that the formel is here in the wrong just as plausibly as one could argue that her suitors are: she seeks an escape from love, an escape from experience, which cannot be granted outside the context of chaste sainthood. Yet that is to impose too heavy an interpretation on this debate, as Nature makes clear in her concluding line: 'This entremes is dressed for yow alle' (665). '*Entremet*' is the French word for an interlude, a play or game. The notion of play here is of enormous importance. Once we put together the fact that the debate achieves nothing, the constant reminders —like Nature's 'This is oure usage alwey fro yer to yeere' (411), or the narrator's 'As yer by yer was alwey hir usaunce' (674)—that we are dealing here with an established, tightly regulated annual pattern, and the final play-connotation of an *entremet*, it becomes structurally plain that the next year's debate will be just as abortive as the one we have now overheard: the three tercels will put their respective cases, Nature will again recommend the first, and the formel will again say 'I don't know'. The inconclusive conclusion to the debate is, on one level, the absurd joke of the recurrent situation. On that level therefore, instead of Chaucer's offering, as we might expect, a sharp alternative to either the *Somnium* or the temple of Venus, he comes up with an inconclusive trifle, a polished inconsequentiality.

He is intent throughout the description of the parliament to underline the artificiality of the proceedings and the artifice of his own rhetoric. Just as the hypostasis of Nature gathers a degree of poetic momentum, Chaucer breaks off with an allusion to his source, Alain of Lille's *De Planctu Naturae*, 'The Pleynt of Kynd'. Instead of bird-characterisations drawn from nature, we have bird-caricatures which owe their elements to a ready wit and bestiary lore. When the smaller birds rise in rebellion against the tedium of the debate, Chaucer mitigates his artifice only to the extent of having cuckoos saying 'kokkow', geese saying 'kek' and ducks saying 'quek quek'. Even at the end, when Chaucer relaxes his artifice enough to give us a gentle stanza of avian love-making which is comically incongruous simply because he takes into account that birds will be birds, whatever their courtly aspirations, he follows this essay in comic naturalism with what appears to be a piece of uncomfortable pedantry:

> And whan this werk al brought was to an ende,
> To every foul Nature yaf his make
> By evene acord, and on here way they wende.
> And, Lord, the blisse and joye that they make!
> For ech of hem gan other in wynges take,
> And with here nekkes ech gan other wynde,
> Thankynge alwey the noble goddess of kynde.

> But fyrst were chosen foules for to synge,
> As yer by yer was alwey hir usaunce
> To synge a roundel at here departynge,
> To don to Nature honour and plesaunce.
> The note, I trowe, imaked was in Fraunce.
> The wordes were swiche as ye may heer fynde,
> The nexte vers, as I now have in mynde.   (666–79)

Yet it is the song which the small birds sing that affords an important key to the poem, for this is the answer to the *Somnium Scipionis*.

I have drawn attention to the imagery of light in the poem. The dreamer may read and find delight while it is day; nightfall induces his original malaise and dissatisfaction with what he has read. The original view of the park shows it suffused with a continual and perpetual light, the perpetuity of art, while the area of the temple of Venus is dark and subject to the sun's rise and fall. The preponderance of artifice is here seen as undermined by time, and the idea that this may be acceptable lies in the shift from Patience's hill of sand to Nature's hill of flowers. The notion that time may indeed touch and transfigure the good artifice of the garden, watched over by Nature, comes to fulfilment when the parliament is foreclosed by the sunset:

> And from the morwe gan this speche laste
> Tyl dounward drow the sonne wonder faste.   (489–90)

I have also noted the significance of harmony in the poem, in the answer to the vast impersonal music of the spheres provided by the song of the small birds.

The two sets of imagery, of light and dark and harmony, converge in the impenitently lyric roundel sung at the end of the parliament:

> Now welcome, somer, with thy sonne softe,
> That has this wintres wedres overshake,
> And driven away the longe nyghtes blake!
>
> Saynt Valentyn, that art ful hy on-lofte,
> Thus syngen smale foules for thy sake:
> Now welcome, somer, with thy sonne softe,
> That has this wintres wedres overshake.
>
> Wel han they cause for to gladen ofte.
> Sith ech of hem recovered hath hys make,
> Ful blissful nowe they synge when they wake:
>
> Now welcome, somer, with thy sonne softe,
> That hast this wintres wedres overshake,
> And driven away the longe nyghtes blake! (680–92)

It is undeniable that the *Parliament of Fowls* concerns love; but the positive aspects of the poem point elsewhere. The dreamer who is not a servant of Love may write his poem, and the small birds who are not servants of Love may sing their song. The small birds, unlike the royal, hunting birds who are servants of Love, achieve their desired partners and fulfil their natural needs. Both the dreamer and the small fowls attain 'ease' and the 'solace' which is harmony; whereas the tercel must, as he says, 'live in pain'. At the start, the poet seeks a formulation for delight and requires 'solace' and 'ease' after the *Somnium Scipionis* and its all too public picture of a rather unfriendly eternity. The poet loves the world too much to find comfort here, and therefore looks to art, as lovers to their beloved, for stasis and fixity, the eternity of the desirable. This much love and poetic imagination have in common. Love is itself a function of imagination; both lover and poet find it hard to come to terms with the fluidity of human experience. Both seek their icons, and an icon is the arrest of time. The *Parliament of Fowls* goes further in its implicit suggestion that in art, if we are skilful and fortunate and wise, we may chance upon the world we wish to inhabit; whereas in love Chaucer is, I think, sufficiently pessimistic to suggest that we do not for long get what we want. Love becomes a metaphor for all human experience. In one sense, art is superior. The poet at the start of the poem seeks his formulation for delight, and is troubled not so much by time itself as by impermanence, the random experience and flux that its passing entails. He therefore experiments with the creation of a poetic world in which there is no time, but by the end of the poem yields even this in return for a delight that is honestly ephemeral. At the end of the poem the small birds make harmony to the poet's own borrowed libretto, and celebrate the renewing power of light (delight) to overcome these 'longe nyghtes blake' that took the dreamer from his library and into melancholy. Nothing could be more straightforward, or more affirmative, than that.

For these reasons I have no desire to complicate this reading with the concept of 'a wintry narrator'.[7] One still hears such comments in Chaucer criticism, and it is nothing short of alarming that academic critics can find something pathetic in the resolve with which the narrator concludes the poem:

> I wok, and othere bokes tok me to
> To reede upon, and yit I rede alwey.
> I hope, ywis, to rede so som day
> That I shal mete som thyng for to fare
> The bet, and thus to rede I nyl nat spare.   (695–700)

Chaucer's dreamer-narrator, restored from 'the soul's / Terrible impotence in a warm world',[8] carries on in a civilised way with exactly what he was doing before he dreamt. The poem's fine opening, after all, postulates a state of creative astonishment and of delight—both drawn from the activity of reading. This is not the only key passage in which Chaucer thus associates delight and reading:

> And as for me, though that my wit be lite,
> On bokes for to rede I me delyte,
> And in myn herte have hem in reverence,
> And to hem yeve swich lust and swich credence
> That there is wel unethe game non
> That fro my bokes make me to gon,
> But it be other upon the halyday,
> Or ellis in the joly tyme of May,
> Whan that I here the smale foules synge . . .
> (*Legend of Good Women*, G, 29–37)

There is much emphasis on the words *book* and *rede* in the first four stanzas of the *Parliament*, and Africanus stresses vicarious experience. Reading is an act of vicarious experience. What is a book but the sum of others' lives and others' dreams? Yet our experience in reading is not passive, as Chaucer's poem itself demonstrates. Private reading is a loss of innocence, a rite of passage, a willed entry of one's own experience into the lists of authority. Though private, it is none the less social; our experience of literature in this respect is little different from our experience of other people, particularly in and by love. To be anything more than our individual selves, we talk and love, write or read. Chaucer's library is a repository not of dusty volumes but of human experience, a resource of new insight. Rather than bathos, Chaucer's return to his library is, in its quiet way, as positive an event as the preceding roundel. Rather than contradicting the dream, the narrator corroborates it.

In the whole of the poem, in the rejected *Somnium Scipionis* as well as in the portrait of Nature, Chaucer highlights hierarchy and order, but these are redefined in the course of the poem. The notion of common profit is grounded upon an ability to discern moral and public priorities, and it leads to a public institutionalisation of these priorities, a parliament. Nature maintains order, in both senses, within this parliament of fowls. But it remains, however wittily, a parliament of fowls: I do not wish to see the parliamentary scenes as in some way a social satire.[9] It is relevant not that Nature orders society, but that she makes love ordered and articulate: that is, she orders experience and emotion. This is exactly what books do too. Indirectly, in the process of Chaucer's poem as in its argument, the act of reading, the ordering of experience and emotion, produces art. The theme of the *Parliament of Fowls* is love and art, apprehended singly and socially. The poem rejoices in the play of mutability; it does not instigate the fear of judgement. It discovers a new, non-penitential value for experience, which tries to accommodate the erotic.

One of the enabling gestures of the *Parliament of Fowls* is the delicate yet forceful association between reading (and so by extension writing) and love-making. Its explicit articulation seems to be Chaucer's original work, a spelling out of the signs of French love poetry. The association has been invented anew by Italo Calvino in a brilliant passage in *If On A Winter's Night A Traveller*. I quote its conclusion: 'every experience is unrepeatable. What makes lovemaking and reading resemble each other most is that within both of them times and spaces open, different from measurable time and space.'[10] The insight, that love and reading (or writing) both offer an opportunity of 'recovering time', is thoroughly Chaucerian. They are both dreamlike. I should like, more crassly, to stress one of its immediate consequences for narratorial tone: any writer who believes this will find in 'himself', as narrator, a multiple amalgam of selves and voices. Medieval dream poetry, with love as its theme or vehicle, always yields this potential for what can be seen as tonal unpredictability. There is no one necessarily appropriate response to a given situation or context: any one unrepeatable experience awakens in a new form or combination a complex of reactions linked to others, past and (for a writer) future. Responses may often be based, for example, on past folly or future wisdom. A narrator is, at once or successively, cynic and idealist. This sort of narratorial range grows out of love poetry, especially dream poetry in which the narrator is both young lover and often older poet; and it provides Chaucer with a masterly technique for sudden and frequent changes of tone learnt, as we shall see, from the *Roman de la Rose*. The technique may sometimes coincide with irony, but is also separate from it. Whereas irony involves a one-for-one substitution, the rejection of the literal meaning and its replacement by another, this use of narratorial *persona* is more frequently a deliberate attempt to keep options open, not foreclose them. The result has something in common with complex allegory.[11] A multiplicity of tones and voices represents a multiplicity of attitudes.

This multiplicity resembles the subject-matter of the *Parliament of Fowls*: the parliament itself; an emphasis on an artifice, a bookishness, that none the less admits the ephemeral to yield delight and ease; the narrator's discounting the authority of the *Somnium Scipionis* on grounds not of truth but of subjective preference; and the assertion, fostered by Africanus himself, of the compensatory value of poetry as serious play, an appreciation of birdsong as equal to the music of the spheres. The experience of Nature, itself based on Authority (Alanus), does not cancel out the 'authority' of Africanus and the *Somnium Scipionis*, which remains true but unpalatable; but authorities, in this sort of thematic universe, are not imposed absolutes but interposed narrative contingencies. They are made subject to what Jill Mann calls 'the determining power of context'.[12] Thus in the *Parliament of Fowls* the real authority, the *Somnium Scipionis*, generates the fictionalised *persona* of Africanus who, by way of brusquely apologetic palinode, licenses the narrator's entry into the garden. Authority is fictionalised, and so shrinks into another apocryphal voice—like the narrator's, or the poet's. If 'every experience is unrepeatable', there are limits to what an authority—or a poet—can usefully decree.

This is not to say, of course, that we cannot determine meaning in Chaucer's poetry—but to do so we must chart a tactful path through the complications sketched here. In my next chapter, I shall try to do this with the *Canterbury Tales*. My concern in the rest of this chapter, however, is with the nature and provenance of those complications, with the questions of why they are there, where they have come from and in what form they appear, rather than, primarily, with how they are used.

By 'complications' I refer to the proliferation of elements that make up Chaucer's narratorial *persona* in the vision poems, the *Legend of Good Women* and in *Troilus*. A typical profile can be drawn from the *Parliament*. Chaucer's narratorial *persona* is pseudo-autobiographical, explicitly so in the *Legend of Good Women* and the *House of Fame*, implicitly so in the *Parliament of Fowls* where the narrator is a nameless scholarly poet. Only in the *Book of the Duchess* is there any doubt of this, as we shall see. The autobiographical stance may in some respects have conformed to historical reality: *L'Envoy de Chaucer a Scogan* identifies Chaucer as a fat man, grey-headed, unlikely to succeed in love (31–5). But this does not make it any less of a fiction when it is used in a fiction. Named or not, the narrator *persona* is always 'dull', lacking in 'connyng'. His anxieties relate to his own craft as a poet, specifically as a poet in the English language; to the European literary tradition, especially European love literature; and to his attitude to authority. He is neither an *auctoritas* nor a lover. As I have suggested, these two aspects are intimately connected: the *persona* is personally detached from, and academically open and receptive to, knowledge and experience. As a Francophone he observes love (that is, courtly love); as an English poet, he does not experience it. This is a standard narratorial posture, including *Troilus*, and it enables Chaucer to combine pessimism about passionate love, even the note of *contemptus mundi* in the *Troilus* conclusion that reverts to the perspective of the *Somnium Scipionis*, with a firm commitment to love as a fitting poetic subject and thus as valuable human experience.

This narratorial *persona*, particularly by virtue of being pseudo-autobiographical, helps to conceal Chaucer as author, and being 'dull' is a revolt, albeit mulish, against authority. Chaucer's narratorial *persona* is uniquely, if passively, open to the multiple possibilities of the poem. In that sense he might be described as a 'naive' or 'stupid' dreamer.[13] Certainly, he is not a reliable arbiter—because he is most reluctant to arbitrate. But does Chaucer in these poems seek to open possible meanings or to close them? If the *persona*'s reluctance to arbitrate is part of the poem's meaning, labels such as 'naive' or 'stupid' are at best irrelevant and at worst misleading. Although highly individuated and wholly fictionalised, the narratorial *persona* supplies not a fully rounded character but a variety of responses and tones. It is an open *persona* reflecting the scope and intensity of the poem for both writer and reader, and of the experience that is in and of the poem.

To explore that *persona* further is to follow Chaucer to his library—to his Latin, Italian and above all French books. For Chaucer's handling of *persona* owes little of its detailed development to English models.[14] His conception of the English romance narrator, not unfairly, is of a voice appealing to lords to listen and, in *Sir Thopas*, offering constant and needless reassurances that he is telling us what he is telling us. In *Sir Thopas*, of course, such tags are used parodically: 'And I yow telle in good certayn, / He hadde a semely nose' (728–9). The intrusiveness and inappropriateness of such tags (compare 713,

749, 758) help create the caricature of a hapless narrator named 'Chaucer'. In a more sophisticated vein, Chaucer's divergence from 'the idea of public poetry' calls for new solutions to questions of *persona*. Chaucer mostly rejects the readily available tones of English voice, homiletic and penitential. He therefore looks elsewhere, to European sources of influence. In characterising these, I draw attention not necessarily to the evident sources of particular poems but to those works from which, directly or indirectly, he learnt most about tone and *persona*.

However, one substantial debt to the English tradition must first be recorded here. It persists as an undercurrent in Chaucer's earlier poetry and resurfaces in his solutions to the question of multiple *personae* in the *Canterbury Tales*. That is his awareness of what Burrow has called 'the older face-to-face relationship between narrator and audience, the relationship characteristic of an age when books were scarce': the mode of address of the *disour* or *geestour* from which the tags of *Sir Thopas* are plucked. This mode is 'the vigorous native stock' onto which Chaucer 'grafted' his sophisticated European forms.[15] It yields not a *persona* but a voice, and the voice is not an author's but a performer's. The performer's relation to the work is, in Rosemary Woolf's phrase, 'naturally anonymous'. It is an articulation of the work's logic of style and subject. This sort of neutral narratorial voice is what Maurice Blanchot calls 'the impersonal "he"', claiming that 'in the narrative form we always hear, like a kind of echo, an indefinable voice which the *genre* as it evolves has gradually, though somewhat misleadingly, brought to our notice'.[16] Historically, the echo, when heard, is that of the *disour*. The European influence upon Chaucer help him to transform this mode drastically, but not quite beyond recognition.

III *The French* dits amoureux, *the Prologue to the* Legend of Good Women *and the* Book of the Duchess

The *dits amoureux* are among Chaucer's most obvious and direct sources, but I do not think that they furnish many of the most important elements in his organisation of tone and *persona*.[17] The parallels between the *House of Fame* and Froissart's *Le Temple d'Honneur*, for example, are quite slight. They do little beyond fostering the peculiar idea that since Froissart's poem was written for an aristocratic wedding, so was Chaucer's. One might have thought that it was too long, and its subject-matter largely unsuitable: the story of Dido and Aeneas is hardly calculated to inaugurate a lifetime of marital bliss. Of the many more sources and analogues to the *Parliament of Fowls*, only two give much indication of a developed narrator-*persona*. One, Jean de Condé's *La Messe des Oisiaus*, contains a late switch towards the poem's end from a narrator who is not characterised, to the poet in person—'I, Jean de Condé'—whose true voice is at odds with the poem's matter, being moral and homiletic. Such a total transition, in one sudden phrase, is not a challenging model. Of far greater resonance among the sources of the *Parliament of Fowls* is Oton de Grandson's uncharacteristic poem, *Le Songe Saint Valentin*, which not only furnishes a bird parliament on Valentine's day but also, at its opening, brief hints towards an insomniac narrator and, at its ending, the best single parallel for Chaucer's non-combatant stance:

Mais du mal des gens me desplet,
La soit ce que je ne suy mye
Nesun de ceulx qui ont amie,
Et si ne suy n'amé n'amis,
Ne oncquez ne m'en entremis
Ne pas ne me vueil acointier
A moy mesler d'autruy mestier . . .
Mais, non obstant ma grant simplece,
Tant est navré qui amours blesse,
Que j'ay pitié de tous amans,
Soyen englois ou alemons,
De France né ou de Savoye.   (389–94, 400–3)

[. . . the sorrows of human lovers upset me, although I am not one of those who have a lover. I am not a lover and never was, and I don't wish to meddle with other people's profession . . . But notwithstanding my own great simplicity, so much is wounded by love that I have pity on all lovers, be they English or German, from France or Savoy.][18]

Grandson hopes that lovers will reap the rewards of loyalty and love with a pure heart; and he speaks of his infinite compassion for lovers and what they suffer. This declaration comes at a very late stage of his poem, but its influence on Chaucer is great: Chaucer makes these central attributes from the start of his narration in the *House of Fame*, the *Parliament of Fowls* and above all, fully developing the notion of compassion, *Troilus*. It is greater single influence on his narratorial *persona* than any of the other *dits amoureux*, in most of which–as in most of Grandson's poems—the narrator is young and a lover.

This may seem to underrate the influence of Machaut. B. A. Windeatt has presented very clearly the parallels between the 'Guillaume' of Machaut's *Le Jugement dou Roy de Navarre* and the 'Chaucer' of the Prologue to the *Legend of Good Women*. The case is substantial. This is the most unusual of Machaut's poems, for the narrator appears not as a stereotyped young clerk or poet-lover but as the poet Machaut reacting somewhat unchivalrously when he is summoned to atone for the judgement given against the lady in his earlier poem, *Le Jugement dou Roy de Behaingne*. The debate occupies the body of the poem but is introduced by an elaborate prologue in which the poet finally ventures forth from his chamber, in which he has remained for months out of fear of plague. James Wimsatt points out that '*Navarre* . . . provides a model for *The Legend* in several ways: in the poet's being accused of offending women in previous works, in his being arraigned before a King particularly sympathetic to ladies, in his awkward attempt to defend himself, and in the penance involving poetic composition.' Moreover, Wimsatt considers that the *Navarre* narrator 'is consistent with the narrator in the other love stories of Machaut', and pleads powerfully for his general influence on Chaucer:

Though he differs in certain respects from Chaucer's timid and docile narrator, yet he is a model for comic individualisation and is a product of poetic problems comparable to those which faced Chaucer. Machaut like Chaucer was not of the nobility, yet he was patronised by powerful royalty and he depicts such patrons in his poems. By presenting his first person narrator in the works as obtuse and comical, Machaut took himself out of competition with his royal audience . . .[19]

It is in this respect that Machaut is especially helpful to Chaucer. He provides a model for appearing comically as narrator *in propria persona* before a court audience. Since this is exactly the situation of the Prologue to the *Legend of Good Women*, the influence is particularly marked. None the less, there are many significant differences between the use of *persona* in this Prologue and that in *Navarre*. Machaut's narrator-*persona* can be seen as 'a cowardly and rather obtuse individual', and so as 'a model of' and an example of 'comic individualisation'; but I think that Wimsatt overstates his general case for seeing 'Machaut's own comic persona' as 'a particularly significant precedent for Chaucer's figure'. Machaut's *persona* is comic in a very different way from Chaucer's figure. Fear of plague, as in the opening of *Navarre*, is not enough to convict a man of cowardice; and elsewhere in Machaut's poetry, as in *Le Dit de la Fonteinne Amoureuse*, reference to the poet-narrator's 'cowardice' works as a witty reminder of Machaut's real-life bravery. The narrator's obtuseness is revealed not so much in others' accusations (and certainly not by his own admission) as by the unconvincing shifts in argument over the three thousand lines or so of the debate in the poem. It seems to me that during its course we are not meant to forget the serious concern for contemporary society shown in the first 458 lines as the narrator's thoughts while he is immured in his chamber; nor do I believe that the prime function of these opening lines is to make the narrator comic. The matter of the whole poem, no less than 4212 lines in length, is the *jugement*. It is not used as a frame for something else, though it ends with the king's sentence of a lay, a chanson and a balade, and the *exempla* of Dido, Ariadne, Medea, Thisbe and Hero occur during the debate itself. The poet makes himself lose, which is a comic (and here, one imagines, a politic) gesture; he loses badly, and in that sense may be convicted as a fool. But the debate is politely maintained throughout: apart from the final defeat, there is no real loss of face or dignity, and for good or ill the *persona* is proudly articulate.

None of this applies to the Prologue to Chaucer's *Legend*. It is a frame only, and its purpose is to explain what for Chaucer seems, at first glance, rather a conventional project:

> But wherfore that I spak, to yeve credence
> To bokes olde and don hem reverence,
> Is for men shulde autoritees beleve,
> There as there lyth non other assay by preve.
> For myn entent is, or I fro yow fare,
> The naked text in English to declare
> Of many a story, or elles of many a geste,
> As autours seyn; leveth hem if yow leste!   (G, 81–8)

This statement precedes the *jugement*, and it is unusual in placing 'the naked text in English' so wholeheartedly at the disposal of 'autoritees'—even if the plain declaration is slightly subverted by the *caveat auditor* of line 88. Already the Chaucer-*persona* has been found in an unusually conventional situation, paying his obeisance—in the manner of a courtly love poet—to the order of the flower. Unfortunately, for one who is about to be brought before a court transformed by Chaucer from a royal court to the court of Love, his service of the daisy marks no new initiation into love's mysteries. The narrator is the same old *servus amatorius* whose place is hopping always behind:

> Allas, that I ne had Englyssh, ryme or prose,
> Suffisant this flour to preyse aryght!
> But helpeth, ye that han konnyng and myght,
> Ye lovers that kan make of sentement . . .
> For wel I wot that ye han her-biforn
> Of makyng ropen, and lad awey the corn,
> And I come after, glenyng here and there,
> And am ful glad yf I may fynde an ere
> Of any goodly word that ye han left.   (F, 66–9, 73–7)

The court of Love pays no denarius to one recruited at the eleventh hour. The consequence of this unregenerate posture is that, unlike Machaut's *persona*, the Chaucer of the Prologue is utterly inarticulate; his one brief effort to excuse himself is met by Alceste with a peremptory 'Lat be thyn arguynge' (475). What in Machaut takes over three thousand lines is collapsed by Chaucer into less than three hundred. Far from being able, like Machaut, to conduct his own case, the Chaucer of this Prologue is unfit to enter a plea. There is nothing for him to choose between Love's censure that Chaucer has begun to 'dote / As olde foles, whan here spiryt fayleth' (261–2), and Alceste's successful defence on grounds of his diminished responsibility:

> This man to yow may wrongly ben acused,
> There as by ryght hym oughte ben excusid.
> Or elles, sire, for that this man is nyce,
> He may translate a thyng in no malyce,
> But for he useth bokes for to make,
> And taketh non hed of what matere he take,
> Therfore he wrot the Rose and ek Crisseyde
> Of innocence, and nyste what he seyde.
> Or hym was boden make thilke tweye
> Of som persone, and durste it not withseye;
> For he hath write many a bok er this.
> He ne hath not don so grevously amys
> To translate that olde clerkes wryte,
> As thogh that he of maleys wolde endyte
> Despit of love, and hadde hymself ywrought.   (G, 338–52)

Authority is always useful when one can claim it. This passage is a wonderful extension of the *Troilus*-narrator's self-effacement behind his book; and it is a brilliant ploy. The *persona* escapes the charges of senility and antifeminist malice by accepting those of folly and rampant pedantry. He is almost wholly passive, a site toured by the court of Love as a silent ruin of intellectual disability. But compared with Machaut Chaucer has radically extended the distance between himself as poet of the *Legend* and the Chaucer *persona* who narrates the Prologue. Unlike Machaut, Chaucer the poet escapes scot-free by pillorying his surrogate. He has accepted no blame and made no apology. He has even, as it were, left with a commission. Neither the strategy nor the *persona* is like Machaut's. Chaucer's debt to Machaut is immense, but it has little to do with the nature or use of his narratorial *persona* and, as I shall argue, it has everything to do with the work to which, in his own translation, he continually gives pride of place in the *Legend*, 'the Romaunce of the Rose' (329). He has learnt little more from Machaut's *persona* in *Navarre* than, in the *House of Fame*, the use of his own Christian name. But he has also had a lesson in dealing firmly but tactfully with an audience from inside the poem.

This conclusion is typical of Chaucer's attitude to the *dits amoureux*. He ransacks them for thematic and structural elements, but—with the sole exception of Grandson's disengaged compassion—he shows little interest in their *personae*. The pattern is created in the very first of his long vision poems, the *Book of the Duchess*, in which the reliance on the *dits amoureux* is at its heaviest. Indeed, reading Windeatt's persuasive presentation of *Behaingne*, the *Fonteinne Amoureuse*, *Remède de Fortune*, *Le Dit dou Lyon* and Froissart's *Le Paradys d'Amours* in what is often virtually parallel text-form with the *Book of the Duchess*, one might easily conclude that Chaucer's poem lacks significant originality. Certainly, so much is plundered from the French tradition that hardly any structural or thematic element is unprecedented. Yet it *is* plundered, rather than borrowed, for it is wrenched quite ruthlessly from its original context. Lines given to Machaut's lady in *Behaingne* go to Chaucer's Black Knight, mixed in with lines on the power of memory given to Machaut's Knight. The Ceyx and Alcyon story as a specific against insomnia and the promise of a featherbed to Morpheus come from the *Fonteinne Amoureuse*, but it is a living lover there who hopes to bribe him into being a messenger to his wife; many of the Black Knight's speeches come from *Remède de Fortune*, as does the chess-game with Fortune—but played for a woman's favour, not her life; a whelp emerges from Machaut's lion; and another parallel for promises to Morpheus and Juno comes from Froissart, as does further sleeplessness and torment—but, again, for the love of a fair lady, not an undiagnosed 'sorweful ymagynacioun'. This sort of chaotic raiding party justifies Windeatt's defence of 'the essentially combinative power of Chaucer's poetic imagination . . . Chaucer's power to innovate-through-borrowing . . . this co-ordinating and re-creating process'.[21] So much is taken from these poems that it is a shock, on reading any one of them, to find a poetic world so completely different from the *Book of the Duchess*—in one case, *Behaingne*, with its slick and rather repugnant denigration of bereavement, a world antipathetic to it. It is a difference that Chaucer has made. It can be gauged, and was in large measure shaped by, Chaucer's radical change of *persona*.

The *personae* of the five *dits* that have contributed to the *Book of the Duchess* are those of clerks, courtiers, lovers who overhear and transcribe, generally —but not always, and not necessarily—in a dream. The question of the truthfulness of dreams scarcely arises here: waking or sleeping, the concerns are the same, Love and Memory. The most that can be said is that by night truth may be veiled: thus the narrator of the *Fonteinne Amoureuse* discovers by day the identity of the lover whose complaint he has already copied—at his portable writing desk, inlaid with ivory—by night. Chaucer's use of the dream, and his questioning of their truthfulness, are by contrast necessary structures: they contribute a good deal to the problematic nature of what he has his *persona* report. The French *personae*, however, do not open themselves to such challenge. They move fairly confidently through a milieu they understand, and they are committed to its main value—the consolation to be found in the experience of gentle love. There is no great distance between the poet, whose signature is frequently present by means of an anagram, and the narratorial *persona*. Machaut in particular may allow some light fun at his own expense—the indecisive narrator of *Behaingne* gets bitten by the lady's dog—but decorum is quickly restored. Often a compliment to the *persona*, and so in immodest fashion to the poet, is worked into the poem: the knight in *Behaingne* is pressed into a somewhat laboured digression in order to describe the narrator as a handsome and capable clerk. The French *personae* play a role in an equivalent of the courtly masques of the Renaissance. They are in disguise but they are nevertheless recognisably themselves, and their sense of themselves is drawn from their secure and reasonably comfortable place in the social hierarchy to which the artefact pays tribute. Furthermore, they are an inevitable complement of their poem's machinery. This machinery itself grows predictably from the constant themes of Love and Memory in a courtly context. A young narrator has little choice but to be a lover or a handsome clerk.

Whatever Chaucer's relation was to this tradition, it was not that of '*grant translateur*'. For he disorients it by destroying the connection between narrative and narrator, poem and poet: his *persona* is not a lover. There is a token attempt at the start of the *Book of the Duchess* to blame the narrator's insomnia on love-longing (35–40), but nothing is made of it, here or elsewhere. Nor, interestingly, does the narrator of the *Book of the Duchess* appear, until the very end, to be a poet. He is presented first and foremost as a sufferer from insomnia that has led to an extreme frigidity of emotion:

> Al is ylyche good to me—
> Joye or sorowe, wherso hyt be—
> For I have felynge in nothyng,
> But, as yt were, a mased thyng,
> Alway in poynt to falle adoun;
> For sorwful ymagynacioun
> Ys alway hooly in my mynde.   (9–15)

This portrait of general numbness, not centred specifically in love, is atypical of the French tradition. One must add that it also makes the *persona* atypical of Chaucer. In fact, this may be the one Chaucer poem outside the *Canterbury Tales* in which the narrator is intended to be a closed *persona*—a narrator, that is, whose psychological state and growth is vital to the meaning of the poem. For psychological growth there surely is. The narrator who begins by admitting that he has 'felynge in nothyng' is led by his dream's end to an expression of compassion—'By God, hyt ys routhe'—and awakes still holding the story of Ceyx and Alcyon with which he read himself to sleep:

> Thoghte I, 'Thys ys so queynt a sweven
> That I wol, be processe of tyme,
> Fonde to put this sweven in ryme
> As I kan best, and that anoon.'
> This was my sweven; now hit ys doon.   (1330–4)

Line 1334, the last line of the poem, brings us for the first time to the poet's present: 'now hit ys doon'. It therefore places the *persona*'s initial insomnia, which we have already seen cured, and his lack of emotional response, in the realm of past history for all that it was told in the present tense. Only in this closing section, then, is the narrator-*persona* fully reconciled with the figure of the poet.

We have been told as much towards the beginning of the Ceyx and Alcyon story:

> Such sorowe this lady to her tok
> That trewely I, which made this book,
> Had such pittee and such rowthe
> To rede hir sorwe, that, by my trowthe,
> I ferde the worse al the morwe
> Aftir, to thenken on hir sorwe.   (95–100)

The making of 'this book' and the feeling of 'pittee' and 'rowthe' are linked in this passage, and they are made a consequence of the dream that has yet to come: the writing and the pity come together, not at this point but 'al the morwe / Aftir' the dream.

Compassion is the product of the narrator's interview with the Black Knight, in which the narrator learns of the poet-lover's grief for his dead wife. As with *Pearl*, many critics have tried to fit this long exchange into the generic shape of the *consolatio*.[22] The first speaker in this short but climactic exchange is the Black Knight:

> 'She ys ded!' 'Nay!' 'Yis, be my trouthe!'
> 'Is that youre los? Be God, hyt ys routhe!'   (1308–9)

The exchange is held to be cathartic for the Black Knight. He has been made to face his loss and state it in plain English: 'She ys ded'. By his cunning pretence of incomprehension, on this reading, the narrator has been responsible for the bereaved lover's rehabilitation. The interpretation claims support from the rapidity with which the narrative is wound up:

> And with that word ryght anoon
> They gan to strake forth; al was doon,
> For that tyme, the hert-huntyng.
> With that me thoghte that this kyng
> Gan homwardes for to ryde
> Unto a place, was there besyde,
> Which was from us but a lyte.
> A long castel with walles white,
> Be seynt Johan! on a ryche hil
> As me mette; but thus hyt fil.   (1311–20)

The punning allusion to 'hert-huntyng' in line 1313 encompasses both the dreamer with the Black Knight, communing in their hidden grove, and the Emperor Octavian who has been hunting in the forests. Since lines 1318–19 contain anagrammatic references to John and Blanche of Lancaster and Richmond, many critics assume that 'this kyng' of line 1314, who returns home after the 'hert-huntyng', is the Black Knight. Kean says that he 'is brought back within the framework of social reference'.[23] The Black Knight in the poem is a figure of John of Gaunt, who was King of Castille; but the 'kyng' of the *Book of the Duchess* is not the Black Knight but the Emperor Octavian, who would naturally return home after the hunt. If the Black Knight is in fact left where he was found, the force of the argument for his consolation by the dreamer is reduced. But my objection to this argument does not depend on this suggestion. Even if it is rejected, the case for consolation—that is, psychological change in the Black Knight—is a frail one, whereas the case for psychological growth and change in the dreamer is a strong one, and has already been made. The Black Knight appears to be in no doubt of his loss, and his plain statement that the dreamer does not understand it runs through the exchange as a leitmotif:

> 'Thou wost ful lytel what thou menest;
> I have lost more than thow wenest.'
>
> (743–4: cf. 1137–8; 1305–6)

It is far from the truth that the Black Knight must be spurred into a statement of his loss in plain English. He has achieved just this with the first five lines he speaks in the poem:

> 'I have of sorwe so gret won
> That joye gete I never non,
> Now that I see my lady bryght,
> Which I have loved with al my myght,
> Is fro me ded and ys agoon . . .'   (475–9)

It seems to me an inescapable inference from this evidence that the turning point of the final exchange lies not in his 'She ys ded' but in the narrator's 'hyt ys routhe!'

As I read this poem, the Black Knight instructs the narrator by example in what it is to feel strong emotion—and, not incidentally, in what it is to write poetry, for he, not the narrator, is the lover-poet of this poem. I have no quarrel whatever with the identification of the Black Knight as a figure of John of Gaunt grieving for his dead Blanche, but we should not allow it to circumscribe the Black Knight's role and attributes within the poem. His is an Orphic role, that of the master-poet lamenting his irrevocably lost wife. I think that this association may have been actively in Chaucer's mind. There is a hint for it, if we need one, in Froissart's *Paradys d'Amours*, where the poet modestly disclaims an excellence comparable to that of Orpheus (1139), and in his conclusion thanks together both Morpheus for his dream and Orpheus for showing him the art and practice of poetry. There is a more obvious source in the *Metamorphoses*, where the Ceyx and Alcyon story is actually one of the tales narrated by Orpheus in his final grief-stricken exile in the wild. Had Chaucer turned over the leaf and chosen another tale, he would have found Ovid's description of Orpheus in a grove leaning against a great tree and singing his heart-rending lament to an audience of animals tamed by his music.[24] This is exactly like the context in which Chaucer's narrator finds the Black Knight, and the Ovidian locale is by far the nearest analogue to the detail of Chaucer's setting (427–47). I do not therefore claim that the Black Knight is a type of Orpheus. He is a figure of John of Gaunt, but this closed *persona* has been given Orphic attributes. By the heart-felt power of his poetry he has educated the callow narrator in pity. Thus he has taught an acolyte to sing.

I believe that this may be a more satisfactory reading of the *Book of the Duchess* than we have had. It has always seemed puzzling, on grounds of social as much as literary structures, that Chaucer should have tried in this way to console one of the most powerful members of the royal family for the loss of his wife, especially as the poem appears to have been composed some considerable time after Blanche's death and there is no strong sense of occasion in the poem. On my reading, Chaucer does not presume to console Gaunt for his loss but presents him with a poetic monument to his grief. The *Book of the Duchess* is a graceful allegory of the power of Love and Memory: 'for be hyt never so derk, / Me thynketh I se hir ever moo' (912–13). It is a tribute to both the living husband and the dead wife. The catastrophe of Blanche's death and the nobility of Gaunt's grief have awakened Chaucer's compassion and have made a poet of him. His narrator is truly a prentice *persona*. Homage is thus paid to Gaunt not as the patron of Chaucer's poetic career but as its inspiration, its 'onlie begetter'. This is an overturning of the *dits amoureux*, and it involves —for, I think, the one and only occasion in Chaucer's poetry—a narrator who is a closed *persona*. He is closed because he is not, until the end of the poem, a poet: he is what Chaucer fears he would have been had he not become one. The poetic initiation which the *Book of the Duchess* celebrates leads to an open narratorial *persona*: hereafter, as in the last line of this poem, his voice will be that of a poet. The writing of the *Book of the Duchess* enables Chaucer to come into his poetic heritage.

That heritage has little to do with the *dits amoureux*, which are never again drawn upon so assiduously. Nor has it much to do with other types of French fourteenth-century poetry: a line from Deguileville may run directly to Langland and Lydgate, but in Chaucer (with the sole exception of his *Prière de Nostre Dame*) it loops back to Jean de Meun. For Chaucer's training in tone and *persona*, that heritage has been lucidly anticipated in the *Book of the Duchess*, where the poet's bedchamber is decorated with the highspots of European culture:

> For holly al the story of Troye
> Was in the glasynge ywrought thus,
> Of Ector and of kyng Priamus,
> Of Achilles and Lamedon,
> And eke of Medea of of Jason,
> Of Paris, Eleyne and of Lavyne.
> And alle the walles with colours fyne
> Were peynted, bothe text and glose,
> Of al the Romaunce of the Rose. (326–34)

This chamber, as Windeatt (p. xiv) aptly puts it, 'is expressive of the dreamer's inner disposition and cast of mind through the influences upon him'. The Troy story, and the claims for England and the English stemming from it, has no influence on Chaucer's development of *persona*, though it will reappear in these pages. The *Roman de la Rose*, however, has an influence that can barely be overstated, and once again—as in the Prologue to the *Legend of Good Women* —it is awarded pride of place. Chaucer's narratorial *persona* begins his career with his colours nailed to the bedroom wall.

IV *Italian and Latin Sources of Influence*

Italian influences contribute little of substance to Chaucer's development of *persona*. There is a handful of ironic analogies drawn in Chaucer's poetry between his narrator *persona* and Dante's pilgrim,[25] but the irony exists in Chaucer's acute sense of the unlikeness of the two. Petrarch is used spasmodically for the odd set piece, as are the *dits amoureux*, but only once, in the Clerk's Tale, is Petrarch a direct source; and there Chaucer's glossing is sometimes at odds with Petrarch's allegory.[26]

It cannot be said for the most part that Boccaccio contributes much more, though his work is used very thoroughly, in the Knight's Tale and *Troilus*. Chaucer's debt is great, but again it has little to do with narratorial *persona*. He found in Boccaccio a stimulating variety of styles, 'a polished rhetoric and poetic that could range from the high style of formal invocation to . . . the relaxed style of relatively natural dialogue'.[27] But this variety is not reflected in the narratorial *persona* of *Il Filostrato*. This is Boccaccio's most developed narrator, but it is hardly very developed: a conventional posture is used in a self-seeking manner, and then abandoned in favour of rank antifeminism. The conventional posture, that of the *servus amatorius*, is established in the prologue to the entire work: Filostrato tells this story to relieve his sorrow in the absence of his lady Filomena. It is to be a perpetual testimony to her nobility and his misery, and Troilo's laments are to be relevant to his own condition. It used to be believed that this frame had a strongly autobiographical cast, alluding to Boccaccio's love for Maria D'Acquino. Vittore Branca, however, has raised strong doubt about this:[28] we are dealing here with a form of disguise and detachment, but one which does not resemble Chaucer's narratorial voice. Whatever the supposed autobiographical content, the tone of special pleading invades the poem. At the beginning of Part I, far from sounding the compassionate note of the *Troilus* narrator, Boccaccio's narrator asks his audience of lovers to pray to Love for himself. There is no more from a narrator's voice until the prologue to Part III, where two stanzas recall Dante's appeal to Apollo in Canto I of the *Paradiso*, but the resplendent light of Dante's Apollo is predictably transformed into the lovely Filomena. This is hyperbole of a major order, and it is there to raise doubt about the narrator's sincerity. The doubt is dramatically confirmed in the twenty-third stanza of Part IV, where the narrator intervenes—identified in the gloss as the author—to say that now he has reached Troilo's unhappiness caused by Criseida's forthcoming departure to the Greek camp, he refuses to appeal as is customary for his lady's aid. For she has herself caused the poet bitter pangs comparable to Troilo's. Although he proceeds to beg her to return to him, the poet-narrator's bitterness is fully evident. This is not a love poem but a poetic revenge. The prevailing antifeminism of the poem is openly revealed by a covert narratorial comment in stanza 86 of Part IV, in a reference to 'the pointless chatter women usually indulge in'.[29] The narrative itself stands by the sincerity of Criseida's grief at her separation from Troilo, and as late as stanza 13 of Part IV is still insisting that she remains in love with him though she is hard pressed by Diomedes. The narrator is absolutely absent from this stretch of the narrative, and the cynicism we may by now suspect to be the poem's design is expressed by Pandaro (for example in stanza 10 of Part VII), whose role as narrator's surrogate is as unambiguous in Boccaccio as it is questionable in Chaucer. The depiction of Troilo's wretchedness proceeds in Part VIII with only implicit markers—he suffers as all jilted lovers do—to remind one of the parallel with Filostrato. Part IX, the ending, has the poet-narrator bring the poem safely into harbour and despatches it once more as a messenger to reproach Filomena: perhaps now she will understand the suffering she has caused. The envoy comes hot on the heels of a scaldingly contemptuous moral exhortation addressed to young men, who are urged to put no trust in women—especially young ones—and to beg Love to grant them 'such clearsightedness in loving that you will not end up by dying for the sake of a wicked woman'.

The narratorial *persona* in this poem is of vestigial extent and venomous intent. The difference in this respect between *Il Filostrato* and *Troilus* is great. This does not mean, however, that we should see in *Troilus* a closed narrator-*persona*. For Howard Schless, the *Troilus* narrator is 'no impersonal voice: on the contrary, he becomes deeply involved in the story, responding, commenting, directing us, the readers, in such a way that we can enter the inner thoughts of the characters and, in turn, respond to the vital emotions of their world'.[30] No first-person narrator is an 'impersonal voice', and the function sketched in the rest of the sentence seems to me an admirable definition of an open *persona*. It is surprising that Schless, following Donaldson's influential view, goes on to characterise this narrator in terms suitable only to a closed one. Yet do the explicit first-person interventions of the narrator-*persona* in *Troilus* achieve more than to break open, in the name of compassion, the easy contempt of women offered as the fruit of Boccaccio's poem? On what grounds do we distinguish the moral or other reactions of the poet from such narratorial interventions? The questions are made very complex by the fact that on the whole passages in *Troilus* in which a narrator is explicitly present in the first-person offer problems no greater than other passages in which there is no first-person. If we are committed to the idea of a pervasive, closed narratorial *persona* we will interpret the latter passages as narratorial commentary; if we are not, we will note them as remarkable shifts in tone. There is little in *Il Filostrato* to parallel such instability of narratorial tone, and there are few significant Italian precedents for Chaucer's development of *persona*.

There are in fact two, both provided by Boccaccio: in the glosses to the *Teseida* and in the authorial addresses of the *Decameron*. The *Teseida* glosses are significant because, through them Boccaccio, as it were, divides himself in two: Boccaccio the poet and Boccaccio the scholar. It is the latter—a sort of Italian E.K.—who supplies the glosses, which sometimes take sharply forensic issue with the poem of his *alter ego*, and whose 'meticulousness and, one would almost say, pedantry' assist Boccaccio in 'displaying the exterior mechanism of his poetry'.[31] Chaucer does not split his literary identity, but if the glosses were contained in his manuscript of the *Teseida* they must have encouraged him to intervene during the course of his narratives, as he does, with clerkly rebuttals.

The *Decameron* passages—the Proem, the lengthy prologue to the fourth day, and the '*Conclusione dell'Autore*'—are an influence very similar to an aspect of that to be traced from Jean de Meun. In some of their detail, they provide a closer analogue than Jean to certain passages of *Troilus* and the General Prologue to the *Canterbury Tales*, but the strategy of the contexts in which Chaucer's defences are deployed makes it probable that Jean is the primary and Boccaccio the secondary influence. The Proem begins on the note of compassion: '*Umana cosa è aver compassione degli afflitti*'. Boccaccio explains that his compassion arises from love, of which he is now cured and so desires to comfort others, especially ladies, the weaker sex with fewer opportunities to dispel melancholy. In the prologue to the fourth day, he notes and answers envious blasts against his relation with his audience of ladies, explaining that his affection for them is carnal (a pretension which Chaucer is not moved to emulate), and citing the precedents of Dante, Cavalcanti and Cino da Pistoia. These can be no more than a very minor influence on a little of Chaucer's narratorial business. The '*Conclusione*' is more important, being a defence against objections that may have been raised by auditors (and readers) in the course of the work. It is a witty defence, though less gentle than comparable passages in Chaucer. Against the objection that some stories are too long, Boccaccio advances the argument, in effect, that no idle female would wish them shorter. Against the objection that they contain too many jokes, he cites the precedent of friars' sermons. Then he immediately proceeds to answer the charge that he is too critical of the friars—by simply stating that most people like his works. Those who do not are under no obligation to read them. The key defences, however, are against allegations of rudeness. He acquits his stories of excessive licence on grounds of generic and stylistic decorum; he is not to blame for others' unhealthy minds. There follows the most important section of all:

Saranno similmente di quelle che diranno qui esserne alcune che, non essendoci, sarebbe stato assai meglio. Concedasi: ma io non poteva né doveva scrivere se non le raccontate, e per ciò esse che le dissero le dovevan dir belle e io l'avrei scritte belle. Ma se pur prosupporre si volesse che io fossi stato di quelle e lo 'nventore e lo scrittore, che non fui, dico che io non mi vergognerei che tutte belle non fossero, per ciò che maestro alcun non si truova, da Dio in fuori, che ogni cosa faccia bene e compiutamente.

In like manner there will be some who will say that there are stories here which 'twere better far had been omitted. Granted; but 'twas neither in my power, nor did it behove me, to write any but such stories as were narrated; wherefore, 'twas for those by whom they were told to have a care that they were proper; in which case they would have been no less so as I wrote them. But, assuming that I not only wrote but invented the stories, as I did not, I say that I should take no shame to myself that they were not all proper; seeing that artist there is none to be found, save God, that does all things well and perfectly.[32]

Boccaccio then adds that there must be diversities of quality in all things, thistles that remain in every well-tilled field:

Senza che, ad avere a favellare a semplici giovinette, come voi il più siete, sciocchezza sarebbe stata l'andar cercando e faticandosi in trovar cose molto esquisite, e gran cura porre di molto misuratamente parlare. Tuttavia chi va tra queste leggendo, lasci star quelle che pungono e quelle che dilettano legga:

Whereto I may add that, having to address me to young and unlearned ladies, as you for the most part are, I should have done foolishly, had I gone about searching and swinking to find matters very exquisite, and been sedulous to speak with great precision. However, whoso goes a reading among these stories, let him pass over those that vex him, and read those that please him.

The Chaucer of the *Canterbury Tales* finds here a doctrine of curtailed responsibility in the shy excuse (not intended to be taken seriously) of being a recorder or translator—whether of his narrators' choices or already existing tales Boccaccio cunningly leaves open. Generally the three passages supply a useful anthology of narratorial byplay with and over the heads of an imaginary audience. Chaucer does not follow Boccaccio, however, in the boisterous arrogance of blaming his imaginary audience for the style and imperfections of his tales. Chaucer's use of antifeminist wit is more like Jean's; but in the General Prologue he couples Jean's defence of the *Roman* (to be discussed below) with Boccaccio's willingness, as a duty based on historical verisimilitude, to justify his own lapses.

Any influence on Chaucer from serious medieval Latin poetry is very small. The strongest examination of Chaucer's possible indebtedness to such poetry is by Peter Dronke, and the majority of the parallels cited are thematic, not tonal. In most of the examples cited by Dronke a developed narratorial *persona* is lacking, and where it occurs, in what Dronke claims as Chaucerian reminiscences of Latin poems, it has generally been added by Chaucer.[33] Examples of the pattern could be multiplied, and the inference is a negative one.

From the Goliardic poems comes an altogether dissimilar influence, and on *persona* a positive one. Jill Mann's essay, in the same collection as those by Schless and Dronke, makes the most of an excellent case by comparing the Goliards (and by implication Chaucer) with Gower: 'The Goliards aim to open up our sense of the contrast and tension between spiritual and worldly values, a sense which in the best of their work leads us to an increased awareness of human complexity; Gower aims to eliminate tension, to establish a firm and unambiguous control over his reader's point of view.'[34] On the question of authority, Mann sees both Chaucer and the Goliards as lined up 'against moral and stylistic rigidity': thus the Wife of Bath is allowed to manipulate texts and Chaucer refuses 'comment in his own person . . . Moreover, by taking texts out of context and assigning them to a radically different one, Chaucer transforms their meaning. The "respectable" arguments become suspicious.' Mann sets the Wife of Bath's Prologue alongside Walter of Châtillon's '*Missus sum in vineam*', which offers a mock defence of the pursuit of wealth. She notes that Walter's citation of authorities is honest; with one exception, Walter does not tamper with his texts. But it is also disingenuous, for by ignoring their original context and placing them in a new and cunningly alien one, Walter ensures that they have a new meaning. His readers are not intended to be uncritically swayed by this new meaning; nor, however, are they called upon to reject it by recovering—as if they were modern scholars—the 'original' context. 'We cannot simply contrast a correct and an incorrect use of texts . . . It is enough for Walter's purpose that the shift to hexameter form proclaims the separateness of his texts, their origin in another literary world, and their borrowed status in this one. The impression given by their use in the mock argument of this poem is of something I can only describe as the promiscuity of argument, axiom, quotation, moralisations, and example.' This is finely put, and it is supported by a good brief account of the influence of the *Speculum Stultorum* on the Nun's Priest's Tale.[35]

It is not exactly a *persona*, then, that Chaucer found in medieval Latin satiric poetry but a highly unpredictable voice expert in equally unpredictable juxtapositions: by aping the techniques of didacticism, this poetry shows the precarious nature of schematic thought. It is an extreme development of debate poetry: art becomes its own irreverent inquisitor, and experience raises an eyebrow at authority. These are such fashionably modern notions that we may be afraid to admit that we have detected their presence in some medieval poems. We should not be, for a failure to grasp the tone of medieval satire will lead to owlish misreadings. This is not a 'self-reflexive artefact',[36] particularly given the fluctuating quality of the satire and the narrative voice: there is a serious concern in many passages, for example, of the *Speculum Stultorum*. Some passages are to be taken seriously; others are not. Neither is a key to the other: this sort of satire is indeed a mixed dish. We are to be aware that texts are being manipulated, and we are supposed to enjoy it without thinking the worse of the texts or sending their manipulators to the headmaster's study. This juxtaposition is not 'irony', if by this we mean—as we should, given the trope's relation to allegory—a literal proposition that we are required to reject in order to substitute the 'real' meaning. Locally, meaning is abundant; but there is no one meaning over all. To demand this is to disqualify oneself as, in this case, a useful critic. So Platonic a notion of truth is no help at all in understanding a tone which includes sophistry.

The Goliardic poets are well versed in Ovid, whom they often quote, and form a line of transmission for Ovidian tone. Chaucer too quoted and used Ovid often, and his tone has much in common with what today we generally think Ovid's tone to have been; however serious a meaning is intended, it is accomplished by or in spite of *epanorthosis*, constant and drastic changes of tone and therefore mood. How much did Chaucer learn from Ovid directly, and how much from intermediaries? This question must be asked, but it can hardly be answered. Two recent books have made sweeping claims for Ovid's influence. John M. Fyler writes shrewdly of Chaucer's and Ovid's counter-pointing of written authority against personal experience, both of which are equally suspect. 'Chaucer no doubt learned from Ovid how to generate irony by opposing the two.'[37] Though the use of the term 'irony' here is flaccid, the claim is otherwise strongly urged: but, as the use of 'no doubt' presages, it is not supported. Chaucer's knowledge of Ovid remains an unknown quantity, in extent and type. It was extensive, Bruce Harbert suggests, but not *that* extensive.[38] Chaucer may well not have known the *Ars Amatoria* and *Remedia*

Amoris, and we do not know whether he had read edited extracts from the *Metamorphoses* or a whole manuscript. (Ovid's greatest influence on Chaucer, as R. W. Frank argues convincingly, was in the development of short individual narratives.)[39] If a whole text, we do not know whether he read it through as a poem or used it as an anthology; we do not know with what kind of *apparatus* he encountered it. The second book to stake a large claim for Ovid's influence, by J. B. Allen and T. A. Moritz, provides much scholarly documentation.[40] These authors emphasise the philosophical Ovid of medieval commentaries and glosses; and these commentaries did not take kindly to ideas of sophistry or pay much impartial attention to tone. This account of the Ovid bequeathed to Chaucer by the thirteenth century does not encourage a belief that narratorial *persona* would have loomed large in Chaucer's appreciation.

Given such uncertainties, it is as well that they may legitimately be bypassed. In whatever form Chaucer received and understood Ovid, the Ovidian narratorial *persona* and *epanorthosis* are beautifully reflected and transmitted in the *Roman de la Rose*. So too are the Goliardic stratagems discussed above. Both possible lines of transmission converge in the *Roman*, the poem to which Chaucer pays frequent and fulsome homage, and it is economical and reasonable to suggest that the great (and certain) influence subsumes the smaller (and uncertain). If Chaucer read much Goliardic poetry or studied Ovid as a poet rather than an authority, he did so through the eyes of Guillaume de Lorris and Jean de Meun, whose precedent is everywhere decisive.

V *What* Le Roman de la Rose *really did to Chaucer*

In remarks foreshadowing the important influence of the *Roman de la Rose*, I have so far tended to stress Jean de Meun's continuation at the expense of Guillaume de Lorris's opening. In the last resort this is just, especially because Jean's continuation is so successful an appropriation that it recasts in retrospect our responses to the poem's beginning—even though there is nothing in that first section of the work antipathetic to an ending, albeit fuller and more competently executed, of the sort represented by the short anonymous continuation. Jean's changes of tone and narrative pace (like his changes of subject) are frequent and peremptory, unlike Guillaume's, but they disguise the first transition by making it one of a long line. The distinction between the two authors should not be made too firmly. Jean's continuation, different as it is, develops hints in Guillaume, and Chaucer's debt to the first part of the poem is immense. Indeed, if modern textual scholarship were to be trusted, the A-fragment of the extant Middle English *Romaunt* is the only surviving part of Chaucer's translation (though it is hard then to explain the extraordinarily close resemblances between Fragment C and the Pardoner's Prologue).[41] The debt extends beyond Chaucer's shaping of a dream frame, opening like Guillaume's with a discussion of the veracity of dreams, to its concomitant, the narratorial *persona*.

In Guillaume's *Roman*, the narrator-poet-dreamer is already a developed *persona*. His status is set in the first twenty lines as on a par with that of the dream. For the poem starts by noting the opinion of 'many men . . . that in sweueninges / Ther nys but fables and lesynges' (I quote from the A-fragment of the *Romaunt*). The poet's dissent is based on the authority of Macrobius' commentary on the *Somnium Scipionis*, and the defence palpably and cunningly fails to distinguish between *somnium* and *insomnium*:

> Quicunques cuide ne qui die
> Que soit folece ou musardie
> De croire que songes aviegne,
> Qui ce vodra, por fol me tiegne,
> Car endroit moi ai je creance
> Que songes soit signifiance
> Des biens as gens et des anuis;
> Car il plusor songent de nuis
> Maintes choses couvertement
> Qu'il voient puis apertement.   (11–20)

> And whoso saith or weneth it be
> A iape, or els nycete,
> To wene that dremes after fal,
> Lette whoso lyste a fole me cal.
> For this trowe I, and say for me,
> That dremes signifiaunce be
> Of good and harme to many wightes,
> That dremen in hir slepe a-nyghtes
> Ful many thynges couertly,
> That fallen after al openly.   (11–20)

This as ever in the *Romaunt* is a close line-by-line translation of the French, which contributes two words used ('signifiance' and 'couvertement'), the 'I' *persona*, and the crucial challenge grounded on the *non sequitur* that what is true of the *Somnium Scipionis* will be true of all dreams of whatever type: 'Qui ce vodra, por fol me tiegne' (14). Since the reasoning is fallacious, this is as good as admitting that the *persona* is 'a fole'; and the nature of his folly is immediately divulged when we are told that his dream occurred

> Ou vintieme an de mon aage
> Ou point qu'Amors prent le paage
> Des jones gens . . .   (21–3)

> Within my twenty yere of age,
> Whan that Loue taketh his cariage
> Of yonge folke . . .   (21–3)

This takes the important step shown by A. C. Spearing to be characteristic of much later dream poetry influenced by the *Roman*:[42] it separates the poet from the dreamer, or rather it posits an indulgent amusement of an older voice at his younger self. The poet remembers himself (or rather, he pretends to) as a callow youth and so places in the poem this earlier self as a character from whom, though he is still 'I', the poet has defined a considerable tonal, because temporal, distance. The *persona* is progressively circumscribed as a character by the allegorical company he keeps: we know precisely what to expect of one so charmed by Idelnesse (Oiseuse) and Myrthe (Deduit). The characterisation

63

is humorously corroborated, and subtly extended, by the actions the dreamer takes, as in the narrative leading up to the Well of Narcissus episode. The account of these actions, and our response to them, is controlled by Guillaume's exploiting the implications of a past tense report by a present voice. The God of Love consults with Swete-Lokyng (Dolz Regart), and decides to stalk the dreamer in order to transfix him with Love's arrow:

> Or me gart Diex de mortel plaie,
> Se il fait tant qu'il a moi traie!
> Je qui de ce ne soi noiant,
> Touz jors m'alai esbanoiant
> Par le vergier tout a delivre. (1315–19)

> Nowe God, that sytteth in maieste,
> Fro deedly woundes he kepe me,
> If so be that he had me shete;
> For if I with his arowe mete,
> It had me greued sore, ywis!
> But I, that nothyng wyste of this,
> Went vp and downe ful many a way. (1339–45)

The prayer is that of the present poet, who knows full well the consequences of the 'deedly woundes' ('mortel plaie'): the contrast is explicit with the earlier self 'that nothyng wyste of this'. When the dreamer comes to the well itself, this potent performance is virtually repeated. The dreamer reads the inscription: 'Here starfe the fayre Narcisus' (1468), and we are then told the story of Narcissus in neutral authorial tones. This is a performance by the present voice, culminating as it does in an appeal to 'ladyes' to take the 'ensample', but it is then attributed to the *persona* who withdraws from the well

> Que de Narcisus me souvint
> Cui malement en mesavint. (1517–18)

> Whan it fell in my remembraunce
> That him betyd suche mischaunce. (1547–8)

Yet in spite of the cautionary tale, and impelled by the misplaced derring-do of the mindly delinquent juvenile, the dreamer overcomes his fears and looks into the well, leaving the experienced present poet to bemoan his past recklessness:

> Mes de fort hore m'i miré.
> Las! tant en ai puis soupiré!
> Cis mirëors m'a deceü:
> Se j'eusse avant cogneü
> Quex sa force ert et sa vertus,
> Ne m'i fusse ja embatus,
> Car mentenant ou las chaï
> Qui maint homme a pris et trahi. (1607–14)

But I may say, in sory houre
Stode I to loken or to powre;
For sythen have I sore syghed,
That myrrour hath me nowe entriked.
But had I first knowen in my wyt
The vertue and the strengthes of it,
I nolde not haue mused there;
Me had bette ben elswhere;
For in the snare I fell anone,
That had bytresshed many one.   (1639–48)

The tone, unlike that of the *dits amoureux*, is consistently humorous, and the dreamer's blinkered limitations are wholly evident long before his formally shrugging off Reason.

This is a relationship not between two voices but between two temporal manifestations of the same voice; and it is by no means as one-sided as the last paragraph may have implied. For the authority of the older self rests wholly upon the experience of the younger self as eye (and 'I')—witness. The right of the older poet to editorialise in the present tense about love's lore and love's pains is compelling only by virtue of the younger dreamer's past report. Take the following transition, which has a vintage Chaucerian sound to it and is actually a very faithful translation from the French:

> Més ne diré pas ore toute
> Lor forces et lor poëtés;
> Bien vous sera la verités
> Contee et la signifiance.
> Nel metré pas en obliance,
> Ains vous dirai que tout ce monte
> Ainçois que je fine mon conte.
> Or revendré a ma parole.   (978–85)

> But though I tell not as blyue
> Of her power, ne of her myght,
> Hereafter shall I tellen right
> The sothe, and eke signyfyaunce,
> As ferre as I haue remembraunce:
> Al shal be sayd, I vndertake,
> Er of this booke an ende I make.
> Nowe come I to my tale agayne.   (992–9)

Here we have the author in the act of writing, and able from his present position to utter 'The sothe and eke signyfyaunce'; but the utterance is made possible by 'remembraunce'. That 'remembraunce' guarantees the poet's claim that his book contains 'al the arte of loue' (40): 'l'art d'Amors est toute enclose' (38). The poet can and does describe more than the dreamer saw: much of the narrative juxtaposition runs along what are now very familiar 'little did I know' lines. But the description would be of secondary value were it not for the dreamer's presence indicated frequently in phrases like 'saugh I' (1273). In other words, the dreamer supplies a text which the poet then glosses:

Qui amer vuet, or y entende,
Car li romans des or amende;
Des or le fet bon escouter,
S'il est qui le sache conter,
Car la matire en est novelle
Et la fin du songe est mout belle.
Qui du songe la fin orra,
Je vous di bien que il porra
Des jeus d'Amors assés aprendre,
Par quoi il vueille bien entendre
(Que je die et que j'encomance
Dou songe la senefiance.)
La vérité qui est couverte
Vous sera lores descouverte
Quant espondre m'orrés le songe,
Car il n'i a mot de mençonge.   (2061–76)

The boke is good at the endyng,
Made of newe and lusty thyng;
For whoso wol the endyng here,
The craft of Loue he shal nowe lere,
If that he wol so long abyde,
Tyl I this Romance maye vnhyde,
And vndo the signyfiaunce
Of this dreme into Romaunce.
The sothfastnesse that nowe is hydde,
Without couerture shal be kydde
Whan I vndone haue this dremyng,
Wherin no worde is of leasyng.   (2163–74)

This is tidy in theory; but the exposition of the two temporal perspectives takes place in a third, the time occupied by the unfolding of the work itself. In that time the two are mixed, and we pass so quickly from one to the other as to become perplexed. In line 1387, for instance (French line 1361), we are with the poet, but by line 1390 we are at least halfway back to the dreamer's sense impression:

Que vous iroie je notant?
De divers arbres y ot tant
Que molt en seroie encombrés
Ains que les eüsse nombrés.   (1361–4)

What shulde I tel you more of it?
There were so many trees yet,
That I shulde al encombred be
Er I had rekened every tree.   (1387–90)

The dreamer speaks out in the present tense—as in line 4136 (French, 3793), 'For I am fallen into hell'—with the author content to defer to the immediacy of his former state as lover, and recalling himself to the authorial present nine

66

lines later. The dreamer's plight is often presented in the present tense, and the English translation perhaps makes even more than Guillaume's French of such tense switches. The English mixing of the two voices is well done. The comment on Male Bouche, for example, is freely amplified from the French, and it combines authorial anger at evil tongues with the dreamer's resentment of a character:

> Malebouche, que nul n'esperne,
> Sor chascun trove quelque herne.   (3909–10)

> Thus Wicked-Tonge (God yeve him shame)
> Can put hem everychone in blame
> Without deserte and causelesse;
> He lyeth, though they ben gyltlesse.
> I haue pyte to sene the sorowe,
> That waketh bothe eue and morowe,
> To innocentes dothe such greuaunce;
> I pray God yeue him yuel chaunce,
> That he euer so besye is
> Of any woman to seyne amys!   (4267–76)

This has the best of both worlds, blending the dramatically involved and circumscribed narrator with the reflective poet, and giving the fiction of the poem an experiential pseudo-validity. The passage is an English embellishment, but the technique is learned from Guillaume.

Guillaume is quite happy to make use of the reported sense-impressions to effect transitions that would otherwise deploy a compositional formula of the type 'Now I have told you about *x*, I shall tell you next about *y*':

> Quant j'oi veües les semblances
> De ceus qui menoient les dances,
> J'oi lors talent que le vergier
> Alasse veoir et cerchier   (1285–8)

> Whan I had sene the countenaunces
> Of hem that ladden thus these daunces,
> Than had I wyl to gon and se
> The gardyn that so lyked me . . .   (1309–12)

About this stage of the poem, indeed, describing activities in the garden, Chaucer makes one of his amplifications of the French to draw out of what looks like an unsigned narratorial comment ('Fox est qui de tel n'a enuie') a first-person comment in the present tense that goes further than Guillaume in scrambling the two voices:

> Diex! cum menoient bonne vie!
> Fox est qui de tel n'a envie.
> Qui autel vie avoir porroit
> De mendre bien se sofferoit.
> Il n'est nus grandres parevis
> D'avoir amie a son devis.   (1295–1300)

> A, lorde! they lyued lustely!
> A great foole were he, sykerly,
> That nolde, his thankes, suche lyfe lede!
> For this dare I sayne, out of drede,
> That whoso myght so wel fare,
> For better lyfe durst him not care;
> For there nys so good paradyse
> As to have a loue at his deuyse. (1319–26)

These lines are interesting as they show Chaucer reacting to a common temptation in reading the *Roman* to extend consciousness of the narratorial *persona* into our response to numerous rhetorical devices (see, for example, *Romaunt* 1067–9, 1171–80) that are not explicitly associated with the first-person pronoun. The narrator's presence in dream poetry encourages this. But as readers we fall into this trap at our peril: the critical history of the *Canterbury Tales* contains many a cautionary lesson. We should not confuse the two; but I think it is fair to say that the doubts raised by the presence of the poet-dreamer-narrator *persona*, and by the interweaving of his two temporal voices, create a context in which we are made to feel confused and disoriented, wary of *sententiae* that may be used here as a form of special pleading.

By these means, authority is undermined. This applied to *auctoritates*, for conventional material is manipulated in such a way that all becomes new, unstable and unpredictable within a decorum defined by the shifting relation of past and present. It applies too to the author, whose arbitrating presence is compromised by his past inanity. That is not all that undermines him. In fact, the author is a fiction—like the dreamer. Or, at least, he is a liar: he vouches for the truth of past dream experience that we know or suspect to be fictitious. Failure to consider this lie, this fiction, accounts for singleminded misreadings of the *Roman* such as Robertson's: for if all is mendacious, there is no point of narratorial reference, no one tone, from which we can begin to explicate 'the truth'.

All these implications are there in Guillaume, but they are realised by Jean. What in Guillaume is discreetly hinted at is by Jean loudly stated and ruthlessly paraded; and Jean makes much capital of the narratorial *persona*. Readers of the Middle English *Romaunt* in Sutherland's parallel text may easily see how Chaucer, or another, responds to this by further amplifications involving the first-person pronoun: it is Jean's practice, I think, that stimulates Chaucer to insert an extra 'I' in the passage from Guillaume last quoted above. Jean's stylistic range is greater than Guillaume's, an advantage colouring his confidence in handling both tone and *persona*. Jean's mastery of *persona* goes well beyond the narrator, for he greatly extends and perfects Guillaume's use of dramatic monologue—with perhaps less respect for allegorical decorum. In Jean's dramatic monologues, which are his main structural mode of amplification, the relation of speaker to theme is variously and variably direct and indirect, major or minor, the voice sometimes defined by allegorical role and at other times the vehicle for much material of wider thematic relevance. Jean begins his continuation by applying this technique to narratorial *persona*, continuing the dreamer's lament with which Guillaume's work finishes, and using it to review the main events of Guillaume's plot. The dreamer's

perversity is shown by twists of thought and tone more abrupt and dramatic
than anything in Guillaume:

> Droit ot Raison de moi blamer
> Quant onques m'entremis d'amer.
> Trop griés maus me couvient sentir;
> Je m'en veil, ce croi, repentir.
> Repentir? las! je que feroie?
> Traïtres, las, honnis seroie. (4151–6)

> Reson had bothe skyll and ryght,
> Whan she me blamed, with al her myght,
> To medle of loue, that hath me shent;
> But certayne nowe I wol repent.
>   And shulde I repent? Nay, parde!
> A false traytour then shulde I be. (4543—8)

From this 'compleynt'—which is a prototype of the 'shrift wythout repent-
aunce' of the *Book of the Duchess*—Chaucer may perhaps derive the identity of
the 'phisicien' that might cure that poem's narrator of his initial wretchedness:

> Et toutefois, por li deduire,
> A vous, Amors, ains que je muire,
> Des que ne puis porter son fes,
> Sans repentir me fais confés,
> Si cum font li loial amant,
> Et vueil faire mon testament:
> Au departir mon cuer li lez,
> Ja ne seront autre me lez.
> Tant cum ensi me dementoie
> Des grans dolors que je sentoie,
> Ne savoie ou guerre mire
> De ma tristece ne de m'ire.
> Lors vi a moi droit revenant
> Raison la bele, l'avenant,
> Qui de sa tour jus descendi
> Quant mes complaintes entendi. (4213–38)

> But first, withoute repentaunce,
> I wol me confesse in god entent,
> And make in haste my testament,
> As louers done that felen smerte:
> To Bialacoil leaue I myn herte
> Al hole, without departyng,
> Or doublenesse of repentyng.
>   Thus as I made my passage
> In compleynt, and in cruel rage,
> And I not where to fynde a leche
> That couthe vnto myn helpyng eche,
> Sodainly agayne comen down
> Out of her tour I sawe Reasoun . . . (4608–20)

The shift in tense here, anticipated in the French, is a signal of what is to come. The complaint has been in the present tense and persuasively relevant to the poem's immediate situation. The poet then reverts to the past tense before the introduction of Reason, whose return Jean has arranged for the express purpose of further debunking the narrator. Before her arrival, Jean has already made the dreamer condemn himself—'I was a foole, 4534 ('Ie fu fox', 4143); 'A foole myselfe I may well call', 4540 ('Tenir me puis pour assoté', 4148)—in a way which seems of immediate relevance but is really the retrospective judgement of the older and wiser poet interpolated into the younger self's complaint. This provides an unequivocal framework for the second brush with Reason (the stichomythic commencement of which is perhaps an inspiration for the climax of the conversation between the Black Knight in the *Book of the Duchess*). When Reason says 'Certes, frende, a foole arte thou' (5185)— 'Certes, biaus amis, fox es tu' (4673)—the narrator has already been seen to agree with her.

After this exchange, as Spearing notes, the detachment of poet from narratorial *persona*, which Jean has accelerated, grows ever greater: the plot is given over to the debasement and humiliation of the lover. He is constantly gulled and does no more to protect himself than protest querulously to such characters as Ami. Eventually, he is brought to the pass of a near-drubbing at the hands of Bel-Accueil's gaolers (15068ff.). At this extreme point, with the old Adam reduced to a shamefully ridiculous position, the new clerk intervenes to speak of his book *in propria persona*. He addresses loyal lovers, who are exhorted to keep listening until they have fully received his Art of Love; and, as Jean bids them wait for clarification of troublesome points, he articulates his sense—or, as I have claimed, what was originally Guillaume's sense—of producing text plus gloss:

> Et se vous y trovés rienz trouble
> Qui vostre conscience trouble,
> Quant le songe m'orrés espondre,
> Bien savrés lors d'amors respondre,
> S'il est qui en sache opposer,
> Quant le texte m'orrés gloser . . .   (15145–50)

[You will have an adequate art of love, and if you have any difficulty, I will clarify what confuses you when you have heard me explain the dream. Then, if someone creates opposition, you will know how to reply about love, when you have heard me gloss the text.]

Jean defends his poem against charges of obscenity, as Chaucer is to defend the *Canterbury Tales*, on grounds of stylistic decorum; against criticism of the portrait of False Seeming, on grounds of fair comment and his own passionate loyalty to Holy Church; and, as Chaucer is to defend *Troilus* and his own translation of the *Rose*, against charges of antifeminism. This last-named defence begins with a disclaimer—Jean wouldn't dream of criticising any living woman, and so forth—but quickly becomes an aggressive apology which Chaucer surely recalled when planning the Wife of Bath's Prologue. If you don't believe me, says Jean, go to the authorities and you'll find that all agree with me; moreover, they do so on grounds of experience:

Cil les meurs feminins savoient,
Car tous esprouvez les avoint,
Et tiex es fames les trouverent,
Que par divers tens esproverent;
Par quoi miex m'en devés quiter;
Je n'i fais riens fors reciter
Se par mon geu, qui pau vous couste,
Aucune chose n'i ajouste . . . (15239-36)

[They knew about the ways of women, for they had tested them all and found such ways in women by testing at various times. For this reason you should the sooner absolve me; I do nothing but retell just what the poets have written between them . . . except that my treatment, which costs you little, may add a few speeches.]

'Blameth nat me'; 'For as myn auctour seyde, so sey I'; and do not be so pedantic as to mind, moreover, my odd little *jeu d'esprit*. The wit of an apocryphal poet is immediately followed by the statement of Jean's readiness to stand correction before Holy Church, in which humour is absent, as we should expect. This is a major source of a Chaucerian repertoire.

But what is the purpose of this defence, placed at a point that seems utterly and authoritatively to differentiate poet and dreamer? In context, it is to absolve the poet, in advance, of responsibility for the ending of his poem. As his *persona* dreamed, and as his dreamer performed, so must he write. The sobriety is maintained for quite some time longer; Nature reprises the Boethian elements of the poem, and with this impeccable authority adds her support to Reason's arguments and stresses self-knowledge as the sole criterion of wise love. There then occurs a very pointed passage on deceptive, distorting mirrors (as in the Well of Narcissus). The moral dimension of these applied optics is clearer still when Nature's discussion moves on, firstly, to a properly sceptical (one might say Pertelotean) treatment of dreams, in which the *insomnium* is foregrounded, and secondly to a fine commentary on *gentilesse*. All this is irreducibly serious, and it culminates in a massively homiletic denunciation of mankind as spiritually corrupt. It is all the more comically shocking, therefore, that Nature's final message, relayed by Genius, should be—as in the *Parliament of Fowls*—an exhortation to fecundity, and courtly folly is waved away by the imperative of impregnation. It is as if high seriousness, and Nature herself, have licensed the poet's decision to let the dreamer get on with it. Ovidian doubts about quite what he is getting on with, which go back as far as Guillaume's Well of Narcissus, are reintroduced by the strategically placed Pygmalion episode. The question raised, mythographically and iconographically, is whether love is really self-love, whether one loves another body and soul or a whited sepulchre; and given such questions, were they seriously posed, one years for an authoritative—an authorial—voice to answer them. What Jean supplies instead is in order an apology for digression, an unfulfilled promise that all will be clarified; and an incongruous statement that the image of his description bears no resemblance to Pygmalion's, which becomes the occasion of a cheerfully extravagant boast in which, once again, the voices of older poet and younger lover are fused:

Mes c'est trop loing de ma matire,
Por ce est drois qu'arrier m'en tire.
Bien orrois que ce segnefie
Ains que ceste ovre soit fenie.
　Ne vous vuel or ci plus tenir,
A mon propos m'estuet venir,
Autre champ me convient arer.
Qui vodroit donques comparer
De ces deus ymages ensemble
Les biautés, si cum il me semble,
Tel similitude i puet prendre:
Autant cum la soris est mendre
Que li lyons et mains cremue,
De cors, de force et de value,
Autant, sachiés en loiauté,
Ot ceste ymage mains biauté
Que n'a cele que tant ci pris.　(21211–27)

[But all this is very far from my matter, and I must draw you back from it.
By the time you have finished this work you will know what it means. But
I won't keep you any longer on this subject; I should return to my story,
since I must plow another field. Whoever, then, would wish to compare
the beauties of these two images could, it seems to me, compare them by
saying that as much as the mouse is smaller than the lion in body,
strength, and worth, and less to be feared, so much was the one image less
beautiful than that which I here esteem so greatly.]

The lover then has his way and his rose; the author has no further overt access
to his poem. In short, we have a highly comic evasion, and a splendidly rough
transition to the climax: henceforth meaning is located in the pilgrim's pole and
his two bags of nails, and all is—at once—obscene mockery and mock
obscenity. This is, finally, an outrageously comic performance (sexual and
poetic), Goliardic and Ovidian in its excess.

Critics are agreed that this poetic performance is ironic; and so helpful does
this critical term turn out to be that we fail to reach general agreement on
anything further. Irony suffers more than most critical terms from the fact that
it can be used in various, and discordant, senses. It can be all things to all
critics; irony's name apparently partakes of its nature. I can think of two ways,
one precise and the other very broad, in which irony can be defined as germane
to the *Roman de la Rose*, though in neither case is it the key to all meanings. The
precise definition, as Wayne Booth insists, involves the rejection of the literal
meaning and a trying out of other possible meanings until the right (or a
consistent) one is found. This is the only sense in which irony can be
categorised as a means of rhetorical expression: most rhetorical expression is
by nature unironical. The rhetorical relation between *ironia* and *allegoria* here
provides a sharp check to the effort to schematise irony in a work that is already
allegorical, in which, that is, one habitually rejects and reinterprets the literal:
it is doubtful whether the same activity can be performed twice over. When one
is engaged with the *Roman de la Rose* in substitution for the literal level, one is
engaged in allegorical exegesis, not—except incidentally—in any systematic

detection of irony. This will reveal much about the design of the poem, and it runs a serious danger of losing touch with its tone. Meaning lies in both design and tone, not in one or the other.

Jean's tone is related to his manipulation of narrator-*persona*. In considering this, we may perhaps speak of irony in the broadest possible sense, that of detachment (Northrop Frye's *eiron* as outsider):[43] to say this may be to say very little, beyond noting that a poet's attitude to his material is rarely one-to-one, passionate and ingenuous commitment—why should it be? Clearly, however, a poem about love in which the author's stance is that of a somewhat acerbic clerk will be different from a *dit amoureux*. Nor should we assume that detachment of this kind is a mode of meaning. It may in fact be the opposite, an evasion of meaning: casuistry pushed beyond the limit of logic, arch-sophistry. Copiousness of tone calls for generosity of interpretation, within limits set by the narrative, and signals inclusiveness of meaning. Here the narratorial *persona* can be seen as one device making for complexity of tone and meaning. And in Jean's dream-poem the *persona* has one other function that could be called ironic: he is the embodiment of dramatic irony. The poet is consciously superior to his audience and to himself as dreamer. Hence in the first instance the banter with imaginary audiences in which Jean promises that all will be explained, and in the second the present-tense commentary on the dreamer's past experience and decisions. The poet, as if *in propria persona*, is endowed with foreknowledge of the work's outcome. This is an extraordinary privilege, all the more so since the present poet is absolved from responsibility for the narrative unfolding of his past self's dream. No wonder that Jean de Meun, and Chaucer, were interested in Boethius: their poet-narrators are shadows of Boethius' God.

To talk of irony, then, will do if by irony we are content to mean a certain distance or detachment, a skilful and progressive intimation of foreknowledge, within a rich variety of tone. To claim that irony is more than this, in some sense both uniform and all-encompassing, is an act of faith, not criticism: it is an appropriation of the poem by the critic's ideology. Irony does not direct the meaning of Jean's work. Like the narrator-*persona*, it serves its tone.

Jean's use of Guillaume's narrator-*persona* is the mainspring of his range of tone. For Jean, as we have seen, capitalises on his inheritance from Guillaume: a narrator-poet who is the reconditioned dreamer, conscious of the distance between the 'I' of the dream's date and the 'I' of its subsequent narration. This is the distance noted above as potentially ironic, but it is only potentially, not necessarily, so: it will always affect local tone but need not reshape meaning. From this distance arise the constant gradations of tone and modulations of voice—some subtle and some sharp—which are especially characteristic of Jean's continuation, because the posture is one not of penitent but reporter. The narrator reports on a younger and wilder self for whom, as a sedate and mature citizen, he disclaims effective responsibility: for Jean, who has made off with the identity of Guillaume's dreamer, it is very close to reporting on someone else altogether. There is a certain amount of editorialising, or glossing, but its occurrence is patchy. There is no reason for the reporter any longer to identify himself with the actions (still less, the dream-actions) of his reported youth. Jean exploits this freedom to the full. He delights to linger in Guillaume's incongruous contexts. He happily stuffs his poem with, at one end of the scale, homily and, at the other, the alarming workmanship of the poem's final scenes, while filling the middle distance with dramatic monologues, stray *sententiae* and exemplary fictions. The narrator's voice is authoritative only when it is clearly that of the poet 'now' rather than the dreamer 'then', but the containment of these two time-scales within that of the work, continuous and sequential, makes the distinction hard to draw. Even when it can be drawn, *epanorthosis* still invades what the present poet has to say: Jean cares less seriously about whether some people will judge his work obscene, or about whether the ladies will be angry, than he cares about misinterpretation of his loyalty to the Church. In any case, as I have argued, the authority of the poet's present-tense utterance is compromised by his presentation of the events of the dream as truthful reporting. An authority based on false experience is an arbitrary authority. Even if we disregard this, we cannot expect the presenter of an *insomnium* to be oracular. In short, the narratorial voice—the present 'I'—is as thoroughly fictionalised as the dreamer's maze. The poem's meaning is therefore made as digressive as Jean's structure. Jean's activity is a form of guerrilla warfare, his meaning a well-camouflaged enemy lurking to ambush its readers with weapons of direct philosophical, moral and social comment at the most unexpected of moments and in the most apparently innocuous of contexts. Its readers are left wondering how such a manifest fiction may inflict such intellectual pain.

Guillaume's narratorial *persona* enables Jean—and after Jean, Chaucer—to discover an Ovidian plurality of tone. It is organised along a sliding scale to do with folly and wisdom worked out in the fictionalised poet's time: all possible reactions of the poet at any age are potentially present in any one comment or in the narration of any one incident. Jill Mann has lately remarked this quality of tone in the *Canterbury Tales*: Chaucer may well have felt sorry for Dorigen on first devising her story, but as an author familiar with its shape and foreknowing its happy outcome why on earth—as narrator, in his comments, covert or overt—should he be expected to waste his sympathy?[44] Chaucer's narratorial *persona*, like Jean's, is temporally unstable: at a particular moment we can rarely be quite sure which of his ages is concealed behind the mask. Moreover, the *persona* is not a constant point of reference; it occurs where it is seen to occur. Having mobilised these formidable convolutions of tone, the narrator is often content to receive despatches in his tent. At times we should be prepared for the mask to drop. The dreamer of the *House of Fame*, who is 'Geffrey', is scarcely portrayed as a dignified figure, as he is first abducted by a garrulous eagle and then deposited amid the hurly-burly of Fame's palace and the whirlwind of Rumour. Yet there is very little distance between the *persona* and the poet when, standing amazed in this universe of possible tones, he produces this ringing declaration:

> I wot myself best how y stonde;
> For what I drye, or what I thynke,
> I wil myselven al hyt drynke,
> Certeyn, for the more part,
> As fer forth as I kan myn art.   (1878–82)

Boitani calls this 'the noble expression of a full and totally human self-awareness and responsibility',[45] a firm statement by the poet Chaucer. The ending of the *Parliament of Fowls* evokes a similar response if, as I believe, the narrator in the final stanza is entirely satisfied and in harmony with his books and his dream. One precedent for the assertion in the *House of Fame* lies in Jean's defence of his poem, but that defence is a digression. By integrating it into his narrative and making it the climax of his plot, Chaucer achieves something entirely new in the process of a dream poem: by the use of a narratorial *persona* he discovers his real self—as an author, and as the mainspring of his own authority.

It is an irreversible step: it negates the need for a dream. One might think, too, that it outgrows the need for a narratorial *persona*. To an extent, as I shall argue, this is the logic of Chaucer's later work; but all he has learnt from the *Roman de la Rose* in the way of tonal variation and the fictionalisation of authority is contingent upon Jean's narratorial *persona*. Thus Chaucer in his later work proposes an original solution. He retains a narratorial *persona* and he abandons the dream. The reconditioned dreamer becomes an apocryphal author.

CHAPTER 4

Voices of Performance: Chaucer's Use of Narrators in Troilus *and* The Canterbury Tales

In the *Roman de la Rose* a complex mastery of tone comes inseparably from a complex narrator-*persona*. The *Roman* gives Chaucer an inspiring precedent which he develops with originality in his dream visions. In his later work, when he moves outside the vision framework, it seems that he does not leave the narrator-*persona* behind him: in *Troilus* many readers detect a highly wrought *persona*, and the *Canterbury Tales* offer what has proved, for modern criticism, an embarrassment of riches. There is continuity in Chaucer's later use of *persona*, but there is also a substantial shift. This chapter's purpose is to assess both.

When the Chaucerian narrator is emancipated from his dreams, he is deprived of an active role in his own narrative. He is even, in *Troilus*, denied the imperfect authority of an eye-witness. If the *persona* is not to be redundant, another role must be found for him. Only one possible role remains: that of the performer of the poem. The narrator is fictionalised, or partly so, as the work's exponent. The proposition is reversible, and probably makes more sense when it is reversed: Chaucer in his later poetry decides to fictionalise, or dramatise, the moments of composition and the act of performance. He therefore retains narratorial *personae*, which enact and sign a fiction.

They also inscribe, in devious fashion, the identity of the performer, at once keeping the author before the eyes of his public and concealing him. He is concealed, in *Troilus*, behind an apocryphal source, 'Lollius', and in the *Canterbury Tales* by a number of *personae* whose words are ostensibly reported by the one pilgrim who also happens to be 'Chaucer'. Authority is thus kept as debatable as in any *insomnium*. As in dream poems too, the narrator's role is not evidently to call into question overt statements or challenge the otherwise obvious meaning of lines. It contributes to the work's tone but it does not determine its meaning, although it complements meaning by insisting that it is contained within a fictionalised performance. This function of the narrator is intrinsic to the poem's subject and its treatment. There is also, however, a partly extrinsic function. Not only does the narratorial *persona* challenge and tease the poet's public, or imaginary audience; he also mediates between the actual and specific poet, Chaucer, and the actual audience of any specific reading that Chaucer could possibly have foreseen. The latter function is one of compliment, not complement: the narrator flatters the audience with his deference, and his sometimes comic characterisation, playing upon his inadequacies, is a modesty-*topos*—that is, a self-congratulation—writ large. Chaucer's treatment of his narrator most resembles that of Jean de Meun, but the attention to an audience is like Machaut's or, better, Grandson's. For Grandson supplies the gesture—a narrator who is not a lover—which most ensures that the poet is seen not to claim social equality, or compete, with his audience. The narrator continues to be the fluctuating presence of dream poetry, by no means a constant point of reference. His interventions also continue to fluctuate in tone and time, responding appropriately to the temporal sequence of the work—and arbitrarily too, as if plucked from a random point in the poet's own lifespan. Such poetry purports, but only purports, to be a form of intellectual autobiography. Such a narrator purports, but only purports, to be more than a rhetorician's surrogate. He promises moral depths, and he delivers wonderfully polished surfaces.

I Troilus

The story of *Troilus* is history, and its matter is supposedly derived from the historical authority of Lollius. Chaucer names this source in Book I, as he introduces the *Canticus Troili*:

> And of his song naught only the sentence,
> As writ myn auctour called Lollius,
> But pleinly, save our tonge difference,
> I dar wel seyn yn al that Troilus
> Seyde in his song, loo, every word right thus
> As I shal seyn; and whoso list it here,
> Loo, next this vers he may it fynden here.   (I 393–9)

The source for the *Canticus* is not Chaucer's usual source, Boccaccio's *Il Filostrato*, but Petrarch's Sonnet 88, and the translation is close enough to justify Chaucer's claim that he translates 'naught only the sentence' but 'every word'. However, both Petrarch and Boccaccio remain unnamed, here as in the rest of *Troilus*, and the effect of this stanza is therefore to construct a fictional gloss on the English poet's general treatment of his proclaimed Latin source. The implication, I think, is that normally he performs an act of abridgement, rendering Lollius' 'sentence'; stencil translation, as here, is the exception. All the matter stems from Lollius, and a few other 'bokes olde' (presumably Joseph of Exeter, Guido, Benoit) that the poet consults for the thought and speech of his characters:

> His resons, as I may my rymes holde,
> I wol yow telle, as techen bokes olde.   (III 90–1)

The reminders of sources cited have in common a self-conscious reference to the poet's 'rymes' or 'vers', and we are to infer from the conjunction of these two that Chaucer lays claim to the credit for the poetic disposition of his poem, not its invention. After the love scenes of Book III have been successfully negotiated, Chaucer thanks the muse Clio and 'myn auctor' (III 1817); and in minor ways (for example, tags like 'as I rede', I 159), the debt has been acknowledged throughout. By the same token, where the book fails him, the poet is powerless: Hector sends a letter to Troilus asking for his counsel

> If swych a man was worthi to ben ded,
> Woot I nought who   (II 1699–1700)

or, when Hector proposes to lead a party against the Greeks,

> Not I how longe or short it was bitwene
> This purpos and that day they fighten mente.   (IV 36–7)

This is not an eyewitness but a book-witness: he can only report what he finds written. He tells us what he cannot say ('Kan I naught seyn . . .' III 967) as well as what he finds ('But wel fynde I . . .' III 971). These may be trivial details of behaviour or graver matters of motivation and understanding:

> But how it was, certeyn, kan I nat seye,
> If that his lady understood nat this,
> Or feynede hire she nyste, oon of the tweye;
> But wel I rede that, by no manere weye,
> Ne semed it as that she of hym roughte,
> Or of his peyne, or whatsoevere he thoughte.   (I 492–7)

At this stage of the work Troilus, and perhaps Criseyde herself, do not know what Criseyde feels. There is therefore a decorum in this ignorance: it corresponds to the time of the work. But these, by and large, are the inevitable gaps that any historian must put up with:

> Nought list myn auctour fully to declare
> What that she thoughte whan he seyde so.   (III 575–6)

The gaps reach to details most authors can take for granted: 'But trewely, I kan nat telle hire age' (V 826). And they bring to mind a narrator who scrutinises his text like a dreamer scans the *mise-en-scène* of his dream. Chaucer adds to his portrait of Criseyde from Joseph and Guido a tag, apparently stressing physical sight, that is expressive of this dreamlike relationship with his apocryphal source:

> And save hir browes joyneden yfere,
> Ther nas no lak, in aught I kan espien.   (V 813–14)

For the apocryphal source takes over the epistemological function of the dream vision, serving in its stead to absolve the poet of responsibility for his narrative, and to mark the necessary limits of the narrator's authority and his perceptions. As in a dream, we should not expect total consistency. The veil is not always overtly present: 'And what she thoughte, somwhat shal *I* write' (II 699), though even here the 'somwhat' signals the normal mode of translation by 'sentence', or abridgement. The narrator thus shares some of the uncertain and fluctuating quality of a dreamer-poet; and it is entirely in keeping with this that he should characterise himself in the terms Chaucer worked out for the narrator of his, earlier, dream poetry. He serves lovers but is not a lover, a role played here not in any dream but in relation to his source: hence in the Proem to Book II he states roundly that he translates from Latin, not out of *sentement*. He professes that he is unable to do justice to the consummation of Book III (1310–11), but pays tribute to its power by confessing to an envy of lovers in mock-blasphemous terms more than usually open to ironic reading:

> Why nad I swich oon with my soule ybought,
> Ye, or the leeste joie that was theere?
> Awey, thow foule daunger and thow feere,
> And lat hem in this hevene blisse dwelle,
> That is so heigh that al ne kan I telle! (III 1319–23)

The narrator proceeds immediately to associate this with his activity as translator:

> But soth is, though I kan nat tellen al,
> As kan myn auctour, of his excellence,
> Yet have I seyd, and God toforn, and shal
> In every thing, al holy his sentence . . . (III 1324–7)

He follows it with a second person plural appeal to his audience of lovers, to be noted below. Like Jean de Meun in the *Roman*, he can profess a detached attitude to love which is not devoid of clerkly suspicion while at the same time invoking the antecedent authority of his text ('After myn auctour . . . / As writen clerkes in hire bokes olde' III 1196, 1199); just as Jean de Meun maintains a pose of fidelity to the prior events of his dream, to license representation of scenes of sexual fulfilment. At the same time the clerkly disengagement from love, like Jean's detachment from his younger self, allows a passage condemning 'feynede loves' in the poem's epilogue (V 1848), and implicitly anticipates the potential for this judgement. The dialectic of the reconditioned dreamer-poet with his youthful dream is transposed into that between the translator-poet and his ancient text. This poet is a reconditioned translator, and the emotion of his first reading is recollected in the wisdom of hindsight.

As with dream poetry, the co-presentation of the poet's initial, absorbing experience (in *Troilus*, of reading) with the wisdom of an older man's judgement unfolds along the temporal axis of the poem itself as the sequence of narration. This is not conducive to a consistency of mood, for the narration must respond according to the local texture of particular stages in its own sequence. We find this reflected in certain types of transition, as in Book III's night of love: 'I passe al that which chargeth nought to seye' (III 1576), or 'Reson wol nought that I speke of slep / For it accordeth nought to my matere' (III 1408–9). We also find it in the framing devices of the various books, especially in the different tones generated in their proems. The proem to Book I, with its compassion for lovers (a stance recalled in Book IV's proem), that of Book II announcing the 'kalendes' of hope, and the cosmic optimism in the proem to

Book III are all manifestly suited to the matter of each book in turn. Lastly we find, in the poet's respect for narrative sequence, a decorum reflected in some of the local comments he permits himself. The presence or absence of a narratorial 'I' makes little difference to such comments, which simply capture —or encourage—the quality of the reader's obvious response. The dramatic question with which Book II ends is of this order: 'O myghty God, what shal he seye?' Similarly, earlier in the same book Criseyde, with Pandarus, has her second view of Troilus riding at the street's end. The structural expectation is that this view will encourage Criseyde to fall in love with Troilus, and so—irrespective of our 'serious' opinions of love or the worthiness of Criseyde —we are surely meant to participate here in the poet's wish: 'To God hope I she hath now kaught a thorn' (II 1272). In Book V, however, we have seen Criseyde transfer her affections to Diomede and even give him Troilus' brooch—'and that was litel nede' (V 1040). Is there any other reasonable reaction to this news? Or any chance of mistaking the sardonic tone of the narrator's comment on Criseyde's final letter to Troilus, that she wrote it 'for routhe—I take it so' (V 1588–9)?

These glosses on single incidents in no way determine our response to Criseyde over all: we are free to judge as we like, just as in life we are free, if we are so foolhardy, to take sides about a friend's marital breakdown. The narrator's attitude is explicit, and will be discussed below. His reportage of the facts is consistent with that limited sense of his own authority already seen to be characteristic of the whole work. She gave Diomede Troilus's brooch and her loyalty. Her lament at the destruction of her own good name is set down as 'the storie telleth us' (V 1051); but it is preceded by a stanza again acknowledging a narratorial consciousness that historical exposition stops short of an exact knowledge of other people's feelings. The stanza begins 'I fynde ek in the stories elleswhere' (1044); it records Criseyde's grief when Diomede is wounded by Troilus; and it concludes: 'Men seyn—I not—that she yaf hym hire herte' (1050). This profession of ignorance is not an ironic way of reinforcing the poet's feeling that Criseyde did indeed give Diomede her heart, though this is the implication of the facts presented; yet it does nothing to soften those implications. Why should it, and how could it? By this stage of the poem the Criseyde whom Troilus has loved, and whom poet and audience have known, is suddenly again a stranger, disfigured by her behaviour. The narrator's comment records this, and abrogates the kind of access to Criseyde's feelings he has had in Books II and III:

> Now myghte som envious jangle thus:
> 'This was a sodeyn love; how myght it be
> That she so lightly loved Troilus,
> Right for the firste syghte, ye, parde?'
> Now whoso seith so, mote he nevere ythe!
> For every thyng, a gynnyng hath it nede
> Er al be wrought, withowten any drede.
>
> For I sey nought that she so sodeynly
> Yaf hym hire love, but that she gan enclyne
> To like hym first, and I have told yow whi;
> And after that, his manhod and his pyne

Made love withinne hire herte for to myne,
For which, by proces and by good servyse,
He gat hire love, and in no sodeyn wyse.   (II 666–79)

This is a narratorial address to the audience, and belongs with others still to be
considered. With the narrator-like hindsight of second reading (after in Book
V we have seen the effect of 'this sodeyn Diomede'), it can be said to be ironic.
The irony is dramatic irony, however, not the verbal irony which requires the
rejection of the obvious meaning. If 'som envious' were to have jangled thus
after II 665, he would have felt foolish to find the rest of Book II filled with the
protracted process of Criseyde's making her mind up. This weighty intervention is another comment of local significance: it belongs at just this stage of the
poem's chronology and no other. The tense and tone of such interventions,
major or minor, changes appropriately with the poem's narrative on a scale of
attitudes ranging from playful to sombre, and a linguistic register from ludic to
religious. The most open example of this kind of decorum is in the proems.
The tone of the poem, however, as distinct from explicit commentary and
narratorial interventions, is less straightforward: the two key registers of
language, ludic and religious, invade the territory appropriate to the other (as
in the mock-blasphemy of III 1319–23: see above, p. 79). They do this most
strongly at times when there is no narratorial *persona* in sight. It will not do to
credit the narrator with the tone.

The sense of the narrator's presence becomes increasingly sporadic from
after the proem to Book IV. In that book we thereafter make do with one stanza
professing incompetence to describe Criseyde's sorrow at the news that she
must leave Troy (IV 799–805) and with a few tags like 'as I devyse' (238, 259,
735), 'I shal yow tellen soone' (1127), as the barest index of the poet's
first-person presence. Book IV ends without a reminder of this presence, and
Book V has no proem. In this book, until the Criseyde portrait (V 814), there is
only one stanza to bring the author explicitly into the poem: its subject is
Troilus' grief (267–73), and it is an exact parallel of IV 799–805. From V 1044
the first-person voice is again much in evidence, dealing almost exclusively
with questions of the nature and extent of Criseyde's guilt. It fades after a
stanza urging every man and woman of chivalry to mourn the death of Hector
(V 1555–61), and resurfaces at V 1765, which marks the start of the epilogue:

> And if I hadde ytaken for to write
> The armes of this ilke worthi man,
> Than wolde ich of his batailles endite;
> But for that I to writen first bigan
> Of his love, I have seyd as I kan,—
> His worthi dedes, whoso list hem heere,
> Rede Dares, he kan telle hem alle ifeere—
>
> Bysechyng every lady bright of hewe,
> And every gentil womman, what she be,
> That al be that Criseyde was untrewe,
> That for hir gilt she be nat wroth with me.
> Ye may hire giltes in other bokes se;
> And gladlier I wol write, yif yow leste,
> Penelopëës trouthe and good Alceste.

N'y sey nat this al oonly for thise men,
But moost for wommen that bitraised be
Thorugh false folk; God yeve hem sorwe, amen!
That with hire grete wit and subtilte
Bytraise yow! And this commeveth me
To speke and in effect yow alle I preye,
Beth war of men, and herkneth what I seye!   (V 1765–85)

There is no question here of a major shift of voice. The first of these stanzas, with its echo of the first line of the *Æneid*, restates that the poet is governed by the pre-existent nature of his story, given the decision to write on love rather than epic deeds. In yet another address to the audience he then moves on, clearly recalling Jean de Meun's apology for antifeminism before the final movement of the *Roman de la Rose*, to the wider implications of Criseyde's guilt, making incidental use of Jean's defence that such material is to be seen in 'other bokes'. Since the narratorial interventions of Book V have almost exclusively arbitrated the matter of Criseyde's guilt, one is not justified in finding here any discontinuity or arguing that a fictionalised *persona* is supplanted by the poet's own voice. In the following stanza Chaucer twists the argument by advice to the women in his audience, who are addressed as 'ye'. There is much room for debating its seriousness or wit, but it expresses an attitude already made manifest in the earlier interventions of Book V: this, unlike *Il Filostrato*, is not to be a book with an anti-feminist moral, and a response resting content merely with blame of Criseyde will be an inadequate response. There follow the two stanzas despatching the book to fame and its public, five stanzas despatching Troilus to the eighth sphere and beyond, two stanzas of exemplary moral recommending to 'yonge, fresshe folkes, he or she' the love of Christ rather than 'feynede loves', and the final three stanzas culminating in Chaucer's great Englishing of Dante's prayer to the Trinity. This is an epilogue (and a conclusion of the narrative) rather than a palinode; its potential has been woven into the fabric of the poem. I cannot see how it can be argued that it, more than or rather than other first-person sections of the poem, is in 'Chaucer's own voice', for it is surely an altogether appropriate response to the poem's sad and sombre ending, as other responses have been to other events, and it is as sharply drawn in its way as earlier interventions were in theirs. It has an advantage that earlier interventions do not: in the commendation of love of Christ it articulates a moral absolute. But, absolute as it is, this sort of absolute could occur only at the end of this sort of poem. It is a radical shift of mood and value, but it is not at all a shift of voice. It does what the first-person narratorial voice has done throughout: it responds appropriately to the particular stage of the work's unfolding.

The majority of the first-person intrusions, in fact, serve very closely the narrative process of the work's unfolding. They arise, as it were incidentally, in rhetorical figures such as *occupatio*, *expolitio*, brevity-*topoi*, *sententia*, *exclamatio* (see, for example, I 141, II 1219, 1264, 1564); and it would be a breach of critical logic to detect in such figures elements characterising the narratorial *persona*, or because of the assumed interposition of such a *persona*, irony. Such figures contain the option of a first person, but the first person is not a *persona* but merely a linguistic feature of the figure: there is little effective difference in respect of the first person between 'What sholde I drecche, or telle of his aray?'

(II 1264) and 'This joie may nought writen be with inke' (III 1693). Like all rhetorical figures they serve as reminders that the discourse is artificial, and thus that behind the rhetoric there is an artificer, a rhetorician.

The rhetorician has many choices open to him. He may, for example, deliberately overdo a figure, or apply it in an incongruous context, so that parody is the end-result, as in the Nun's Priest's Tale; but there is little sign of such inflation in *Troilus*. One of few exceptions, I think, appears in the content of the *exclamatio* 'But O Fortune, executrice of wyrdes' (III 617), applied as it is to a shower of rain. The rhetorician can also signal irony by including an ironic statement in the figure, but the conjunction of irony and figure is fortuitous. The one thing that a rhetorician cannot do is to signal irony by the very use of a rhetorical figure. If rhetorical figures were by nature ironic, they would cease to be rhetorical figures. Moreover, except in the abnormal circumstances outlined (and they would have to be very clearly signalled), we cannot speak of a narrator-*persona* as the rhetorician who decides to use the rhetorical figures. This, irreducibly, is the role of the poet. Therefore we should refuse to entertain any criticism inviting us to see an unreliable narrator as responsible for the rhetoric of *Troilus*. And if the narrator is reliable, there is little or nothing, rhetorically, to distinguish him from the poet in performance.

Much of the first-person narratorial intervention in *Troilus* directs our attention specifically to the performance of the work: not least in the large number of appeals to the audience. The poem's audience is invited, as it were, onstage, into the poem. Sometimes this is done in small and orthodox ways:

> Now lat us stynte of Troilus a stounde   (I 1086; cf. II 687)

> Now lat hire slepe, and we oure tales holde
> Of Troilus . . .   (II 932–3; cf. II 1709)

> What nedeth yow to tellen al the cheere
> That Deiphebus unto his brother made . . . ?   (II 1541–2)

Sometimes it is done more peremptorily:

> But al passe I, lest ye to longe dwelle
> For for o fyn is al that evere I telle.   (II 1595)

Sometimes the audience is the direct foil of a joke: on getting to know Troilus' good qualities, Criseyde was 'namore afered, / I mene as fer as oughte ben requered' (III 482–3). The joke here, like many other comments, revolves around the narrator's characterisation as 'withouten sentement': he defers to his audience directly as the experts in matters of love. In Book II, Criseyde lies in bed thinking of Troilus, 'the manere and the wise / Reherce it nedeth nought, for ye ben wise' (II 916–17); and in Book III, when they are reunited in bed,

> Nought nedeth it to yow, syn they ben met,
> To axe at me if that they blithe were.   (III 1681–2)

The most important example in Book III occurs when the narrator has excused himself for any ineptitude in his handling of love scenes (reinvoking the loveless *persona*), but promises to do his best to follow his author (III 1317–30; see above, p. 79):

> For myne wordes, heere and every part,
> I speke hem alle under correcioun
> Of yow that felyng han in loves art,
> And putte it al in youre discrecioun
> To encresse or maken dymynucioun
> Of my langage, and that I yow bisech.
> But now to purpos of my rather speche.   (III 1331–7)

As the last line suggests, the poet of Book III is less than thoroughly daunted. Indeed, he is not so loveless that he cannot include himself in a comment on Criseyde's reception of Troilus: 'With worse hap God lat us nevere mete!' (III 1246). Even so, a hint of the loveless *persona* persists, I think, in a self-deprecating comment on Troilus' grief in Book V, though the plural audience here has temporarily given way to a singular reader:

> Thow, redere, maist thiself ful wel devyne
> That swich a wo my wit kan nat diffyne.   (V 270–1)

Not a specific audience but every imaginable type of public is incorporated into the process of the written performance. That public, as audience, is consulted, cajoled, hurried along, flattered, mollified (if they are women), warned against jumping to hasty conclusions (if they are envious janglers), and—most important of all—involved in the rhetorical decisions in such a way that they too share the poet's struggle with his 'auctour':

> But now, paraunter, som man wayten wolde
> That every word, or soonde, or look, or cheere
> Of Troilus that I rehercen sholde,
> In al this while unto his lady deere.
> I trowe it were a long thyng for to here;
> Or of what wight that stant in swich disjoynte,
> His wordes alle, or every look, to poynte.
>
> For sothe, I have naught herd it don er this
> In story non, ne no man here, I wene;
> And though I wolde, I koude nought, ywys;
> For ther was som epistel hem bitwene,
> That wolde, as seyth myn autour, wel contene
> Neigh half this book, of which hym liste nought write.
> How sholde I thanne a lyne of it endite?   (III 491–504)

This is a bravura performance for a mere transition to summary narrative ('But to the grete effect', 505): but during its course the reader/auditor has been called upon to ransack his knowledge of literary structure and modes of narration, and to consider the difficulties of a translator. It is one of the several points in the work where, at some length, the audience participates in direct discourse with the narrator. That discourse extends to shared values, like the chivalrous grief at Hector's death, and shared wisdom—particularly proverbs and sententious commonplaces:

> For ay the ner the fir, the hotter is,—
> This, trowe I, knoweth al this compaignye.   (I 449–50)

Longer variants of this pattern are common; a proverb is supported by an authorial 'I', applied and then thrown open to the audience for approval (compare, for example, II 1338, III 1058–64 and III 1212–25, which culminates in an exhortation of 'every womman' to be as generous in bed as Criseyde was to Troilus). They are indices of an ongoing performance, and regulators of the audience's responses appropriately to the time of the poem. They are mainly deferential and confidential in tone until the epilogue, when the tone of the address becomes instead magisterial. Throughout, the audience is actively invited to share, and sometimes instructed in, a variety of responses.

The numerous modes of narratorial and audience engagement, of activating the poem as a living performance, naturally occur in clusters. In Book I, Troilus is toppled from his initial scorn of lovers (a shallower version of the distrust of love to which the epilogue will return), and this fall is recounted by a blend of complex changes of tone without narratorial signature, explicit narratorial interventions, rhetorical set pieces and appeals to the audience. After Troilus, like the dreamer in the *Roman de la Rose*, has succumbed to the God of Love's arrow, the poet breaks into an *exclamatio* ('O blynde world, O blynde entencioun!' 211), then develops an oblique and unflattering reference in the style of the *Roman* to Troilus and all lovers ('alday faileth thing that fooles wenden' 217) into the highly unflattering comparison between Troilus and 'proud Bayard' (218–31). The audience is then directly apostrophised as 'Ye wise, proude and worthi folkes alle' (233) and urged to take 'ensample' from Troilus of the *sententia* that 'may no man fordon the lawe of kynde' (239). Line 240 states flatly that this *sententia* has ever proved true. Only then, again in an appeal to the audience, is there a use of the first-person pronoun:

> For this trowe I ye knowen alle or some,
> Men reden nat that folk han gretter wit
> Than they that han be most with love ynome.   (I 240–2)

This is what I have described as a largely incidental 'I', generated by the *sententia* and the address, not by the wish to interpolate a fictionalised *persona*. The next two stanzas assert that since the effect of love is to ennoble, and since in any case love cannot be withstood, the audience, apostrophised again, should not refuse to love; 'and therfore I yow rede / To folowen hym that so wel kan yow lede' (I 258–9). We do not understand this 'I' if we inquire whether it belongs to the poet himself or to a narrator-*persona*. Clearly, it is a narratorial or authorial 'I', as the next stanza confirms by returning to the immediate telling of the immediate tale ('Of hym thenke I my tale forth to holde' 263); but it is no more than one of several linked devices by which within 100 lines the poem may pass from Troilus' distrust of love to a comment which, while it must be categorised as narratorial, is not explicitly so: 'Blissed be

Love, that kan thus folk converte!' (I 309). The tone throughout is witty and elastic, and the narratorial 'I' is but a small contributor. The whole passage, however, conforms to the time and stage of the work: Troilus' fall is sudden and, so, initially funny, but the audience probably does not need the long instruction it receives in order not to shun his example. Locally, the humour adds richness to the tone; structurally, it is important that love and its effects should be both watched with detachment and taken seriously. A variety of responses is simultaneously invoked.

So it is, too, in the Proem to Book II. This proem runs the first-person pronoun through six of its seven stanzas and brings together all the different characteristics of the narratorial *persona* that I have described. The first stanza announces a new phase in the time of the poem: the poet, having barely steered his course through the sea of Troilus' despair, can now publish the 'kalendes' of hope. In the second and third stanzas, he invokes Clio's help and addresses his audience, excusing himself for lacking *sentement* and announcing his Latin source as his alternative strategy:

> Wherfore I nyl have neither thank ne blame
> Of al this werk, but prey yow mekely,
> Disblameth me, if any word be lame,
> For as myn auctour seyde, so sey I.   (II 15–18)

The famous fourth stanza begins with linguistic change and ends with a statement of cultural and historical relativism, itself an encouragement to plural viewpoints: 'Ek for to wynnen love in sondry ages, / In sondry londes, sondry ben usages' (27–8). This argument undoes a lot of the advantage held by 'any lovere in this place' (30) who might question Troilus' speech or conduct: the modern lover may be surprised by what he hears, but the poet-narrator-historian will not be (35). There are as many ways in love as there are roads to Rome (36–42), just as there will be many differences of behaviour and viewpoint in the poet's present audience. As for this poet, he will carry on following his author:

> Ek scarsly ben ther in this place thre
> That have in love seid lik, and don, in al;
> For to thi purpos this may liken the,
> And the right nought, yet al is seid or schal;
> Ek som men grave in tree, some in ston wal,
> As it bitit; but syn I have bigonne,
> Myn auctour shal I folwen, if I konne.   (II 43–9)

In this brief summary of the proem I have moved from speaking of the narrator to speaking of the poet. I believe that this is the bias of the proem. It opens with the fictionalised Chaucer-*persona* familiar from his earlier poems and to that extent extraneous to *Troilus*, a reprise of the narrator who is not himself a lover but one 'that God of Loves servantz serve' (I 15). This fiction is of use, perhaps, to Chaucer in his contemporary situation, preventing any clash of amatory interests with his audience, just as the naming of a fictitious source may have been, as R. F. Green suggests, a serious expedient adopted to gull an audience who may not have been over-impressed with citation of Boccaccio as source-authority.[2] In the situation of the proem, however, the first of these two fictions is useful for two lines, and its main role is to introduce the second. It is the resource of an apocryphal copybook which dominates this proem; in the 'classical' ring to a Latin source which anticipates the book's despatch to the steps of Homer, Lucan and Statius, and in the freedom from responsibility, 'thank ne blame', that it confers. The naming of a real source would achieve something of this, but it would not also ensure, as 'Lollius' does, that Chaucer is able to do as he likes while translating, from Boccaccio, what he wants.

Only when the source is fictitious does it offer the freedom of a dream. Jean de Meun reports on his dreamer, Chaucer on his text: both with the (fictional) justification of reluctant veracity. But while Jean defends his style from a charge of obscenity on grounds of decorum, Chaucer can defend 'al this werk' from a charge of stylistic lameness on grounds of accurate translation. His apparent inferiority to his audience in 'sentement' is more than balanced by his historian's awareness of other 'usages'. Just as some fourteenth-century French love debates (and Jean) proclaim the clerk's superiority over the courtly man, so the three final stanzas of the proem delicately hint at the poet's superiority over the lover. He knows more, and he knows better than to scribble on trees or walls. This implies not a dramatic advantage—for the poet shares his foreknowledge with his audience in the first stanza of the poem (and repeats it in I 52–6)—but a dramatic relation between poet and audience, which is to be that of friendly adversary. The poem dramatises its own performance in order to contain a direct challenge to any audience, present or future. This does not mean that the poem is 'self-reflexive'. Rather, it holds the promise of meaning which is located exactly in the challenge to the audience. The challenge is that each member of the audience must arrive at a meaning by means of his or her own moral values, selecting from the multiple tones of the poem. When we enter into dogmatic debate about the poem's meaning, we are doing just what Chaucer intended: 'Ek scarsly ben ther in this place thre / That have in love seid lik'. The fictional narrator-*persona* helps to launch this enduring challenge, but the fictional aspect of the narrator is useful only because it serves a greater fiction about 'myn auctour'. The lie—like in dream poetry the poet's basic lie about the dream as historical event—keeps us from identifying the 'present poet' as Chaucer. But the absence of a dream-role for a younger version of the *persona* makes his fictional attributes of far less relevance. There is no appreciable distance here between narrator and poet, as long as we accept that the poet is caught in mid-performance and in mid-lie: he is seen writing a poem.

There is a vast difference between this reading of the *Troilus* narrator and many to which we have been subject. I see no evidence for distinguishing between Chaucer and a wholly fictionalised and unreliable narrator who has fallen in love with Criseyde, strives to extenuate her, and only succeeds in making matters worse for her owing to the poet's cunning acts of sabotage. The inventor of this sentimental incompetent is E. T. Donaldson, whose views I have already discussed in Chapter One. I have already looked, too, at many of the passages on which Donaldson's portrait is based; but there are two passages outstanding which demand quotation. The longer occurs in Book V:

But trewely, how longe it was bytwene
That she forsok hym for this Diomede,
Ther is non auctour telleth it, I wene.
Take every man now to his bokes heede;
He shal no terme fynden, out of drede.
For though that he bigan to wowe hire soone,
Er he hire wan, yet was ther more to doone.

Ne me ne list this sely womman chyde
Forther than the storye wol devyse.
Hire name, allas! is punysshed so wide,
That for hire gilt it oughte ynough suffise.
And if I myghte excuse hire any wise,
For she so sory was for hire untrouthe,
Iwis, I wolde excuse hire yit for routhe.   (V 1086–99)

The first of these two stanzas is simply another dramatic presentation of the historian's gaps, and it reaches out to 'every man' in the audience: its closing couplet cannot be read as verbal irony in the light of the preceding lines. The chronology of Diomede's wooing of Criseyde has been quite precise: he states his case on the tenth day after Criseyde's leaving Troy, and takes her glove away with him. That night Criseyde revolves her friendless predicament and begins to incline towards remaining with the Greeks. The next day Diomede returns to continue his suit, and 'refte hire of the grete of al hire peyne' (V 1036). Thereafter—but when exactly is unclear—Criseyde begins to shower him with presents. But this is not what this stanza is about: it is about when Criseyde actually 'forsok' Troilus, when, that is, in all this auspicious wooing Criseyde irrevocably dishonours her good name by sleeping with Diomede. The second stanza is not the starry-eyed pity of a jilted lover but the measured 'routhe' of the translator-historian for 'this sely womman'. He does not refuse to blame her: if he 'myghte excuse hire any wise' he would like to, but (the subjunctive is plain) he can't. Only, he places a limit on his blame: he will not blame her 'Forther than the storye wol devyse' (and actually does blame her less than Boccaccio). I read this as another contribution in the first-person to the reader's understanding of the poem: it won't do just to blame Criseyde. Chaucer shows no further interest in her, and it is left to the righteous Henryson to visit a literary vengeance upon her. This passage occur on Criseyde's last appearance in Book V, and it is Chaucer's last word on her. As such, it supplements and supplants the three lines in the proem to Book IV from which Donaldson's reading presumably evolves:

For how Criseyde Troilus forsook,
Or at the leeste, how that she was unkynde,
Moot hennesforth ben matere of my book,
As writen folk thorugh which it is in mynde.
Allas! that they sholde evere cause fynde
To speke hire harm, and if they on hire lye,
Iwis, hemself sholde han the vilanye.   (IV 15–21)

88

This stanza sounds chivalrous in the extreme, or would sound so were it in Book V, but it is dramatically and tonally appropriate to its existing place in the poem's temporal structure—less than twenty lines after Troilus, at the end of Book III, has been left 'in lust and in quiete' with Criseyde, 'his owen herte swete' (III 1819–20). The change of mood is sudden and regretful, but it is also resolute; and we have already seen how in Book V the narrator too has cause 'to speke hire harm'. There is no final judgement in these lines, which prepares for the poet's defence against antifeminism at the end of Book V: they are holding devices, restraining too easy and too early condemnation of Criseyde by the poem's audience.

The idea of the *Troilus* narrator as a fourth major character in the poem must be rejected in its entirety. It leads to a misreading of the way in which *Troilus* quizzes its audience, and is based on a misunderstanding of Chaucer's adaptation in *Troilus* of a narrator developed in dream poetry. The result of this inquiry is paradoxical. In *Troilus* Chaucer transfers many aspects of the narrator-*persona* of dream poetry to what he presents as a work of history. He gives to this narrator only one fictional attribute: though he is a servant of lovers, he is not a lover himself. This attribute is used partly as an extrinsic defence in relation to the poet's original audience, but also intrinsically, as the instrument of Chaucer's enabling lie about his source. It is the combination of apocryphal source and narrator that enables the author to inscribe his audience in the poem. Both are part of the work's tone. Most important of all is *epanorthosis*, frequent changes of tone. Though developed in dream poetry, in this new context it has little to do with narratorial interventions which until the epilogue are in fact more stable than the rest of the poem's tonal texture. They are stable because they are constant indices of the poem's process and performance. It is unclear to what extent one may justifiably talk of a narratorial *persona* at all: unexpectedly, Chaucer retains a closed figure of some complexity, and makes it simple, open, virtually transparent. It becomes the voice of performance, stressing both the fact and the fictional nature of the poem. It is not the author's voice, but it is very near to being a neutral voice. It is the voice of an apocryphal author commenting on his own composition, almost the voice of the poem itself speaking from the time and continuum of its own performance. Through it, poetic fiction marks out its own context. Writing of all kinds means 'translating an invisible text containing the quintessential fascination of all adventures, all mysteries, all conflicts of will and passion scattered throughout the books of hundreds of writers'.[3] History proves as intractable, and as powerful, as dreams.

It seems doubtful whether the idea of the narratorial *persona* in *Troilus* can be acceptably modified outside this context of fictionalised performance. In a highly intelligent attempt to do so, Piero Boitani discusses the *persona* as 'a narrative device that reveals, in the ambiguity between what he says, what he does not say, and what he accidentally lets drop, the first extraordinary self-consciousness in English literature'.[4] There is much to be said for some such frame of reference: Chaucer is self-conscious, bookish and concerned with the act of fiction, and to know this is enough to see the fallacy in Robertsonian efforts to force the abundance of tone into one narrow and factually orthodox channel. But it does not seem to me that even this qualified conception of the *Troilus*-narrator is correct. I am not at all sure that medieval poets would have esteemed this sort of ambiguity as we do (its main advantage for modern criticism is that it is virtually indefinable); and I do not think that ambiguity is a useful term for the active challenging of the reader's responses. In Boitani's analysis, the 'he' who 'says, . . . does not say, and . . . accidentally lets drop' seems to point to the poet as narrator, not to a fictionalised *persona* who, Boitani claims, is 'a competent, rather pedantic individual'. Yet Boitani's words are a sensitive modification of one standard line of *Troilus* criticism. In the haste to appreciate Chaucer's sophistication in *Troilus*, we have character-ised its narrator in terms that grossly insult Chaucer's own textual perform-ance. That indeed is a 'Chaucerian irony'.

II The Canterbury Tales: *High Style and Voice*

Chaucerian irony has been a growth industry in *Canterbury Tales* criticism, though there are some welcome signs that it may have reached its apogee.[5] Over recent years more and more claims have been made for the ironic relation of tale to teller, not just in terms of local tone or the juxtaposition of tales and frame; rather, we have been invited to see the narratorial voice of individual tales—even the Parson's Tale—as unreliable, its authority undermined by the poet Chaucer. Yet such work has been ill-supported by any systematic examination of Chaucer's use of narratorial voice and *personae* in the *Canterbury Tales* as a whole—an issue which is persistently raised by the claims made about individual tales and their tellers. For we have been invited to think of an over-genteel Franklin, or a misogynist Merchant, or an insincere Monk, or a suspect Knight as narratorial voices whose supposed moral flaws are integrated into the narration. The irony presented is generally not stylistic or structural, but psychoanalytical. Not all ironic criticism of the *Canterbury Tales* depends on this premise; much does. I cannot see how the premise can credibly be entertained. What follows is not a critical essay on the *Canterbury Tales* but a brief review of the evidence about narratorial voices in the light of the approach to Chaucer's use of *persona* so far described in this book. I shall not take issue with individual critical interpretations, but concentrate on the primary evidence and what it should do to focus the direction of critical study.

In the high style poems of the *Canterbury Tales* we find a narratorial voice—a constant voice—consistent with that portrayed in *Troilus*. I shall use the Man of Law's Tale to characterise it, in spite of the fact that the status of the tale's pairing with its teller is uncertain. Its prologue provides a highly inventive frame in which legal language is bandied between the Host and the Man of Law, who proceeds to list many of Chaucer's works: since Chaucer has told all the stories around (if not particularly well, and with the exception of nastily incestuous material peddled by Gower), what is left for a humble lawyer? The conclusion, 'I speke in prose', may just be an outrageous Chaucerian joke but very probably reflects an original assignment of *Melibeus*, not Constance, to this teller. This in a sense makes the existing tale rather too easy a case for refuting a close narratorial relation of tale and teller. However, if this is so, the situation is not unique: the Shipman is thought by some to be under the delusion that he is the Wife of Bath, and the Merchant that he may perhaps be the Friar (though, as I shall argue significantly, the evidence for both is in one line near the start of the tale). It is true too that, irrespective of the textual difficulty with the Man of Law, some critics have detected a strange quality in the style of the tale's narration. It is certainly a slightly more flamboyant high style than we find in the Clerk's or Second Nun's or Prioress's tales. This is what makes it a useful example. If the strangeness proves to be apparent, not real, we may with reasonable confidence apply whatever conclusions we draw about this tale to others in high style.

The unusual quality of the narration in the Man of Law's Tale comes from Chaucer's use of Innocent's *De Miseria Humanae Conditionis*. As in the excerpts used in the Pardoner's Tale, this treatise employs *exclamatio*, one of Chaucer's favourite figures, in a manner that modern critics may find bombastic: 'O foule lust of luxurie, lo thyn ende!' (925). But if it is to be judged overwrought, it must be as a serious exhibition of style, not of hysteria; and given the strength of Innocent's moral fervour, it would be hard to judge it stylistically indecorous. Why Chaucer should choose to weave elements from Innocent's treatise into Trivet's tale of Constance is another, and interesting, question; but the answer leads away from narratorial *persona* and towards *dispositio*.[6] In the following passage, denouncing the second of the Tale's evil mothers-in-law and the King's messenger tricked by alcohol into abetting her plot, the first stanza comes directly from Innocent and the rest is Chaucer's:

> O messager, fulfild of dronkenesse,
> Strong is thy breeth, thy lymes faltren ay,
> And thou biwreyest alle secreenesse.
> Thy mynde is lorn, thou janglest as a jay,
> Thy face is turned in a newe array.
> Ther dronkenesse regneth in any route,
> Ther is no conseil hyd, withouten doute.
>
> O Donegild, I ne have noon Englissh digne
> Unto thy malice and thy tirannye!
> And therfore to the feend I thee resigne;
> Lat hym enditen of thy traitorie!
> Fy, mannysh, fy!—o nay, by God, I lye,
> Fy, feendlych spirit, for I dar wel telle,
> Thogh thou heere walke, thy spirit is in helle!   (771–84)

I suspect that the second stanza alarms or amuses some modern readers: its style seems overdone, somewhat in the manner of the artisans' play in *A Midsummer Night's Dream*, and it is tempting to label it parodic. The context, however, firmly discourages any such resort: it would seem rather that Chaucer, having adapted Innocent's attack on the typical drunkard to the luckless messenger, himself succumbs to the temptation of trying to outdo Innocent's *exclamatio*. This is no occasion for parody: Constance and her child are about to be cast adrift because of Donegild's substitution of the messenger's letter. There is no possible case for irony: whatever the narrator means, it is not that Donegild is an angel in disguise. A stance of passionate narratorial involvement cannot be read, in the case of a lay saint, as a direction to audience disengagement. There is therefore no alternative to accepting these lines at their face value, and noting that their dramatically black-and-white language is in line with the characterisation of Donegild elsewhere: she was an elf, and everyone hated her company (754–6). Evil is *very* evil, especially in the generic shape of pagan mothers-in-law. The characterisation of Donegild is paralleled by an earlier *exclamatio* against the Syrian Sultaness:

> O Sowdanesse, roote of iniquitee!
> Virago, thou Semyrame the secounde!
> O serpent under femynynytee,
> Lik to the serpent depe in helle ybounde!
> O feyned womman, al that may confounde
> Vertu and innocence, thurgh thy malice,
> Is bred in thee, as nest of every vice!
>
> O Sathan, envious syn thilke day
> That thow were chaced from oure heritage,
> Wel knowestow to wommen the olde way!
> Thou madest Eva brynge us in servage;
> Thou wylt fordoon this Cristen mariage.
> Thyn instrument so, weylawey the while!
> Makestow of wommen, whan thou wolt bigile.
>
> This Sowdanesse, whom I thus blame and warye,
> Leet prively hire conseil goon hire way.
> What sholde I in this tale lenger tarye?   (358–74)

The 'I' who 'thus blame and warye' is not there to raise a knowing smile but to draw discreet yet forceful attention to the narratorial presentation of the tale, as in the straight transition of the last line quoted. Line 372 accepts responsibility for what has been a very effective *exclamatio*, emotive in its use of semantic collocations to do with the Fall's undoing of 'Vertu and innocence'— collocations entirely in tune with an account of the tribulations of a female saint. The vehemence with which evil is condemned, as actively Satanic in its inspiration, is exactly balanced by similarly ornate chains of rhetorical questions establishing that 'No wight but Crist, sanz faille' (501) actively looks after the persecuted righteous (477–504; 931–45, where the previous stanza is again drawn from Innocent and again prepares for the highest of high styles). The 'I' is integral to the *exclamatio*.

   These are the only problematic uses of the 'I' narratorial voice in this Tale, and here as elsewhere the 'I' proves to be no more than a product of the Tale's rhetoric. Elsewhere, the use of the first person is arrogated by such rhetorical devices as the overdoing *topos* (288, 400, 419), and frequent brevity *topoi* which ensure that the Tale remains within the bounds of summary narrative: 'What nedeth gretter dilatacioun? I seye . . .' (232–3: cf. 175, 205, 219, 410–11, 428, 990). These brevity *topoi* are close to open narratorial commentary on the process of narration:

> Me list nat of the chaf, ne of the stree,
> Maken so long a tale as of the corn.
> What sholde I tellen of the roialtee
> At mariage, or which cours goth biforn;
> Who bloweth in a trumpe or in an horn?
> The fruyt of every tale is for to seye:
> They ete, and drynke, and daunce, and synge, and pleye.   (701–7)

This polished stanza contains two references to the first person (701, 703) which make its interests inseparable from 'the tale'. As well as the central brevity-*topos*, they serve as a transition, and are therefore of the same order as other examples which involve the first-person plural ('But now to purpos lat us turne agayn', 170: cf. 953–4) as well as the first-person singular ('And forth I lete hire saille in this manere, / And turne I wol agayn to my matere', 321–2: cf. 410–11, 581, 900, 938–6). They are performance markers, signs of the poet's unfolding of the narrative, serving a role similar to that of tags like 'as I shal yow devyse' (154), 'this place / Of which I speke' (575–6: cf. 877), 'if I shal nat lye' (694: cf. 1007), 'as I guesse' (1088: cf. 1143). Unlike these tags, however, which stress the solo performance of the narrator ('I ne seye but for this ende this sentence', 1139), they also engage the audience of the poem as active witnesses. Addresses to the audience are frequent, comprising short structural promises ('so as ye shal heere', 238: cf. 329, 249, 749, 910), reminders ('As heerbiforn that ye han herd devyse', 613: cf. 881), assurances ('I yow heete', 1132), inclusion of the audience in a Boethian or religious moral ('Allas we been to lewed or to slowe', 315; 'Sathan, that evere us waiteth to bigile', 582: cf. 126), the sharing of a joke ('Housbondes been alle goode, and han ben yoore; That knowen wyves—I dar sey yow na moore', 272–3), and the anticipation of a possible response:

> Men myghten asken why she was nat slayn
> Eek at the feeste? who myghte hir body save?
> And I answere to that demande agayn,
> Who saved Danyel in the horrible cave
> Ther every wight save he, maister and knave,
> Was with the leon frete er he asterte?
> No wight but God, that he bar in his herte.
>
> (470–6: cf. 246–7)

Chaucer also anticipates all possible audiences: 'riche marchauntz' (122), the 'noble, . . . prudent folk' apostrophised in line 124, and the 'queenes', 'duchesses' and 'ladyes' who are asked to have 'routhe' on Constance's 'adversitee' (654). These are no part of the audience of Canterbury pilgrims to whom the Tale's valediction is addressed, 'us alle that been in this place' (1162). The appeal to 'routhe' as a key reaction is evoked by many of the narrator's interventions. The Roman people's opinion of Constance is solemnly endorsed ('And al this voys was sothe, as God is trewe,' 169): she is apostrophised as 'my Custance' (446, 803: cf. 631); the poet prays for her welfare when she is *in extremis* (243, 873–5), and once includes the audience in his prayer for Alla's soul (1146); the reactions of poet and audience are combined in an impersonal curse on Alla's steward ('God yeve hym meschance', 914) and in honour of 'Cristes mooder—blessed be she ay' (950). The poet is partly the equal of his audience. As in *Troilus*, he is dramatically presented as a translator (see, for example, 1095), ignorant of certain facts: how much gold the Romans granted to Syria (242), how King Alla found out his mother's guilt so that he slew her (892), the name of the 'hold' in Northumberland where Constance's ship was cast up (507) and the heathen castle 'Of which the name in my text noght I fynde' (905). The source is itself fictionalised: what in the last quotation is a 'text' was first introduced in the Prologue as a 'tale' taught by 'a marchant, goon is many a yeere' (132). Above all, the act of its performance is also fictionalised. On the sadness of the reunion of Alla and Constance, the narrator addresses a request to his audience that vividly captures likely circumstances of medieval performance:

> I pray yow alle my labour to relesse;
> I may nat telle hir wo until to-morwe,
> I am so wery for to speke of sorwe.   (1069–71)

And the one real breach or incongruity of tonal decorum in this poem comes in a stanza on Constance's marriage which is surely addressed to an audience in a jocular reminiscence of diurnal reality. The tone still owes something to Jean de Meun:

> They goon to bedde, as it was skile and right;
> For thogh that wyves be ful hooly thynges,
> They moste take in pacience at nyght
> Swiche manere necessaries as been plesynges
> To folk that han ywedded hem with rynges,
> And leye a lite hir hoolynesse aside,
> As for the tyme,—it may no bet bitide.   (708–14)

This is indulgence in narratorial byplay with the poem's imaginary audience; but it is of only local effect. Like the use of narratorial voice in *Troilus*, that of the Man of Law's Tale evokes praise and blame, anticipates audience objections and directs its response. It makes possible a range of tones; it dramatises the performance as if for the audience included in the poem; it stresses its own fiction (and that of its narrator); and it nevertheless demands the engagement of all possible audiences with its subject.

What holds for this tale holds for the others in the high style: a sketch in these terms of the narratorial voice of the Clerk's or Prioress's Tale would simply duplicate the conclusions reached, except perhaps in a slightly less complex form. The major difference is to do with the naming in the Clerk's Tale of the real or ultimate source—Petrarch—in order that Chaucer may exercise an unusual freedom, open only to a poet-translator, of dissenting from the neat allegory of his source in the name, once more, of 'routhe'. In the Second Nun's Tale, the quite vestigial narratorial voice is so unmatched to the teller that there is no effort to disguise the serious act of pious translation, even in the Prologue:

> I have heer doon my feithful bisynesse
> After the legende in translacioun.   (24–5)

In the Marian invocation, even the illusion of performance to an audience is surrendered. The context is that of reading, and the voice of apology is that of the translator-poet, as in *Troilus*, not that of the Second Nun:

> Yet preye I yow that reden that I write,
> Foryeve me that I do no diligence
> This ilke storie subtilly to endite,
> For bothe have I the wordes and sentence
> Of hym that at the seintes reverence
> The storie wroot, and folwen hire legende,
> And pray yow that ye wole my werk amende.
>
> (VIII: *Second Nun*, 78–84)

Similarly, there is nothing to distinguish the narratorial voice of the Monk's Tale from that of the legends (not the Prologue) in the *Legend of Good Women*: it is the serious and learned historian-poet reporting on his sources (see, for example, Monk's Tale, 2255); on the return to the frame, the Host confirms this impression by complaining that 'therinne is ther no desport ne game' (2791).

In the case of the Knight's Tale, the situation is more complex but similar.[7] A mention of the prize supper 32 lines into the narration constitutes the only real matching of tale with frame. The narratorial *persona* is otherwise the poet-translator-historian whose concern is with what 'olde stories tellen us' (859), 'olde bokes seyn' (1463), who is both thoroughly in command and, within the limit of his competence, at the disposal of the narrative and stylistic registers of the poem:

> Who koude ryme in Englyssh proprely
> His martirdom? for sothe it am nat I;
> Therfore I passe as lightly as I may.
>
> (I, *Knight's Tale* 1459–61)

The only real tonal shock in which the narratorial first-person pronoun figures prominently occurs when Chaucer deliberately omits the account from his source (transferred to *Troilus*) of the dead Arcite's ascent to the eighth sphere:

> His spirit chaunged hous and wente ther,
> As I cam nevere, I kan nat tellen wher.
> Therfore I stynte, I nam no divinistre;
> Of soules fynde I nat in this registre,
> Ne me ne list thilke opinions to telle
> Of hem, though that they writen wher they dwelle.
> Arcite is coold, ther Mars his soule gye!
> Now wol I speken forth of Emelye.   (2809–16)

It is Chaucer, not the Knight, who chooses to turn over the leaf of the *Teseida*. This is Chaucer's lie, not the Knight's, and no light will ever be shed on this passage by asking why a genteel elderly knight refuses to indulge in theological speculation. In the same way, it is Chaucer, not the Knight—here as elsewhere —who pretends to be a plain and clumsy English versifier while forging the new and consummate high style of a master rhetorician. The problem of the passage quoted is one of the translator's attitude, not the Knight's; it is a question involving the narratorial voice, but it is essentially one of tone, not one of narratorial *persona*. We are 2000 lines away from the faint echo of a Canterbury pilgrim who recalls that he may win a dinner, and who awakes as from a long sleep to resume the narratorial role in the last line of the Tale: 'And God save al this faire compaignye' (3108). The metaphor of sleep is appropriate: the poem's narratorial voice has slipped into the idiom of dream poetry when following Boccaccio in describing the three temples of the third part. Somewhat disconcertingly, the narrator becomes an eyewitness in ancient Athens:

> Ther saugh I first the dirke ymaginyng
> Of Felonye   (1995–6)
> The sleere of hymself yet saugh I ther   (2005)
> Yet saugh I Woodnesse   (2011)
> Yet saugh I brent the shippes hoppesteres   (2017)
> And al above, depeynted in a tour,
> Saugh I Conquest, sittynge in greet honour   (2027–8)
> Now to the temple of Dyane the chaste,
> As shortly as I kan, I wol me haste,
> To telle yow al the descripsioun   (2051–3)

(see also 2056, 2062, 2065, 2067, 2075). It is as if Chaucer feels that, generically, high-style tours of exotic courtly landscapes must be conducted tours; and as if by reflex the narratorial first-person pronoun is thrust into the role of guide. There could be no more emphatic demonstration that it is a cipher, an empty pronoun, functioning as a voice to serve the poem's unfolding. Nothing justifies the use of such a voice to forward a critical argument about the true character of the Knight or the Prioress, the Man of Law or the Monk.

To put it bluntly: the 'I' of narration is demonstrably not the 'I' of the ostensible teller.

This statement about narratorial voice seems to challenge some common critical assumptions; and it is open to a number of objections. Firstly, it appears to ignore the fact that there is a fluctuating relation of tale to teller throughout the *Canterbury Tales*: some tales may be much more revealing of their tellers than I have yet implied. Secondly, the account I have offered seems to overlook the fact that Chaucer took the trouble, and his posthumous editors a little more, to assemble the *Canterbury Tales* within a fairly developed frame, for which I have so far proposed no function. Thirdly, the account seems to imply that the surface style of the tales must normally be taken at face value: what of the cases when it is parodic, and are there no grounds on which it can ever be seen as ironic? These are substantial objections, and I propose to consider each in turn.

III The Canterbury Tales: *Voice, Frame and Tone*

It is perfectly true that the relation of tale to teller in the *Canterbury Tales* is highly variable. One genre in particular demands an extremely close match: the dramatic monologue. The Canon's Yeoman's Prologue and Tale is the most complete display of this genre, for the quasi-autobiographical subject of the narrative—the history of the voice—dominates both Prologue and Tale. With the Pardoner and the Wife of Bath the autobiography is restricted to the Prologue, and less evidently, if at all, informs the Tale: I have argued this view in detail in Chapter Two, on the Pardoner's Prologue and Tale, and I suspect that something similar is true of the Wife. The voice of the Tale is not that of the Prologue, except at the very beginning and the curse on old husbands at the very end; elsewhere in the Tale there is no stylistic or formal sign of a dramatic *persona*, and if an argument is to be made, for instance, that the Tale reveals the Wife's deepest wish (to be transformed like the Loathly Lady into a beautiful girl), is must be made on grounds other than those of narratorial voice, and has no place in this study. Be this as it may, the dramatic monologue is a special case. At same other times, Chaucer appears to have taken little interest in the match of teller and tale: the legend of St Cecilia, for example, was probably incorporated from matter already to hand and was not designed for the Second Nun. The same may well apply to the tales given to the Man of Law, the Clerk, the Knight and the Prioress. In each case the ascription is very suitable: not evidently to the nuances of portraiture and characterisation found in the General Prologue or in the links, but to what might in such circumstances be expected of a typical knight, lawyer, prioress and monk. It is a literary version of social hierarchy: a matter of decorum. The solemn and serious historical tragedies of the Monk's Tale are not designed for the particular monk of the General Prologue who 'leet olde thynges pace, / And heeld after the newe world the space' (175–6). The sort of monk suited by this anthology of a tale is the satiric opposite conjured up in that portrait, one who loves 'Upon a book in cloystre alwey to poure' (185). The sort of Prioress who speaks a fine and eloquent Marian prologue is one who reserves her pity for more than dead dogs and bleeding mice. The Serjeant-at-Law of the General Prologue, officious, pompous, full of self-importance and legal jargon, recurs in the prologue of the Man of Law's Tale, in conversation with the Host, but has no significance in the Tale's narration. There is not such patent inconsistency with the Knight and the Clerk, but then these portraits—unlike the three cited before—are not composed in the style of ironic commendation. We should not strain unduly to see in character sketches of the General Prologue a blueprint for the narratorial *personae* of individual tales. This is not to deny a connection between portraits and links on the one hand and the ascription of tales on the other: an example that springs to mind here is the Nun's Priest, whose lonely male position in a convent is a less virile equivalent of Chauntecleer in his roost. However, we turn the tale into wish-fulfilment at our peril; and I do not know how we can proceed from noting the witty and apt relation to arguing that because of it 'the attitude of the teller thus becomes an ingredient of the story',[8] except in broad—and bland—terms of decorum, here a brilliantly comic decorum, a kind of structural conceit.

The Nun's Priest's Tale itself belongs alongside the rhetorically extravagant burlesque of *Sir Thopas* and the Squire's Tale (which I shall consider below). The idea that it is the Priest's 'humorous revenge' on his nuns seems an acceptable insight, but a marginal one; but it does serve to emphasise, I think, how extrinsic the 'quytyng' structures of the *Canterbury Tales* are to the narratorial voice of the tales they frame. Where we might most expect a dramatically developed narratorial *persona*, we are given hardly anything. The narratorial voices of the Friar's and Summoner's Tales are utterly neutral, and there is no use at all of the first-person pronoun in the narration of these two tales except in their opening and closing lines. Much the same is true too of the Miller and the Reeve. In the Miller's Tale, a token attempt at a drunken lilt ('Now sire, and eft sire', 3271) may conceivably affect one line of the tale, and it is only in the conclusion of the Tale that we return to the voice of the link. In the Reeve's Tale, the first-person interventions in the story consist of an assurance that the story is true (3924), a sarcastic endorsement of the miller's wife's ugliness ('But right fair was hire heer, I wol nat lye', 3976), a reminder that the two students dwelt in the hall 'of which I seye' (4003), a note of geographical ignorance about the town where the students were born, which is 'Fer in the north, I kan nat telle where' (4015); and the connection is far from secure between these uses of 'I' and the 'I' of the Tale's last line, 'Thus have I quyt the Millere in my tale' (4324), which reclaims the voice for the frame. 'Quytyng' constitutes an obvious decorum and ensures a lively frame. It does not authenticate the narratorial voice, which is conceived not dramatically but rhetorically and stylistically: the narratorial use of the first-person is infrequent in these *fabliaux* because it is rhetorically licensed more often in high style than in low. There is a dividing line between frame and narration.

To my mind this is the logical interpretation of the evidence. It is a failure of logic that, for example, would see, as the narratorial *persona* of the Franklin's Tale, a socially climbing Franklin who disingenuously asserts that he is 'a burel man' who 'learned nevere rethorik, certeyn', and proceeds to stun his audience with his rhetorical genius.[9] For some critics, this is charming modesty: for others, it is downright dishonesty, the mark of a jumped-up gentleman too clever by half. The modesty or dishonesty is then associated with the preceding link in which the Franklin praises the Squire's 'wit' and 'eloquence' and expresses the wish that his own son were 'of swich discrecioun / As that ye been' (V, 685–6). Since the Franklin of the frame reveals *gentilesse* to be a central social pretension, and since the *demande* posed by the Tale is one of *gentilesse*, the whole of the Tale is held to reveal, even by some to exist in order to reveal, something of its teller's social attitudes. On the level of decorum, this is a truism; and by those who feel that the Franklin is genuinely modest, his narration is seen as trustworthy and his tale is taken seriously. No great harm is done. For those, however, who like Robertson suspect dishonesty, the Tale's moral content is seen as perverted: the tale is held to reveal altogether different things about its teller (whether by means or in spite of the narratorial *persona* is never entirely clear). Even on their own dramatic grounds, some of these readings seem somewhat doctrinaire: what the Franklin actually says is that the Squire has done quite well 'considerynge thy yowthe' (675), and that none of the company will be his equal in eloquence 'If that thou lyve' (679): these reflections could conceivably be *gentil* demurrals. But this is not the central flaw of the two types of critical approach to the Franklin's Tale sketched here. As delicate critical probes they resemble Schliemann's excavation of Troy: distinct strata are indiscriminately ploughed up in the certainty of reaching what proves to be the wrong destination. The Franklin's Tale is a vintage performance of the standard high-style narrator delineated in this chapter: the Tale is attributed to a spurious source, a Breton lay; the narration is a treasure chamber of *epanorthosis*, the more so since authorial foreknowledge and an audience's pseudo-generic expectations (of a lay) conjoin to promise a happy ending; the audience is constantly cajoled and teased with unanswerable riddles (who *was* 'the mooste fre'?; and the narrator, who enjoys proclaiming his rhetorical incompetence, parallels this game with another in which he condemns astrology (1131, 1272), professes ignorance of it ('I ne kan no termes of astrologye', 1266), and then blinds his audience with science (1273–93). As, I think, in the Merchant's Tale, there proves to be nothing here for dramatic or psychological reading of narratorial *persona*. There is everything for the study of theme and tone, which the narratorial voice serves and indicates. The level at which this is the Franklin's Tale is still that of structural decorum. The frame does not occlude or inhabit the picture.

What, then, is the purpose of the frame? This objection is best met by recourse to the General Prologue, in which one type of narratorial *persona* is set up and practised. It is a familiar one: Chaucer, the present author of the *Canterbury Tales* (34–42), reports the evidence of his own senses while a pilgrim in a past time (20–34). The closest resemblance is to the narrator *persona* of the *Roman de la Rose* and Chaucer's own dream poetry, but with crucial differences. If the *persona* is familiar, the context is not. This is not a dream, though the General Prologue opens as if it were going to be. It is rather what Donald R. Howard has recently asked us to recognise as travellers' tales, an on-the-road version of an *insomnium* with a similarly dubious claim to credibility.[10] The General Prologue provides not only the framework but the first traveller's tale. By placing an earlier self in the company, Chaucer achieves the distance of the dream-vision poet in a naturalistic context, and brings to the presentation of a verse *novelle* collection the full range of tone made possible by the temporal interaction of his two ages. He is before his public as author ('as I yow devyse', 34):

> But natheles, whil I have tyme and space,
> Er that I ferther in this tale pace,
> Me thynketh it acordaunt to resoun
> To telle yow al the condicioun
> Of ech of hem, so as it seemed me . . .   (35–9)

He is also there in his prologue as eyewitness ('so as it semed me'). The eyewitness speaks in the past tense, but also in the historical present: the Prioress had an elegant cloak, 'as I was war' (157), and her forehead was almost a span broad, 'I trowe' (155). The pilgrim vouches for the veracity of the poet's description; and the narratorial first-person pronoun appears most often in the more complex portraits, confirming the strong interest felt by both poet and pilgrim. The portrait of the Monk contains what might be called a signed opinion: the monk takes little notice of the Benedictine rule or of the text 'That seith that hunters ben nat hooly men' (178)—'And I seyde his opinion was good' (183). The past tense, 'I seyde', controls the irony of this line. It would still be possible to have irony with a line like 'I seye his opinion is good', but it would be a different kind of irony which would involve the poet directly; as the line stands, it is the younger self whose folly is implicated and from whom the poet keeps a discreet distance.

The variation of the narratorial *persona*'s two voices turns observation into evaluation and description into indirect speech. Of the friar, we are told —without any overt narratorial engagement anywhere in the portrait—that 'Unto his ordre he was a noble post' (214). The irony is unmistakable, and the details of the portrait support it at every turn: the only reading of the friar is that he is a scoundrel who thinks well of himself. And here lies the problem, a source of uncertainty in the reader that is a fertile resource in the tone of the General Prologue. The line could be an antifraternal sarcasm directly on the poet's part, but given the presence as observer of the younger and foolish poet, the quasi-dreamer, to whom are we to attribute this comment: should we see it as indirect speech, and if so should we ascribe it to the 'Chaucer' pilgrim or to the friar himself? Context informs us unequivocally that this opinion is untrustworthy, but we cannot tell *whose* it is. It is not news but rumour. The device shows up quite often: of the Prioress, in whom 'al was conscience and tendre herte' (150), of the Franklin who 'was Epicurus owene sone' (336), the Reeve whose management is defeated by 'noon auditour' (594), and the Pardoner who 'was in chirche a noble ecclesiaste' (708). Its great strength is that it is not always allied to irony, rumour being an unstable phenomenon, so that as readers we must be ever watchful. It enables report to be made, without overt display of authorial omniscience, of all kinds of facts the poet-pilgrim cannot conceivably know at first hand, like the Franklin's pantry provisions. Either as pilgrim or poet, the narrator-*persona* rarely commits himself: hence the notoriously teasing line in which the poet attempts a consultant diagnosis based on the pilgrim's records of the Pardoner, 'I trowe he were a geldyng or a mare' (691). The pilgrim narrator is quite ready to throw in his epistemological hand: of the Shipman, 'For aught I woot, he was of Dertemouthe' (389); of the Merchant, 'But sooth to seyn I noot how men hym calle' (284), though this line is strategically placed by the poet to undermine the preceding line's confident testimonial that 'he was a worthy man with alle'. Where he offers a specific assurance, it is liable to be inconsequential (the Clerk was not fat, 'I under-take', 288—an elementary irony), or unsarcastically humorous (of the Wife's kerchiefs, 'I dorste swere they weyeden ten pound', 454). Only once does he act as worthwhile glossator, on the Summoner: 'But wel I woot he lyed right in dede' (659). The same is true of the poet-narrator, who makes one ex-plicit, important, and wholly reliable value-judgement, on the Parson: 'A bettre preest I trowe that nowher noon ys' (524), and otherwise restricts his appearances to accepting responsibility for the narration: 'of which I telle' (571, the Reeve); 'Of his array telle I no lenger tale' (330, the Man of Law).

The foregoing short account has in fact mentioned every instance of the overt narratorial 'I' in the pilgrim portraits. From these very few uses of the first-person pronoun an enormous variety of effects has grown. They are sufficient to underscore the duality of the narratorial *persona*, and this duality, in the style and tradition of the *Roman de la Rose*, is the *sine qua non* of the generous and unpredictable tonal range. It pays due comic tri-bute to Geoffrey Chaucer. Beyond that, however, far from concentrating attention on the narratorial voice it breaks up into what, mindful of the *House of Fame*, I have called rumour. A dual register of narratorial voice promises and prepares to swell into multiple and unidentifiable voices of performance.

What is true of the General Prologue is true in general of the frame. Its function is not to narrow and concentrate attention on the narratorial *persona* but to disperse it into a scattering of fictions. Given this narratorial diaspora, the narratorial voice of the individual tales can remain surprisingly constant, responding as is appropriate to genre and subject, the tone and time of the tale. This is why I am loth to follow Piero Boitani's conclusions from the General

Prologue, though his reading of it in many ways anticipates my own.[11] Boitani speaks of 'the Narrator, Chaucer' as present in all the *Canterbury Tales*; he then distinguishes between Chaucer as majuscule Narrator and 'Chaucer' as miniscule 'narrator': Chaucer is 'the Narrator of the other narrators; he is a fictive narrator among the other narrators' (p. 240). 'The experience of the real world . . . is doubly mediated: by the character as an individual and by the Narrator . . . The tales provide an experience of the world that is doubly reinvented (by each pilgrim and by the Narrator)' (p. 266). This is thoroughly logical, and it fairly represents the concept behind the strategy of the frame (if not the practice behind the narration of the Tales). But I am not at all sure that Chaucer wants us to lose much sleep over this complexity, or much wakefulness over such double reinvention in our reading of the *Canterbury Tales*; and any such argument has its flaw. The flaw is revealed in Boitani's careful argument when he has to discriminate between 'Chaucer's own voice', which 'returns' in the Retracciouns (p. 239), and 'the *persona* of the Narrator' which 'lies behind the stories purportedly narrated by the pilgrims' (p. 238). It would be fairer to say that Chaucer's prose voice returns in the Retracciouns; but for that, I cannot see—as with the *Troilus* epilogue—how they can be said any more or less genuinely in Chaucer's own voice than anything that has gone before. There is a decorum in the Retracciouns too: they are perfectly suited to the time of the work at which they appear, at the moment of the confession in Canterbury for which the Parson's Tale is the preparation; at least, they would look most odd anywhere else. I sympathise with Boitani's feeling that Chaucer is the Narrator of the 'stories purportedly narrated by the pilgrims', but I cannot see in what sense his narratorial voice 'lies behind' these tales: it is exactly, and vitally, where we would expect a narratorial voice to be, on the very surface. Therefore I cannot see how, except in the General Prologue and the frame, it is worth calling this Narrator a '*persona*' at all. A voice of narration is not a narrator-*persona*: it is the index, and prime mover, of a performance. The General Prologue, and the links, are there to insist on the tales as performance and as fiction.

This means that the narrator-*persona* of the General Prologue is instrumental in setting up the performance framework but must otherwise be of limited influence and restricted significance. That this is so is confirmed, I think, by a key passage of the General Prologue that I have not yet considered, in which the first-person pronoun is prominent. The passage occurs just before the General Prologue, and with it the frame of the *Canterbury Tales*, is energetically hijacked by the Host. It begins with ten lines of what might be termed administration by the poet-narrator-pilgrim:

> Now have I toold you soothly, in a clause,
> Th'estaat, th'array, the nombre and eek the cause
> Why that assembled was this compaignye
> In Southwerk at this gentil hostelrye
> That highte the Tabard, faste by the Belle.
> But now is tyme to yow for to telle
> How that we baren us that ilke nyght,
> Whan we were in that hostelrie alyght;
> And after wol I telle of our viage
> And al the remenaunt of oure pilgrimage.   (715–24)

This is straightforward enough (granted a liberal definition of 'a clause'), but the tidying up of the poet's desk-top is followed by his first elaborate address to the audience of the *Canterbury Tales*. The passage is crucial, and must be quoted in full:

> But first I pray yow, of youre curteisye,
> That ye n'arette it nat my vileynye,
> Thogh that I pleynly speke in this mateere,
> To telle yow hir wordes and hir cheere,
> Ne thogh I speke hir wordes proprely.
> For this ye knowen also wel as I,
> Whoso shal telle a tale after a man,
> He moot reherce as ny as evere he kan
> Everich a word, if it be in his charge,
> Al speke he never so rudeliche and large,
> Or ellis he moot telle his tale untrewe,
> Or feyne thyng, or fynde wordes newe.
> He may nat spare, althogh he were his brother;
> He moot as well seye o word as another.
> Crist spak hymself ful brode in hooly writ,
> And wel ye woot no vileynye is it.
> Eek Plato seith, whoso that kan hym rede,
> The wordes moote be cosyn to the dede.
> Also I prey yow to foryeve it me,
> Al have I nat set folk in hir degree
> Heere in this tale, as that they sholde stonde.
> My wit is short, ye may wel understonde.   (725–46)

This is the most important use of the narratorial *persona* in the General Prologue, and it is the final and climactic one. As well as some cheerfully blasphemous abuse of authority (the Miller's Tale is hardly comparable to the New Testament), it contains flattery of the audience and the familiar stance of poetic incompetence ('My wit is short'), and it entails a shift in the relation of poet and pilgrim. The pilgrim aspect of the *persona* matters here only as the guarantor of the poet's authority: he was there, he knows what these folk were like and how they spoke. The authority of the *Canterbury Tales*, like that of the *Roman de la Rose*, is therefore wholly fictionalised. However, the narrator as poet presents his transcription of the pilgrim's pretended experience as an act of *translation* (730–6), a task no different from that of *Troilus*. All writing, so apprehended, is indeed a matter of 'translating an invisible text'. The author's apology centres primarily on style (and so, but only incidentally, to matter). The true reporter, in seeking to translate 'pleynly', must reproduce others' words 'properly': the theory is conventional, and it is one of stylistic decorum. The defence is borrowed from Jean de Meun's Raison. It is repeated just where we might expect it, before the first *fabliau* of the collection, in the famous conclusion of the Miller's Prologue (3167–86): the author must speak churlishly 'or elles falsen som of my mateere' (3175), and the blame for any distress caused falls not on the poet (who here sounds very like Jean de Meun) but on the reader ('Blameth nat me if that ye chese amys', 3181).

It is the same voice, of a 'burel man', as provides a decorous comment on the consummation of the Merchant's Tale:

> He stoupeth doun, and on his bak she stood,
> And caughte hire by a twiste, and up she gooth—
> Ladyes, I prey yow that ye be nat wrooth;
> I kan nat glose, I am a rude man—
> And sodeynly anon this Damyan
> Gan pullen up the smok, and in he throng.   (IV 2348–53)

The hilarity of the excuse, as in Jean, lies in the deliberate misunderstanding: members of the Festival of Light are not prone to be impressed by a defence of four-letter words on grounds of stylistic decorum when they are really objecting to copulation alfresco. Nevertheless, the 'vileynye' defended is that of style, not matter. The theory is one of general stylistic decorum, and in my view the theory largely determines the attribution of tale to teller and wholly controls the narratorial voice of each tale in turn. It is the most rudimentary and token kind of stylistic decorum that provides an echo of the ostensible narrator's voice at the very beginning and end of most, not even all, tales. Apart from these echoes, it is misleading to speak of narratorial *persona* at all in the tales themselves, with the one exception of the Canon's Yeoman. Only in the General Prologue, where it furnishes the programme for the work's multiplicity of theme and tone, and sometimes in the links is narratorial *persona* in itself a fruitful or interesting topic of critical study.

To meet the third possible objection I raised at the end of the last section of this chapter, I need note here only that style, with absolute rhetorical propriety, may sometimes be burlesque and that all style is capable of conveying irony of content. On burlesque and parody, I have nothing to add here to others' enjoyment of *Sir Thopas* and to Donaldson's superb essay on the Nun's Priest's Tale as an example of the comic rhetorical anatomy of rhetoric.[12] The Squire's Tale is discussed in detail in Chapter Five below, and is an excellent test case for knowing when to stop.

As for irony, it should be analysed in its own terms and in the manner already proposed. Efforts to yoke it to narratorial *persona* are profoundly misconceived. The Merchant's Tale is a good example. Over-attention to the misogynistic Merchant's Prologue (not found in the Hengwrt manuscript) has led to some preposterously dark readings of a *fabliau* in which, at the end, everyone—including the wife, whom the ostensible narrator could be supposed to hate—escapes scot-free and with his or her desires at least adequately fulfilled. This Tale is far more suitably examined as an ironic performance: the Christian view of marriage, for example, is put into a context which makes its use—to justify January's senile lusts—clearly ironic, but the irony is at January's expense, not Christ's or the Merchant's.[13] The irony brings to mind Jill Mann's remarks about 'the determining power of context': but it is only when we stop shaking our heads over the imagined nastiness of the ostensible narrator that we can enjoy it. It is justifiably approached as irony, one might add, because, just as rhetorical burlesque draws blatant notice to itself, it is explicitly signalled; if the signals are absent, there can be no irony, and no amount of contrary claims and ingenious reading should ever persuade us to overlook their absence. But the study of narratorial *persona* can contribute to that of irony: in, for example, the remarkable passages of provocatively antifeminist commentary and address in the Physician's Tale (72ff.) and the Manciple's Tale (187–222),[14] whose tone cannot be understood without some recollection of Jean's manipulation of narratorial *persona* in the *Roman de la Rose*.

With the *Canterbury Tales*, however, I should claim no more than that the historical study of narratorial *persona*, and Chaucer's use of it, makes a salutary contribution to what should be a central topic of Chaucer criticism: tone. The *Canterbury Tales*, which seem to offer most for the study of narratorial *persona*, in fact offer least. Or rather, they offer, as fiction should, a marvellous illusion. It is essential to our appreciation of illusion that we should not mistake it for reality. In looking at the tales themselves, we are better off speaking of narratorial voice than narratorial *persona*: as the long address by the narratorial *persona* of the General Prologue makes clear, the voice is thereafter stylistic and rhetorical, a function of decorum. The corollary is that lines using a narratorial 'I' in the body of any of the tales *cannot* be used to demonstrate a point about the attitude of the ostensible teller. The standard presumption must be that neither characterisation nor irony is to be invoked unless, with the latter, the proper case can be made from the particular context. The narratorial voice of the tales may not be inherently trustworthy, for it is entirely open to other literary purposes and devices; but it is certainly not inherently suspect. It is a mainly neutral voice. It takes its colour from the interaction of style and theme, and the interest of passages in which it is identified by the first-person pronoun is that such passages, if examined *in extenso*, form one valid approach towards a much-needed analysis of Chaucer's tone: a complex interplay of contexts—voices and styles, language and themes, writer and all possible readers and audiences—that is not reducible to 'character'.

We have seen, for example, how by means of narratorial *persona* in the General Prologue eyewitness report is translated into indirect speech from another to become an unidentifiable voice, a tone, a rumour. In the energy it has expended on narratorial *persona* in the tales themselves, some modern Chaucer criticism has paid too little attention to rumour. It has, in fact, remained admiringly beside the House of Fame:

> Loo, to the Hous of Fame yonder,
> Thou wost now how, cometh every speche;
> Hyt nedeth noght eft the to teche.
> But understond now ryght wel this,
> Whan any speche ycomen ys
> Up to the paleys, anon-ryght
> Hyt wexeth lyk the same wight
> Which that the word in erthe spak,
> Be hyt clothed red or blak;
> And hath so verray hys lyknesse
> That spak the word, that thou wilt gesse
> That it the same body be,
> Man or woman, he or she.
> And ys not this a wonder thyng?
>
> (*House of Fame*, 1070–83)

In writing these lines, Chaucer could have been predicting the course of much Chaucer criticism. We need now to pass from the illusory 'body' in Fame's stratosphere to 'the word in erthe': not, in this literary case, to real men and women, but to the fictional channels for 'speche', the voices of performance.

CHAPTER 5

The Literary History of the Squire's Tale

The Squire's Tale has been treated unkindly by modern criticism. It has either been neglected, as by Donaldson and Robertson,[1] or, worse, exposed to reductive reading. 'What is certain', claims one critic, 'is that the Squire's Tale contains in miniature many of the symptoms of the waning of the middle ages'.[2] With such a lethal infection around, Chaucer must be rescued. It is perceived that the Tale has faults: 'occasional lapses in taste and a very primitive conception of narrative',[3] 'rambling narrative',[4] a repeated pattern of 'elaborate inconsequence, incongruity and downright bathos'.[5] Then let these be faults of the teller, not the author. Attention duly shifts to Chaucer's creature, the Squire. To benign eyes, he is 'a very young, young man' whose 'intellect . . . is limited'.[6] More censorious scrutiny shows him to be 'a trivial person',[7] a dyed-in-the-wool lecher (the General Prologue admits that he dances and sings)[8]—hence thoroughly unreliable, an accident-prone narrator, at best a figure of fun. Chaucer is detached from the teller. 'Thus, in one way, the Squire's Tale is a chaotic and fragmentary failure; but in a more important way it proves to be another one of Chaucer's complete and engaging master-pieces . . . In the end it would seem that the most wonderful thing about the Squire's Tale is that we have missed its delicate humor for so long.'[9] 'Delicate humor' is an unexpected product of such aggressive criticism; but then, delicacy is a subjective property. The sort of method that impresses McCall as satisfactorily tactful is judged by J. B. Severs to be 'an exaggerated and unconvincing argument'.[10] A slightly fuller protest has come recently from J. A. Burrow, who reminds us of Milton's praise in *Il Penseroso* of Chaucer as poet of the Squire's Tale, and comments: 'This is not our Chaucer. Critics in the later age of the novel were even to suggest that the poet deliberately aborted the Squire's Tale, as he did *Sir Thopas*, out of sheer impatience with its insipid marvels. Yet a more attentive and unprejudiced reading, such as Milton may prompt, will put that suggestion out of court.' Burrow links the Squire's Tale with 'precisely those sides of Chaucer's work which we are least well-placed to see in our particular period'.[11]

This study, a re-assessment of the Tale's critical reception, is in part a response to Burrow's remarks. I shall argue that the historical disagreements between 'our Chaucer' and the Chaucer of previous ages do not depend on a wondrous modern rediscovery of Chaucer's humour, though modern studies have done much to define questions of his tone; they depend rather on the literary framework different ages provide to accommodate their appreciation of that humour.

Four main phases may conveniently be distinguished in the reception of the Squire's Tale: the Renaissance view, from Spenser to Milton, marked by its reverence for Chaucer and regret that the Tale was left, in Milton's phrase, 'half-told'; the late Augustan and Romantic view, emphasising sublime and romantic aspects of the first part of the Tale, set in Cambyuskan's court, and generally deprecating the second, to do with Canace and the falcon; the scholarship typical of the late nineteenth and early twentieth centuries, engaged in a conscientious and undogmatic search for sources; and the criticism of the last forty years or so in which preconceptions derived from the novel have joined forces uneasily with sustained close reading. I shall consider each briefly, postponing until last questions of how Chaucer's contemporaries and immediate successors responded. I should note, however, that the very first notice received by the Squire's Tale was exceptionally unfavourable. A professional scribe, John Duxworth, copied what is now Bibliothèque Nationale, Paris, MS Anglais 39, probably between 1422 and 1436, for and under the supervision of the royal French prisoner in England, Jean d'Angoulême. On what Manly and Rickert take to have been Angoulême's instructions, Duxworth left off copying the Squire's Tale after line 28 with the following comment: '*Ista fabula est valde absurda in terminis et ideo ad presens pretermittatur nec ulterius de ea procedatur.*'[12] The judgement is singular (if I understand '*absurda in terminis*' correctly as referring to style) in two respects: it leaves no room for possible appreciation of humour and it takes no account of the fact that the Tale is incomplete.

Renaissance comments on the Tale do not highlight its comedy, though I shall argue that this does not mean their authors failed to enjoy it. They do persistently focus on the Tale's fragmentary nature. Spenser is alone in implying, ambiguously, that it may once have been complete. He voices an epic conviction that 'wicked Time' has 'robd the world of threasure endlesse deare' in the shape of Chaucer's complete Tale; he therefore apologises to Chaucer's 'most sacred happie spirit / That I thy labours lost may thus reuiue'.[13] The common and almost certainly correct feeling is Milton's, that the Tale was left incomplete by Chaucer himself. Similarly, John Lane refers to Chaucer's 'lost, or rather suppressed, tale', the implication here being that Chaucer himself suppressed it, and playfully presents his continuation of Chaucer's 'Master-peece' as that 'which hath binn loste allmost three hundred years and sought by manie'.[4] I shall consider the testimony of Spenser, Milton and Lane at greater length below, for there is much to be learned from their agreement on the 'warlike' nature of a Tale in which the only blood spilled is a falcon's.

More than one scholar has noted the continuity between Renaissance and late Augustan views of the Squire's Tale as, in Warton's phrase, 'one of our author's noblest compositions': Warton was influenced by Milton.[15] Yet it is a significant shift in cultural perspective that enables Warton to add 'that Milton, among Chaucer's pieces, was most struck by his SQUIER's Tale. It best suited our author's predilection for romantic poetry. Chaucer is here ranked with the sublime poets'. Warton is also the first to lament on behalf of 'every reader of taste and imagination . . . our author's tedious detail of the quaint efforts of Canace's ring, in which a falcon relates her amours', at the expense of 'the notable achievements we may suppose to have been performed by the assistance of the horse of brass'. Richard Wharton's 'free imitation of Chaucer's fragment' (1805) amplifies the censure: 'The story of the Falcon, in the second book is so void of interest, even in Chaucer's hands, that, had it not been pointed out in the above lines as a constituent part of his fable, I should have left it entirely out of *mine*; and should have taken my departure from the more interesting and magnificent circumstances . . . in the first book'.[16] The Renaissance enjoyment of the grandeur of the first part of the Squire's Tale is here augmented by distaste for a second part which the later commentators wish to take equally seriously, but cannot. It is also augmented by late eighteenth-century canons of sublimity, which give place naturally to the romantic love of vitality and spontaneity seen in Leigh Hunt's praise of the brass horse as 'copied from the Life. You might pat him and feel his brazen muscles'.[17] Burrow quotes and endorses this remark. Certainly, it is wonderfully appreciative of the brass horse, more so than modern critical preconceptions would readily allow; but it is thoroughly conditioned by the aesthetic preconceptions of its own time.

It is from this admiringly post-Romantic vantage point that the first serious modern Chaucerian scholars, armed with Skeat's text,[18] approached the Squire's Tale. They did so with an eye for detail quite unlike that which informs 'practical criticism'; indeed, the weakness of much of their work is that it does not address itself directly to matters of tone. Its great strength is its concern with structure, and its preparedness to ask how the Tale would have developed had Chaucer continued to write it. The question requires a good deal of source-hunting, and recent critics have sometimes been too quick to dismiss its results. Kahrl, for example, notes: 'one of those most active in searching for sources or analogues for the Squire's Tale, H. S. V. Jones, was still forced to admit that Chaucer apparently "worked inventively with a free hand".'[19] Kahrl's suggestion that Jones was 'forced to admit' this, as if against his will, is unfair. For Jones presented his view as a summary of 'the best critical opinion'.[20] The view was formed out of an earlier debate, in which Skeat proposed a source in the Marco Polo material and Manly, in rejecting Skeat's opinion, stated that he himself could 'hardly resist the conviction that Chaucer found all his characters named and his scene laid in the source—written or oral—from which he derived his plot'.[21] Jones, and others such as Lowes, sought to demonstrate that if Chaucer had one source, it has not survived, and that, given the mixture of materials in the Squire's Tale and the numerous existing analogues to different parts of it, such a single source is improbable.[22] The negative conclusion is persuasive and valuable. It suggests that in the Squire's Tale Chaucer tried to combine a vast array of disparate elements gleaned from various sources, written and oral: 'there are facts which seem to point with some distinctness to the view that Chaucer himself may have been the one responsible for the story as it stands . . . , that the whole tale as it now stands may be a composite of Chaucer's own.'[23] Some of the matter relating to Cambyuskan and his court is indebted, as Lowes showed, to accounts of the empire of Prester John. For that relating to Canace and the falcon, no direct source is proposed (the nearest thing would be Chaucer's own *Anelida and*

Arcite), but analogues, in Indian and Persian poetry and the *Arabian Nights*, are explored by Jones, Braddy[24] and in 1970 by Albert C. Friend, who adds to understanding of the captive bird motif with precedents from two authors writing in England in the late twelfth century, Neckam and Berechiah. Friend provides an accessible model for a tale in which two separated birds are reunited by human agency.[25] It disposes, as we shall see, of Braddy's worry about incest in the source story, which is fanciful, thinly based and has been unduly influential. Chaucer's choice of a Tartar setting was well explained by Lowes, who domonstrated that 'Chaucer did not lack opportunity of knowing a good deal about both Tartary and Russia' and stressed the significance of Armenian visitors to London in Chaucer's time: 'it cannot be too strongly emphasised . . . that sources other than the *books* Chaucer read—sources that he in his intercourse with men and in his reaction upon the interests, the happenings, the familiar matter of his day—entered likewise into "that large compasse of his", and must be taken into account in estimating his work'.[26]

The most important contribution to this kind of study is probably that of Jones, in two articles evaluating the source-material collected by W. A. Clouston in 1889[27] and concentrating attention on the romance *Cléomadès*, by Adenès le Roi, and to a lesser extent the *Méliacin* by Girard of Amiens. Both poets visited the English court in the reign of Edward I, and Jones surmised that 'though dead for a hundred years, they were remembered' there;[28] more to the point, perhaps, is the inference that their works remained part of a court repertory. The provenance of the *Cléomadès* story is Arabic by way of Spain, and it appears to provide a model for magical gifts to royal daughters and, above all, for 'a wonderful horse'. Jones claims *Cléomadès* as a model, not as a source: he claims, that is, that Chaucer remembers the outline and some details of the romance but does not work with it in front of him.[29] The case for this kind of use is a strong one: it furnishes details of the motion and operation of the horse (made, in *Cléomadès*, of ebony) by means of pins; for speculation, about its manufacture, by 'Gent de petit entendement' (1639); for the setting, a royal birthday feast; and for the magic mirror that reveals treason.

By this account Chaucer has considerably rationalised his model. Instead of three kings, each bringing one present for one of three daughters, he supplies the one knight bearing several gifts for the Tartar king and his one daughter. In *Cléomadès* the magic horse is brought by the ugly suitor Crompart, who demands in marriage the king's most beautiful daughter, and the operation of the horse is known to Crompart alone. This enables Crompart, who resents opposition to the match by the princess's brother, Cléomadès, to dispose of the prince by suggesting that he mount the horse, and then despatching him to the skies. Cléomadès, however, has seen that Crompart works the horse by means of pins, and is able to gain control; he lands in Tuscany and finds the bedroom of the beautiful Clarmondine with whom he falls in love. He is condemned to death by Clarmondine's father, asks leave to die sitting on his horse and, when it is granted, promptly escapes. The rest of the poem deals with his successful pursuit of his love, and his rescue of her from the evil Crompart. Jones draws attention to an episode in which Cléomadès is persuaded to fight two brave knights at 'the castle of the discourteous custom', and proposes that this may shed light on Chaucer's final reference to Cambalo, 'That faught in listes with the bretheren two' (660).

Jones is quite outspoken in his assessment of some of these differences between the Squire's Tale and *Cléomadès*, and his evaluation of them leads him to consider Froissart's *L'Espinette Amoureuse* as another possible resource for borrowing, or plundering, of occasional details—much in the way that Froissart's poetry is used in Chaucer's dream-poetry. It seems to me that one of the crucial differences is not assessed adequately: the mysterious visitor to Cambyuskan's court is the reverse of ill-favoured (88–101), and he readily divulges all the mechanism for working his magic horse (126, 314–34). This difference has sometimes been taken by modern critics—appropriating source-studies without reflecting on them— as a sign of artlessness in Chaucer's version. It is rather, I think, an evident guarantee of guilelessness on the part of Cambyuskan's mysterious visitor: he is to be no wicked Crompart, though—given the precedent of *Cléomadès*, his partiality with his gifts, and the idealised *descriptio* he receives—he is well set to become Canace's suitor. This, of course, is the kind of speculation to which Jones's work leads, as Jones himself was well aware: 'Stories of this cycle . . . suggest the kind of plot which Chaucer may have had in mind for the part of his story that was never written.'[30] Such work is based on, and does much to confirm, the premise that the Squire's Tale could have proceeded. It does not accord with the confidence of much later modern criticism that the Tale runs itself into the ground.

In examining the later criticism, we find ourselves confronted with another order of evidence than that considered by students of sources and analogues, critical questions in large measure either neglected or taken for granted by the older generation of scholars. These are really questions of tone, and they were first aired fully in an admirable and important essay by Gardiner Stillwell, 'Chaucer in Tartary'. Stillwell writes with an eye to correction, not total dissent: 'That romance is present, I should be last to deny.'[31] His argument, however, is that what makes the Squire's Tale more interesting than most romances—'sagacious realism, humour, critical intellect, subtlety of mood, and natural human gusto'—'prevent Chaucer from achieving a uniformly romantic tone . . . His excessive use of whimsical *occupatio* betrays a certain skittishness, an uncomfortable awareness that all is not well with him in these strange regions' (p. 188). There is an element in this shrewd criticism of wisdom after the event: the fact that Chaucer leaves the Tale unfinished 'indicates that he is not altogether at home in Tartary' (p. 179). There are other possible explanations, and it is odd that Stillwell's has won largely unquestioning acceptance. A splendid analysis of the opening of Part Two, and a lively appraisal of its comedy, is oddly truncated by the conclusion: 'The Canacee-falcon episode cannot hold his interest. He leaves it unfinished' (p. 181). Yet Stillwell's great achievement is his analysis, and collecting together, of tonally disingenuous passages in the Tale; and Stillwell is the first critic to claim humour in the frequent use of *occupatio* in the Squire's Tale.

This is the first passage he cites, on (or, rather, off) the subject of Canace:

> But for to telle yow al hir beautee,
> It lyth nat in my tonge, n'yn my konnyng;
> I dar nat undertake so heigh a thyng.
> Myn Englissh eek is insufficient.
> It moste been a rethor excellent,

That koude his colours longynge for that art,
If he sholde hire discryven every part.
I am noon swich, I moot speke as I kan.   (34–41)

Stillwell argues that Chaucer is tilting at the rather mechanical *effictio* com-
mended by the rhetorical handbooks: 'Chaucer seems here to avoid the
tedious, itemised descriptions of the rhetoricians. He may also have had his eye
humorously cocked at conventional descriptions in romances . . . Canace is for
the moment a colourless romantic ingénue, and he lets her alone until he comes
to Part Two, where he sees an opportunity of doing something with her'
(p. 182). This is nicely observed, and such insights are supported by several other
examples. Stillwell sees the long passage in which Chaucer describes the
people's theorising about the horse—a passage which, we have already seen, is
prompted by *Cléomadès*—as unromantic and incongruous, and feels that
Chaucer's delight in idle jangling keeps him too long from his story. This really
depends, of course, on the projected duration of the narrative, and is vulnerable to the reminder that the poet of the *House of Fame* and the Nun's Priest's
Tale is eminently interested in idle jangling and incongruity; but it is subtly
argued, especially when compared to later versions of the argument in
which the lines are seen as redolent of anti-intellectualism (which hardly
explains their presence and scientific intricacy), and of snobbery which 'arises
from the squire's distaste for "lewed" people and their chatter'.[32] The
lines cited by Derek Pearsall to support this view (220–4) are certainly un-
kind to 'lewed peple', and they are not the only such lines in Chaucer's
poetry; but the significance of Pearsall's comment is that the judgement is
not now seen as playful (as it was by Stillwell), and it is now ascribed to the
Squire.

There is therefore a world of critical difference between Stillwell and his
successors. Here are Stillwell's and Pearsall's glosses on a key passage:

> Heere is the revel and the jolitee
> That is nat able a dul man to devyse.
> He moste han knowen love and his servyse,
> And been a feestlych man as fressh as May,
> That sholde yow devysen swich array.
>   Who koude telle yow the forme of daunces
> So unkouthe, and swiche fresshe contenaunces,
> Swich subtil lookyng and dissymulynges
> For drede of jalouse mennes aperceyvynges?
> No man but Launcelot, and he is deed.
> Therfore I passe of al this lustiheed;
> I sey namoore, but in this jolynesse
> I lete hem, til men to the soper dresse.   (278–90)

Stillwell italicises 'Who koude tell yow', and comments: 'The lines call to mind
a delightful scene, but at the same time there is the subtly humorous refusal to
go into detail, seen especially in the reference to the narrator (who may be
thought of as either the Squire or Chaucer) as a dull man' (p. 184). Pearsall's
account comes from a radically reformed critical universe:

No one could fail to draw the inference, that the man who is 'as fressh as is the month of May', who knows all about love and his service, the 'subtil lookyng and dissymulynges', is none other than the Squire himself. The imaginary or impossible narrator who alone could do justice to such 'revel and jolitee' is, whether the Squire realises it or not (certainly, we are meant to), himself: he could describe just this scene, but does not, out of 'modesty'. The implicit comparison between himself and Lancelot ('and he is deed') gives to the Squire's assumed modesty more than a tinge of fatuously admiring self-regard.   (pp. 293–4)

One should supplement this with Joyce E. Peterson's criticism of Stillwell's statement that 'the narrator may be thought of as either the Squire or Chaucer'.

Critics subsequent to Stillwell tend to identify the narrator solely with the Squire, arguing that the artistic lapses, the confusion, and the general unevenness of the tale are purposeful imperfections used by Chaucer, the over-narrator, as methods in his ironic characterisation of the Squire.[33]

What Stillwell claimed as humour has become irony, and his emphasis on the mode of narration as an adjunct to the Tale has been supplanted by a moral critique of its ostensible teller. Peterson's essay is in fact devoted to a neo-Robertsonian reading, especially of Part Two of the Tale, of such ferocity that it leaves no room for humour in confronting the exegetical enormity of the Squire's failings:

He who can ask pity for a falcon but remain insensitive to the feelings of men, who can go on a crusade for the grace of a lady not for the grace of God, who can create a sacrilegious identity between his courtly-lady Falcon and Christ, is "ongentil" for all his gentillesse.   (p. 74)

It would be hard to find a tale less suited to such value-judgements: which is why, presumably, Robertson himself left it alone. In a spectacular and by now wholly familiar reversal of critical priorities, the tale is subordinated to its teller. Pearsall's reading is less harsh, but it is no less grounded in 'dramatic reading'.[34] It has also located the best lines in the whole Tale on which to build, given the connection with the portrayal of the Squire in the General Prologue (I, 92): 'He was as fressh as is the month of May'. This is why I have called this a key passage in the Squire's Tale, for if, as I have wondered (and propose below), the connection formed no part of Chaucer's intentions when writing the passage, the 'dramatic principle' would be hard-pressed to survive in a reading of the Squire's Tale.

There is no need to repeat at length here the reasons for believing that its demise would be timely. The dramatic principle arose out of the attempt to find coherence in the *Canterbury Tales* as a whole;[35] it is one result of asking interesting questions about a tale's 'function in the Canterbury scheme'.[36] These questions occur quite early (1951) in Marie Neville's essay on the Squire's Tale, and it must be recorded that the Squire's Tale's stocks have fallen as dramatic readings have grown strong. There are particular reasons for seeing the dramatic principle as the major factor in the Squire's Tale's decline, and as a major cause of distortion in critical appreciation of it.

To begin with, dramatic readings are a response to a printed edition of the *Canterbury Tales* (generally, as here, Robinson's), not to a Chaucer who composed for manuscript and oral publication. The boundary between frame and tales, which seems to me a mainly temporal one in the latter contexts, is redrawn by dramatic readers and a rather uniform relation is imposed. The tales are treated as if all are potentially dramatic monologues. All sorts of questions about the varying status of links, and the varying strength and quality of relation between tale and teller, are flattened out or put aside—as they have to be for the method to work as an organising structure. At the same time, such reading is curiously selective about the passages it assigns to the ostensible narrator and those it reappropriates for Chaucer as, in Peterson's phrase, 'over-narrator'. What seems to be good is often still Chaucer's; what is bad usually belongs to the dramatic narrator. Lest this seem an unduly jaundiced inference, it is worth considering a certain surface parallel between Part Two of the Squire's Tale and the Nun's Priest's Tale. Both are concerned with talking birds; in both, the rhetoric is inflated considering its context; and incongruity coupled with frequent bathos is a common effect. Yet nobody has argued that the Nun's Priest is at best immature and at worst immoral, and few feel that the Nun's Priest's personality has much to do with the success of the performance. True, the content of the two is vastly different, but there is a similarity of technique, and this is commonly misrepresented in Squire's Tale criticism. Peterson, for example, notes the splendidly anthropomorphic lines which have the tercelet falling to his knees and being taken by the hand when farewelling the falcon. She adds: 'in the skilful fable, such as the Nun's Priest's Tale, the animals perform only those acts which are consistent with their anatomy' (p. 71). This is untrue, unless thinking, talking and reading (Nun's Priest's Tale 3064–6) were once accomplishments of medieval cocks. A real indecorum occurs in the Nun's Priest's Tale when after Chauntecleer's splendidly learned speech on the interpretation of dreams 'he fley doun fro the beem' (3172), feathered and trod Pertelote 'twenty tyme' (3177) and 'chukketh whan he hath a corn yfounde' (3182). The bathos resembles that of the Squire's Tale when the marvellously overwrought high-style of the well-bred falcon's lament of betrayed love dwindles from its pretensions of *gentilesse* to a plain statement of the avian facts of the case: 'He saugh upon a tyme a kyte flee' (624). The 'other woman' has rarely seemed less enticing.

Modern criticism is surely right to feel that 'it would take a very sober reader to accept this bird-tale with an entirely straight face'.[37] Augustan and romantic readers thought so too; they judged it indecorous, and disliked Part Two in consequence. My complaint is that, having claimed the prerogative of a sense of humour, dramatic readers frequently fail to use it. The falcon alludes to Boethius, and her use of the *Consolation* is about as logical as Chauntecleer's translation of *Mulier est hominis confusio*: 'Womman is mannes joye and al his blis' (3166). The misapprehension has been exegised patiently by modern dramatic readers; it occurs in the falcon's speech, not in the narrator's commentary, and one would expect it to be recognised as the falcon's error, not the narrator's. Not a bit of it. 'By having the Squire quote Boethius, Chaucer invites a comparison between the Squire's values and the values expressed in the *Consolation*', maintains Peterson, offering further proof of 'the profanity of the Squire's nature' (p. 70). The heavy-handed application of proper Boethian values is close to a standard element in dramatic readings of the Squire's Tale.

Kahrl blames the Squire for turning Boethius' *exemplum* 'on its head' (p. 206); Haller thinks that 'the moral applies to himself (the Squire) as well as the hawk . . . the Squire is as disordered philosophically as he is poetically'.[38] Absurdity prevails outside, as well as within, the tale. The Squire is required to take responsibility for the falcon's speech, but given no credit for the very clear indications that it is not to be taken entirely seriously. Very few readers miss those indications: expert exegesis is scarcely needed to realise that the falcon may well be misinterpreting *gentilesse*. Nevertheless, she is genuinely— if melodramatically—distraught, and Canace does the 'gentil' thing, which is to feel sorry for her. It is hard to see why the Squire should be blamed, or denied an excuse like the Nun's Priest's when he too wades into heavy Boethian waters: 'I wol nat han to do of swich mateere; / My tale is of a cok' (3251–2).

That several dramatic readers concur in this palpable illogicality seems to show that the appropriation of Tale by dramatic teller in their reading is absolute. All the Tale's perceived faults are to be laid at the Squire's door, and all the good things praised by earlier readers are brushed aside, if they are considered at all, as involuntary flashes of Chaucerian genius from behind the mask. There is a progressive crudification here of Stillwell's insights. Not only are the frequent incongruities and instability of tone to be imputed to the Squire, but also the Tale's rhetoric—figures, disposition and even invention. Disturbing issues of critical method and logic are raised by such criticism. It is one thing, with Stillwell, to question 'the straightforwardness of the narrative voice'; it is quite another, with Haller, 'to take a further step, and to assume that Chaucer . . . is making fun of his Squire' by offering a kind of rhetorical satire. Haller studies the Squire as rhetorician, 'assuming throughout that the Squire's faults of rhetoric come from deliberate calculation on Chaucer's part'.[39] The case is provocative, but it can hardly be *assumed*. No argument is presented, however, and the inference must be that if the critic manages to complete his essay the assumption will somehow have proved correct. It leads to some sad revaluation. For example, the exuberantly inventive and comic personification of sleep 'with a galpyng mouth' at the opening of Part Two is found to be 'ridiculous' and 'farfetched' (pp. 290–1). One wonders how a good conceit can ever be otherwise. One wonders too why the Squire's Tale is censured for such elaboration (in speeches, in narration, in astrological references) when, again, the Nun's Priest's similar essays, such as the apostrophe to Friday, are relished as affectionate rhetorical parody, an authentic signal of the mock-heroic.

This last explanation has many advantages over Haller's 'rhetorical satire'. It is difficult to see how figures such as *occupatio*, *exclamatio* and *diminutio* can ever, in themselves, be satirical: how, that is, their very use can reveal psychological or moral shortcomings. They may of course be parodic, as in the Nun's Priest's Tale; but I doubt that it is in the nature of rhetorical figures for their badness in itself to be designed as an index of incompetence, or any other failure, on the part of a fictitious narrator. In the one unequivocal case where Chaucer wishes to achieve something like this effect, *Sir Thopas*, he does not trust to rhetorical figures; he provides not only a succession of incongruities but also, and primarily, the metrically incompetent use of a verse-form that he elsewhere eschews. There are no comparable clues in the Squire's flawlessly smooth pentameters. The notion of parodic tone looks better than that of psychological maladjustment, or simple incapacity, in the face of passages such as the following:

> The knotte why that every tale is toold,
> If it be taried til that lust be coold
> Of hem that han it after herkned yoore,
> The savour passeth ever lenger the moore,
> For fulsomnesse of his prolixitee;
> And by the same resoun, thynketh me,
> I sholde to the knotte condescende,
> And maken of hir walkyng soone an ende.   (401–8)

These lines seem heavily portentous, and some critics have taken them to mean that a key node in the plot has arrived: Canace's interview with the falcon is to be 'the knotte' of the tale.[40] It seems to me that this is a misreading. The moment sounds meaningful, but the narrator is playing with his audience, sonorously commiting the very faults he identifies ('For fulsomenesse of his prolixitee'), and the whole subsides into bathos; the performance has been in aid of nothing more than a stop to Canace's morning constitutional. The passage is by no means incompetent, for the effect is deliberately protracted and cleverly gained. I can see no possibility of its revealing anything of its narrator's psychology, except that he enjoys playing poetic games with his audience—in other words, he sounds like a poet, or like Chaucer when he self-consciously plays the poet. The tone is a problem, but it is not susceptible to psychological or satiric solutions. The key to the game must be found in the tone itself, not in some external reference.

The contributions made by close reading over the last thirty years or so have been substantial. It has at least identified many tonal problems, without resolving them satisfactorily. The main value, however, lies in its detail rather than its thesis. One of the unpardonable features of dramatic readings is their resolute refusal to contemplate that the Tale is actually—rather than 'dramatically'—unfinished; for if the admission is once made it defeats any dramatic reading. We have therefore seen the phenomenon of the 'finished fragment', and the Epilogue to the Tale, generally in the Ellesmere version, is raised to the status of a merciful interruption:

> 'In feith, Squier, thow hast thee wel yquit
> And gentilly. I preise wel thy wit,'
> Quod the Frankeleyn, 'considerynge thy yowthe,
> So feelyngly thou spekest, sire, I allow the!
> As to my doom, ther is noon that is heere
> Of eloquence that shal be thy peere,
> If that thou lyve; God yeve thee good chaunce,
> And in vertu sende thee continuaunce!
> For of thy speche I have greet deyntee . . .'   (673–81)

This may or may not damn with faint praise ('considerynge thy yowthe'; 'If that thou lyve'). But it does not read like an interruption, at least by the standard of other interruptions: 'Hoo!' quod the Knyght, 'good sire, namoore of this! / That ye han seyd is right ynough, ywis' (VII, 2767–8). Several scribes seem to have expected further copy, and some find the transition so sudden that they carry a statement to the effect that 'Chaucere made noo end of this tale'.[41] Manly and Rickert believe that '672 is certainly an astonishing place to end, unless the author had a stroke of apoplexy'.[42] The fact is that the lines quoted do not bear the weight of an interruption; they would be suitable at the real narrative conclusion of the Squire's Tale or, come to that, any other tale assigned to the Squire. Moreover, we cannot avoid a decision on whether the fragment is 'finished' or otherwise. We can and must decide what to make of the narrator's highly unusual prospectus:

> Thus lete I Canacee hir hauk kepyng;
> I wol namoore as now speke of hir ryng,
> Til it come eft to purpos for to seyn
> How that this faucon gat hire love ageyn
> Repentant, as the storie telleth us,
> By mediacion of Cambalus,
> The kynges sone, of which that I yow tolde.
> But hennesforth I wol my proces holde
> To speken of aventures and of batailles,
> That nevere yet was herd so grete mervailles.
>   First wol I telle yow of Cambyuskan,
> That in his tyme many a citee wan;
> And after wol I speke of Algarsif,
> How that he wan Theodora to his wif,
> For whom ful ofte in greet peril he was,
> Ne hadde he ben holpen by the steede of bras;
> And after wol I speke of Cambalo,
> That faught in lystes with the bretheren two
> For Canacee er that he myghte hire wynne.
> And ther I lefte I wol ayeyn bigynne.   (651–70)

According to Pearsall, this is a 'staggering synopsis'. Citing Robinson's remark that 'the plot is obscure', he continues: 'it would betray a certain lack of humour to attempt to penetrate its obscurity. The point hardly needs labouring: the only person who is confused is the poor Squire'.[43] The judgment would have astounded Jones, Lowes and at least two generations of source-scholars; and its disregard of these scholars' work is rather surprising. It is true that the passage presents many difficulties. Not least is the very existence of a prospectus: as it stands, the passage is like finding notes for a speech by 'a man of gret auctorite'. 'Nowhere else in any of his tales does Chaucer announce his plan for the continuation of it', note Manly and Rickert, adding the caution that 'we should bear in mind that he did not prepare his work for publication' (III, 484). The lines read like the poet's own notes, jotted down at the time when he laid the work aside.[44] Then there is the name 'Cambalo' in 667, with the variant 'Cambalus' in 656: the name is that of Canace's brother, who in 667 seems to have no business winning his own sister. Much has been made of this apparent incest. What we have here, however, I am all but convinced is no more than an archetypal scribal error; I shall discuss the problems of early textual history below. I think it entirely probable that for the name 'Cambalo', had the Tale continued, we should have been able to substitute the name of

116

Canace's suitor, who may well have turned out to be Part One's well-favoured visitor to Cambyuskan's court: whose speech is so pleasing (especially in contrast with Crompart in *Cléomadès*), whose manner is so gracious, who brings two presents for Cambyuskan's daughter and none for his wife, and whose dancing-partner is Canace (277). The 'bretheren two' with whom he was to fight may well have been Cambalo and Algarsif, especially since the winning of Canace may have had a dynastic significance (as John Lane thought); misunderstanding may well have led to the lists, and the lists to mutual respect. They will not have led to tragic consequences, given the property of the magic sword to heal fatal wounds. Spenser manages something of the kind in the battle between Cambell and Triamond.[45] The Eastern analogues suggest another motive for the brothers' defence of their sister: Canace's sympathy with the falcon may have led her to a general distrust of all men, from which she has to be won. The falcon's recovery of her 'repentant' tercelet may have been meant to be achieved in the manner brought to light by Friend: Cambalo in his travels overhears the tercelet's lament, repeats it on his return, and is deceived by the falcon's promptly feigning death into opening her cage door so that she is able to make her escape. Or it may be achieved by means of the magic mirror, which shows false lovers; in which case Cambalo's mediation may have been to recover the tercelet in order to persuade Canace to give up her aversion to men. The mirror has also a political significance, revealing enemies of the King, and this property may well have been planned to trigger Cambyuskan's 'batailles'. Algarsif's winning of Theodora with the brass horse's help is wholly explicable along the lines of *Cléomadès*, with the difference already observed that he is not tricked into riding it.

The foregoing paragraph is not put forward as a perfect disencoding of an unwritten continuation. That would be impossible. It is no more than speculation, informed however by the work of two generations of critics who never once dreamed that the Squire 'is finished even if he does not know it'.[46] Every point of the prospectus is accounted for, as is the supposedly excessive number of gifts brought by the 'strange knyght'. True, the resulting poem would be very long, 'longer even than the Knight's Tale';[47] but this has always been admitted, though its implications are not always explored. However others may wish to modify my speculation in their own imaginings, I believe that it demonstrates what it has to: that at one stage Chaucer designed a complete plot for what he left as an unfinished fragment. If this is so, it follows that in a vital respect scholars such as Jones and Lowes were right, and later critics who maintain that 'the Squire is in Wonderland' are wrong. This raises once again problems to do with the Tale's early textual history, and it definitively rules out answers provided by dramatic readings. For these are based on a false premise: that the Tale is as good as complete. Proponents of such readings are right to insist that questions of tone are also crucial. These questions are all the more pressing because they need to be resolved in a new way.

I believe that the historical review of criticism, as briefly practised here, gives an important clue about what Chaucer was doing. This lies in what the sixteenth and seventeenth centuries thought he had been going to do.

I do not mean by this just the content of Spenser's and Lane's continuations, though these are interesting and justify a few observations. They are quite unlike what I have rashly proposed; moreover, they are not successfully Chaucerian. In Spenser's case, this is because his continuation is successfully Spenserian; in spite of the homage to Chaucer, Spenser makes no effort to keep hold of all the strands Chaucer left behind. Like Lane, he accepts the precedent of a joust for Canace, but he switches the power to heal wounds from the sword to the ring. Spenser's continuation is centered upon Canace and her brother. The latter duly acquires a new wife, as if in an effort to remove the possible embarrassment I have put down to textual corruption. Chaucer's bird motif is left to Book IV, and Canto viii for the adventures of Spenser's Squire—about whom Spenser has no moral qualms. Lane's continuation is altogether fuller, as befits a true continuation with no ulterior literary purpose. His version is packed with jousts, battles and conquest, its main theme being the rebellion of the unworthy Algarsif against his father when Cambyuskan decides that his kingdom should go to the winner of a tournament for Canace's hand. Civil war ensues, with Camballo finally successful. Cambyuskan is killed in battle but revived by the magic sword, Algarsif is forgiven, and in a final tournament Algarsif duly wins Theodora (with no help from the brazen horse), Canace is won by a new character, the admiral Akafir, and tercelet and falcon are reunited by means of the magic mirror and at Camballo's request. Lane complicates his version unnecessarily with extra characters: two 'bouncing girls' are brought into his Part XI for no other purpose than to lose a singing contest with Canace and the rather tardily introduced Theodora; as Spenser requires a *dea ex machina* (Cambina)[48] so Lane in Part X (to revive Cambyuskan), calls upon a *deus*—in this case King Thotobun, who turns out to have made mirror, ring, sword and horse; and an unexpectedly large role goes to Cambyuskan's wife, somewhat intimidatingly called Queen Ethel. Lane is Spenserian in his liking for 'Faerie' and a good deal of witchcraft as motivation for Algarsif. He only just manages to return to the falcon and the tercelet in Part XII and, while he is clearly fascinated by the horse of brass, can find little to do with it beyond ride to war. The pleasantly fanciful result is that Cambyuskan and Canace go for a ride to the sun and moon. Lane's work is not altogether serious. He tries to imitate Chaucer by presenting public opinion —the views of 'The Vulgar' (VI, 307ff.), and by the odd self-consciously extravagant *occupatio*.[49] There is also much direct narratorial intervention, as in Spenser. In spite of these redeeming touches, there is no disputing Furnivall's sour evaluation of Lane's work nor his sense of Lane's love for the Squire's Tale: 'he'd have written a better poem if he had been able'.[50] But literary quality has little to do with the interest of Lane's work. At the least, it testifies that length was no object; at most, it provides a real clue to the nature of Renaissance interest in the Squire's Tale.

It is fruitful at this stage to recall Milton's tribute to Chaucer as poet of the Squire's Tale:

> him that left half told
> The story of *Cambuscan* bold,
> Of *Camball*, and of *Algarsife*,
> And who had *Canace* to wife,
> That own'd the vertuous Ring and Glass,
> And of the wond'rous Horse of Brass,
> On which the Tartar King did ride.

Gardiner Stillwell asks why Milton mentions the Tale in *Il Penseroso* rather than *L'Allegro*:

> In *L'Allegro* he exhibits great interest (literary in its associations) in the high life of chivalric persons (117–30). Yet Canacee's bright eyes, and Cambyuskan and his barons, are reserved for *Il Penseroso* (109–15), where the Squire's Tale is associated with the more elevated and tragic strains in poetry, sung 'In sage and solemn tunes' (117).   (p. 12)

There is good reason for the 'sage and solemn tunes', and it does not seem to me to lie where Stillwell thought it did: 'for a just and accurate appreciation of Chaucer's tone qualities it is unfortunate that Spenser, Warton and above all Milton have been our chief guides in the reading of the Squire's Tale'. The idea here is that the modern age has made a sudden discovery of humour in the Squire's Tale, unseen by Spenser or Milton. This would not be true of Lane, who refers to 'yonder warrlike Squiers tale, tragecomicalie handled': this makes quite a shrewd distinction between matter and tone. Nor do I believe it to be true of Spenser or Milton, though the critical vocabulary of their day left little room for recording smiles. They see the Squire's Tale as a fragment of something that would have been very long, would have treated of wars and marvels, love and chivalry, and of a serious but delicate tone (with, to judge from Lane's narrational interventions and use of *occupatio*, occasional lightening). The setting is to be vast in range, exotic, and unavoidably, being Tartary, foreign: though we have seen Spenser and Lane, and one could suspect Milton too (who contemplated an Arthurian epic before deciding on *Paradise Lost*), do as much as they can to annex Tartary into Faerie Land.

In short, what lies behind Milton's placing of the Squire's Tale in *Il Penseroso* is what also lies behind Lane's description of it as Chaucer's 'Master-Peece' and Spenser's incorporation into the *Faerie Queene* of his tribute to the 'renowned Poet' who wrote the Squire's Tale

> With warlike numbers and Heroicke sound,
> Dan *Chaucer*, well of English undefyled.   (IV, II, xxxii)

It is what J. L. Lowes rediscovered when he asked in 1913: 'may not Chaucer in the Squire's Tale have attempted seriously what in *Sir Thopas* he had thrown off as a *jeu d'esprit*, a romance of his own into which should be woven motives from various sources?'[51] The high place given to the Squire's Tale in *Il Penseroso*, among 'sage and solemn tunes', is dictated by considerations of genre and 'Heroicke sound'. All three authors regarded Chaucer in the Squire's Tale as the true father of English epic.

The unstable tone of the Squire's Tale would have been no impediment. We must remember Spenser's chief epic model, which he aspired to overgo; a model objected to by Tasso on the grounds that it was really romantic, sometimes frivolously so, not epic at all. A clue to Lane's awareness of the same model is provided by his manuscript divisions of his poem. What Furnivall, out of pedantic loyalty to Chaucer, reproduces, for example, as 'Part XII' was written in Lane's holograph as '*Canto duodecimo*'. The divisions were in Italian, not English. And it is unlikely to have been a chance association that leads Spenser to pay passing tribute to this model in the course of his continuation of the Squire's Tale, one canto after his homage to Chaucer. The immediate context is the arrival of Cambina, carrying with her a cup brimfull of the divine drink, Nepenthe:

> Much more of price and of more gratious powre
> Is this, then that same water of Ardenne,
> The which *Rinaldo* drunck in happie howre,
> Described by that famous Tuscane penne.   (IV, iii, 45)

The reference is of course to the *Orlando Furioso*. For all three authors, Chaucer in the Squire's Tale was one hundred and fifty years ahead of his time. He was the English Ariosto. It is an anachromatic parallel, and self-consciously so—charged with national pride in, after all, having been first. It is also extraordinarily illuminating. There could hardly be a better historical vantage point from which to value the tone of what we have of the Squire's Tale, and the structure of what we have been denied.

This chapter is not to transform itself into a study of Ariosto, but some parallels must be drawn. However anachronistic, they gloss a Renaissance reading of the Squire's Tale. If the Squire's Tale has too much plot, *Orlando Furioso* has a plethora. Ariosto speaks of the many wefts of his tapestry (for instance II 30, XXII 3)[52] and of the many instruments he must play. He therefore develops a pattern of artful interlacing (see, for example, in XXXIII 78, 92, 96) and a series of slick narratorial transitions:

> Di questo altrove io vo'rendervi conto;
> ch'ad un gran duca à forza ch'io riguardi,
> il qual mi grida, e di lontano accenna,
> e priega ch'io nol lasci ne la penna.   (XV, 9)

(Later I shall relate to you what happened; now I must turn my attention to a great duke who is calling and beckoning to me from a distance, entreating my pen to release him onto the page).

Yet the narratorial voice apparent here is unstable, and sometimes the transitions are wonderfully artless, anticipating Byron's *Don Juan* or Frere's *Monks and Giants*. Some of these deal humorously with the narrative complications of the subject-matter:

> Soviemmi che cantare io vi dovea
> (già lo promisi, e poi m'uscì di mente)
> d'una sospizion che fatto avea
> la bella donna di Ruggier dolente . . .

> Dovea cantarne, et altro incominciai,
> perché Rinaldo in mezzo sopravenne;
> e poi Guidon mi diè che fare assai,
> che tra camino a bada un pezzo il tenne.
> D'un cosa in un'altra in modo entrai,
> che mal di Bradamente mi sovenne:
> sovienmene ora, e vo' narrarne inanti
> che di Rinaldo e di Gradasso io canti.

> Ma bisogna anco, prima ch'io ne parli,
> che d'Agramente io vi ragioni un poco . . .   (XXXII, 1–3)

(I remember that I was to relate to you a suspicion (I did promise but then it slipped my mind) which had embittered fair Bradamant against Ruggiero . . . That was to be my song, but I started on another, for Rinaldo intruded, and then Guidono, who kept me busy as he held up Rinaldo's journey awhile. And so I went from one topic to another, quite oblivious of Bradamant. But now I have remembered, and I shall take up her story before continuing that of Rinaldo and Gradasso. But before I start I must talk to you a little about Agrament.)

There is an ironic antifeminism which Ariosto shares with Chaucer, and which both derive from Boccaccio; though the following example strikes as more Chaucerian than most because of the use of an imaginary source, Turpin, behind which Ariosto shelters as in *Troilus* Chaucer shelters behind 'Lollius':

> Donne, e voi che le donne avete in pregio,
> per Dio, non date a questa istoria orecchia,
> a questa che l'ostier dire in dispregio
> e in vostra infamia e biasmo s'apparecchia;
> ben che né macchia vi può dar né fregio
> lingua sì vile, e sia l'usanza vecchia
> che 'l volgare ignorante ognun riprenda,
> e parli più di quel che meno intenda.
>
> Lasciate questo canto, che senza esso
> può star l'istoria, e non sarà men chiara.
> Mettendolo Turpino, anch'io l'ho messo.   (XXVIII, 1–2)

(Ladies, and ladies' devotees, by all means disregard this tale which the innkeeper is preparing to relate to the disparagement, to the ignominy and censure of your sex—not that a tongue as common as his can either sully or embellish your image. The ignorant herd will always carp at everything; the deeper their ignorance, the more they will talk. Skip this canto: it is not essential—my story is no less clear without it. As Turpin included it, so have I).

There are larger parallels, hinted at in this passage, between Ariosto and Chaucer's treatment of the various layers of audience in the *Canterbury Tales*; and there is a close parallel between Ariosto's reference to ''l volgare ignorante' and Chaucer's treatment of 'lewed people' in the Squire's Tale:

> Of sondry doutes thus they jangle and trete,
> As lewed peple demeth comunly
> Of thynges that been maad moore subtilly
> Than they kan in hir lewednesse comprehende.   (220–3)

Stronger yet is Ariosto's contempt for '*vulgo sciocco e ignaro*', 'the ignorant and mindless rabble' (VII 2).

There are other quite precise parallels with the Squire's Tale. Firstly, we find a large number of occasions on which Ariosto uses *occupatio* to deliberately obtrusive effect (see, for example, IX 93–4; XXIX 30, XXXVII 21–2). The last cited deserves quotation, as it shows Ariosto both refusing to dilate further in praise of a woman, as in Squire's Tale (34–41), and concerned, as in Squire's Tale (401–8), with a knot of the tale:

> Se quanto dir se ne potrebbe, o quanto
> io n'ho desir, volessi porre in carte,
> ne direi lungamente; ma non tanto,
> ch'a dir non e restasse anco gran parte:
> e di Marfisa e dei compagni intanto
> la bella istoria rimarria da parte,
> la quale io vi promisi di seguire,
> s'in questo canto mi verreste a udire.
>
> Ora essendo voi qui per ascoltarmi,
> et io per non mancar de la promessa,
> serberò a maggior ozio di provarmi
> ch'ogni laude di lei sia da me espressa . . .

(If I proposed to set down on paper all that could be said about this lady, or all that I could wish to say, I should go on and on and still leave a great deal unspoken. And the pleasant tale of Marfisa and her companions, which I promised I should pursue if you came to hear me in this canto would be neglected. Now since you are here to listen to me and I to fulfil my pledge, I shall reserve till greater leisure my efforts to give full expression to her praises . . .)

This kind of *occupatio* is very like Chaucer's in the Squire's Tale: it guilefully takes almost as long to refuse to do something as it would to do it, it takes pleasure in the 'fulsomnesse' of its own 'prolixitee', and it involves a teasing contract with an audience grounded in '*ozio*'. Such virtuoso turns occur less in the final cantos of Ariosto's poem as the wefts of the tapestry are brought together, and one assume they would have occurred less towards the end of Chaucer's design. Secondly, Ariosto has an eye for scientific detail and is prepared to turn aside for it, as in the attack on muskets in Canto XI. Lastly, Ariosto is not afraid to cultivate romance bathos for the sake of the mock-heroic:

> S'in poter fosse stato Orlando pare
> all'Eleusina dea, come in disio,
> non avria, per Angelica cercare,
> lasciato o selva o campo o stagno o rio
> o valle o monte o piano o terra o mare,
> il cielo e'l fondo de l'eterno oblio;
> ma poi che 'l carro e i draghi non avea,
> la già cercando al meglio che potea.   (XII, 3)

(Had Orlando possessed not only the zeal but also the powers of the Eleusinian goddess, he would not have left a single wood, field, pond, stream, valley, hill, plain, land or sea unsearched, nor even the heavens or the pit of eternal oblivion, in his quest for Angelica. But since he did not have the chariot with the dragons, he sought her as best he could.)

Such parallels build up a picture of tonal affinity between Ariosto and Chaucer's Squire's Tale. Ariosto is detached from the chivalric world he describes, both in its fighting and its lovemaking; his conception of it is self-consciously literary, fictionalised, even at times zany. He works within a tradition in which 'the comic element is increased, sometimes to the point of parody',[53] and the narratorial tone conveys his mood of detachment in its sudden twists from tragic to comic; or, as Professor Brand puts it, 'the grandiose and the pedestrian exist side by side' (p. 155). Yet Ariosto is not cynical: neither arms nor love is 'merely a butt for his facetious wit' (Brand, p. 94), so that the romance narrative is never undermined in the enjoyment of its near-absurdity. Perhaps Chaucer's narratorial control in the Squire's Tale is less assured: he is more like Boiardo, entertainingly loquacious and never really planning more than one move ahead.[54] But then, we have only 670 lines on which to judge from what must have been in conception a massive enterprise. If only the first two Cantos of *Orlando Furioso* survived, we might well reckon it a highly talented, mercurial and overburdened failure. Judgements of this kind on the management of plot and the control of tone are highly dependent on length. We should be careful not to over-read apparent failures in these areas within the Squire's Tale, for if it were as long as its closing prospectus indicates that it should have been, on completion, their impact might well have seemed very different.

We may have to encourage a more widespread reading of Ariosto among students of English literature before we can hope to improve the general esteem of the Squire's Tale. None the less, my conclusion is that we have much to learn from Spenser, Milton and the humble Lane. In the light of their reading of Ariosto, neither tonal disturbance nor fantastic plot would have deterred them from seeing in the Squire's Tale the first seed of the English epic. Nor would the fact that it is really a romance: Milton, after all, contemplated an Arthurian romance-epic before deciding on *Paradise Lost*. In the same way, Chaucer seems to have set out to write in the Squire's Tale a romance of truly epic proportions—and stopped; preferring perhaps to write *Troilus* or the Knight's Tale. Neither of these satisfied Renaissance criteria as a completed Squire's Tale might have done: the one because it is too romantic and inadequately warlike, the other because it is the reverse. Spenser and Milton saw the Squire's Tale as heroic, as a sage and solemn tune, because of what it could have been had it not remained half—(or probably, had the line scanned, one-tenth)—told. They saw it as a noble ruin of lost opportunity. In medieval England, however, the high Homeric horse went riderless. For it was made of brass, and 'vanysshed, I noot in what manere'.

The rest is pure speculation. Yet speculation appears unavoidable in an essay on the literary history of the Squire's Tale; at least, it would seem a failure of critical courage not to consider the poem's earliest history, from composition to its appearance in *Canterbury Tales* manuscripts, even though speculation is the only resource available. There are three major questions. When did Chaucer write his fragment? Why did he stop? And when, and under what circumstances, did his fragment become the Squire's Tale? I repeat that my responses must be seen as tentative and insecurely grounded. If they are worth making at all, it is because they raise credible possibilities that have not always received a decent hearing by those who adopt a 'generally agreed' position that is in some respects no less precarious. What follows is devil's advocacy.

As for the date of composition, the Squire's Tale is commonly ascribed to the last major period of Chaucer's life or the penultimate one: to some date, then, in the 1390s. I cannot see that the grounds for this are strong; and certain factors point in another direction, to the 1380s. For one thing, if I am right in my suggestion about the tone of certain narratorial interventions, that they have a mock-heroic intent, then I should be inclined to date the Squire's Tale before the Nun's Priest's Tale, where the touch is so much surer. I have been tempted to date the handling of the falcon in Part Two before the *Parliament of Fowls*, where the handling of avian lovers with 'gentil' pretensions is more subtle; but who is to say what might have happened in that poem had one of the tercelets glimpsed a passing kite? For another, Jones made a respectable, though not an overwhelming, case for influence from Froissart's *Espinette Amoureuse*, or poems of that tradition; this sort of influence marks the 1380s rather than the 1390s. A more telling point altogether, however, is the affinity between Part Two and *Anelida and Arcite*, which is quite an early poem. Since *Anelida* treats the complaint without much humour, and the Squire's Tale does not, one would expect the Squire's Tale to be the later poem, but not so much later that the *Anelida* had ceased to be alive in Chaucer's mind. All in all, there is a reasonable possibility that the Squire's Tale may belong to the 1380s, and perhaps to the earlier period of '*Saint Cecilia* (the Second Nun's Tale); the tragedies afterward used for the Monk's Tale, *Anelida*'.[55] In other words, like the Second Nun's Tale, it may not have been designed originally for its place in the *Canterbury Tales*.

Why did Chaucer stop? There can of course be no confident answer. Chaucer did not hesitate to leave works unfinished, and Furnivall's famous answer still seems plausible, though it is more robustly expressed than (by no means to our credit) we would allow:

> The completion of the Squire's Tale would have taxt Chaucer's utmost power, even when he was at his best. The subject is one into which he could have imported little humanity. The Continuation would have been a constant strain on his invention and fancy. The work wouldn't have repaid the effort, and so the Poet tùrnd it up, as he did the *Good Women* when he'd done nine of them out of the proposed nineteen. Who of us, in his own line, has not done the like? Man is mortal; and when a fellow-man doesn't see his way thro' a bit of work, it bores him, and he drops it.[56]

However, the question is worth asking in conjunction with a possible revised dating. At least we may establish another reason why the Tale remained unfinished, if the extant two parts were written by the mid-1380s. Such redating would reflect on the Introduction to the Man of Law's Tale (II,

77–80), a passage in praise of Chaucer in which incest genuinely does raise its ugly head:

> But certeinly no word ne writeth he
> Of thilke wikke ensample of Canacee,
> That loved hir owene brother synfully;
> (Of swiche cursed stories I sey fy!).

Instead of wondering why Chaucer should have sought to rehabilitate the name 'Canace' in the wake of Gower's *Confessio Amantis*, we may perhaps interpret these lines as a humorous protest against Gower's making it notorious—at a time when Chaucer may have been using it seriously for his heroine in the Squire's Tale. The name is bound into the metre and the rhyming position of several lines. True, Chaucer could simply have changed it; but if he had already set the Tale aside, Gower's unwelcome intervention could have been enough to guarantee its permanent abandonment.

If the Squire's Tale, like the Second Nun's Tale, was an existing fragment before Chaucer began to assemble the *Canterbury* Tales, at what stage and under what circumstances was it brought into the collection and attributed to the Squire? The dramatic principle has encouraged over-confident criticism, obscuring the relevance of such textual questions. A recent essay and edition by N. F. Blake have restated these questions in an extreme form.[57] There will be many, including myself, who dissent from some of Blake's major conclusions, but the critical justice of his challenge must be accepted. Blake follows the order of Hengwrt, in which the Squire's Tale follows the Man of Law's Tale, rather than Ellesmere. Here is the gist of Blake's introductory note to

[*The Squire's Tale*] The square brackets indicate that the allocation of this tale to the squire was almost certainly made by the editor of Hengwrt rather than by Chaucer himself, for this tale introduces a group of four tales which share this feature. These four may have been in process of writing when Chaucer died . . . Scribes did invent links to follow the Squire's Tale, but these are spurious and were introduced to maintain the continuity of the poem . . . (p. 286)

The other tales whose attribution is editorial, in Blake's view, are the Merchant's Tale, the Franklin's Tale, and what Blake retitles the Nun's Tale. The last is of no further concern to this argument, though it is true that there is no attempt to attach it to its teller or indeed adapt it to the *Canterbury Tales* framework ('Yet preye I yow that reden that I write', VIII 78). The Merchant's Tale bears some indications of having been composed with another narrator, perhaps the Friar, in mind; in Hengwrt it stands without a prologue. The Franklin's Tale raises other considerations: in Hengwrt, the speech after the Squire's Tale, attributed to the Franklin in Ellesmere, is given to the Merchant, and the Host's comment on the Merchant's Tale leads into an invitation to the Franklin, not, as in Ellesmere, the Squire. Blake relegates both links to an appendix, arguing that 'they appear to be later' than Chaucer's original work, and that 'in later manuscripts with the new order' they were adapted to act as the Squire-Franklin link and the Merchant-Squire link (p. 667). The first of these claims is much stronger than the second. It seems in fact that the Hengwrt editor adapted the links as they are found in Ellesmere: in the first case, this is shown by the clumsy substitution for 'frankeleyn' of 'marchant certeyn' in the line '"That knowe I wel, sire," quod the Frankeleyn' (V 699), and in the second case, a line ('And seye somewhat of love . . . ,' V 2) is made defective when 'of love' is omitted in Hengwrt as being, presumably, less appropriate to the Franklin than the Squire. However, the fact that the Ellesmere version is correct does not establish that Chaucer wrote these links (as I shall discuss below), or, if he did, that he left clear instructions about which Tales were to be inserted within them.

There is some doubt that Chaucer left much indication at all of the ascriptions to be given to most of the high style tales except Knight and Clerk, and as Blake shows, the order of the canon is particularly problematic in the case of the tales now ascribed to the Man of Law, Clerk, Merchant, Squire and Franklin: 'We may state that these five tales each formed an independent group. That means their order in relation to other tales had not been decided by Chaucer, though some may have had prologues and/or endlinks from the pilgrimage frame attached to them' (p. 4). The problem with the Clerk's Tale is merely one of relative position. The Man of Law's Prologue is ill-suited to the following Tale, since it promises to avoid rhyme and 'speke in prose' (II, 96). It is suited only to *Melibeus*, which is, after all, a translation of a treatise by a famous Italian lawyer. The endlink to the Man of Law's Tale also goes wrong.[58] The disorder in the sequence of the *Canterbury Tales* in the various manuscript traditions begins here, and has most to do with the placement of the five tales Blake indicates. Blake argues that the three remaining Tales—Squire, Merchant and Franklin—had neither original prologue nor endlink and were not allocated to a teller by Chaucer. This cannot be taken as proven, but the theory has much logical force and merit. Certainly, we cannot be sure that the ascription of the Squire's Tale to the Squire is Chaucer's own.

One need not accept all Blake's deductions from, or his special pleading for, Hengwrt to agree with this: it is consistent with the process traced by Parkes and Doyle,[59] and in the main with the situation envisaged by Manly and Rickert. Chaucer would have had more than one original of the pieces of the *Canterbury Tales*, as well as cancelled versions. Scribes searched for copy after his death, and were faced with the question of ordering the various groups they found. The internal order of the groups was largely decided, as were many of the ascriptions to tellers. The whole order probably was not, and there are grounds for suspecting that a number of the high-style tales were not dedicated to tellers. Chaucer's editors therefore had a number of unattached tales to assign to a number of unattached tellers; they had to assign material to the Man of Law, the Merchant, the Squire, the Second Nun and perhaps the Franklin. They then had to align these with existing links, or even compose new ones (for instance, the Merchant's Prologue?), and order the parts as best they could. This is only one possible scenario, but given the wide range of disagreement in the early manuscripts it is a plausible one.

For the sake of argument, then, let us conceive that the early editors found themselves faced with the need to find a tale for the Squire, and matched him up with a fragment of a romance set aside by Chaucer; perhaps adding a couple of lines for '*pars tercia*' in the hope of pulling off the effect of an 'interruption', and perhaps one couplet to indicate a more specific occasion of performance ('I wol nat taryen yow, for it is pryme', 73). Chaucer could conceivably have done this himself, but there is some reason to think not. My view is based on a passage I have already quoted and called a key passage: the narrator's (very Chaucerian) profession that he is 'a dul man' unable to describe 'the revel and the jolitee':

> He moste han knowen love and his servyse,
> And been a feestlych man as fressh as May,
> That sholde yow devysen swich array.   (280–2)

This is either what Pearsall says it is, an ironic manipulation of the Squire based on his depiction in the General Prologue ('He was as fressh as is the month of May', 92)—a narratorial irony of a kind for which I can find no other evidence; or it is the justification for Chaucer's beleaguered first editors' decision to ascribe this fragment to the Squire, mindful of the cliché-connection with the General Prologue and disregarding the fact that this passage actually disclaims the 'lusty' freshness that characterises the Squire. If this were so, the connection between the Squire and his Tale would be fortuitous: it rests on the coincidence of one phrase. I cannot prove this; indeed, it is not a matter of belief but one of possibility. The very doubt is damaging to dramatic readings, and confirms the wisdom of earlier generations that concentrated on the Tale, not the teller.

There is one last step in this speculative listing of neglected possibilities. It has long been accepted as a possibility that some small additions in Ellesmere may not be Chaucer's. Manly and Rickert say that they are 'either improvements by the author or emendations by a highly intelligent reader'. They offer 'no guarantee that the changes may not have been made by someone else'. In the end, 'the only test is the knowledge and taste of the reader'.[60] I venture to suggest that the knowledge and taste of modern readers could be influenced more than they commonly are by the identification by Parkes and Doyle of Scribe C of Trinity College, Cambridge MS R.3.2—working alongside Scribe B, of both Hengwrt and Ellesmere—as Thomas Hoccleve. The discovery that Hoccleve belonged to the circle of Chaucer's first editors is treated with caution by Parkes and Doyle;[61] but it seems to me far-reaching. Hoccleve's poetry is only now being rescued from neglect and undervaluation. He claims to have known Chaucer, and acknowledges him as his master—not least by affecting Chaucer's own stance of dullness:

> My dere maistir—God his soule quyte!—
> And fadir Chaucer, fayn wolde han me taght,
> But I was dul, and lerned lite or naght.[62]

If Chaucer in the 1380s and 1390s ever had such a thing as a 'workshop',[63] the young Hoccleve would have been a likely member. In spite of E. P. Hammond's strictures to the contrary,[64] Hoccleve is the best writer of Chaucerian lines after Chaucer. He would have been perfectly capable of improving, amending or forging links. His one great metrical weakness is the expansion of the pentameter to contain a vocative or a name: 'I, Hoccleve, in swich case am gilty, þis me touchith.' The weakness appears most conspicuously in the *Canterbury Tales* in the Franklin's address to the Squire: 'So felyngly thou spekist, sire, I allow the.'

With this in mind, I should like to examine the curious and cursory 'Introduction to the Squire's Tale':

> 'Squier, com neer, if it youre wille be,
> And sey somwhat of love; for certes ye
> Konnen thereon as muche as any man.'
>   'Nay, sire,' quod he, 'but I wol seye as I kan
> With hertly wyl; for I wol nat rebelle
> Agayn youre lust; a tale wol I telle.
> Have me excused if I speke amys;
> My wyl is good, and lo, my tale is this.'   (1–8)

What interests me here is the relentless emphasis on 'wille', and its context. It is unparalleled in Chaucer's work. The phrase 'hertly wyl' appears in the Clerk's Tale (176), and 'good wyl' appears in a context much like the present one in the Franklin's Prologue (715). Elsewhere in Chaucer, 'good wil' appears only in the context of love and dedication to one's lover.[65] The present use may be a joke, since the Host has asked the Squire to say 'somwhat of love', but it would be a weak one. On the face of it, the use does not look quite Chaucerian. As for 'rebelle' as the infinitive of a verb, this occurs nowhere else in Chaucer's work: 'rebelleth' occurs three times as the third person singular of its present tense, but except in this passage the form 'rebelle' is always a noun. Hoccleve, however, uses it as an infinitive, modified by 'wil': 'but þou be obstinat / And wilfully rebelle . . .' (Regement 189–90).

It is Hoccleve, not Chaucer, who harps on will, sometimes associated with 'lust' ('of his owne fre wil and lust', Regement 1152), and who tends to pit his heart and will against his poetic deficiencies: 'swich as is my smal konyng, / Withal so treewe an herte, I wole it oute' (2066–7); 'Now noble prince, though I be nat wys / Wel-willed am I' (2186). For Hoccleve, like the Squire ('My wyl is good'), is over-apologetic: 'But how I speke, algate I mene weel' (1986). The quotations are all from the Prologue to the Regement, in which Hoccleve's pose is that of youth ('in myn age grene', 834; 'I am so childissh ay', 2058) being directed by age, the beggar, as the Squire is governed by the Host. For Hoccleve this is a favourite topos, maintained by him well into middle age; for Chaucer, who prematurely adopted the posture of advanced and portly middle age, it is rare. It is demonstrable that the Regement contains sections of pastiche from the Man of Law's Tale and a versification of parts of the Melibeus. Might one not detect a similar quality of Chaucerian pastiche in the introduction to the Squire's Tale: 'Have me excused if I speke amys'? Again, the evidence is not conclusive, but I find it suggestive. I would claim that Hoccleve could have written these eight introductory lines to the Squire's Tale; and there is a possibility that he did in fact write them. If this is so, then it is also possible that he wrote the Epilogue to the Merchant's Tale, for the Merchant's endlink and the Squire's headlink always appear as one unit; and he would then be favourite for authorship of the Merchant's Prologue, described by Manly and Rickert as 'rather late' (IV 266)—so much so perhaps that it was supplied in time for Ellesmere but not for Hengwrt.

It is worth remembering that the Merchant's Prologue in its turn is preceded in Ellesmere by a textually problematic stanza immediately following the

Envoy to the Clerk's Tale. This is accepted as authentic by Fisher, but printed in square brackets by Robinson:

> This worthy Clerk, whan ended was his tale,
> Oure Hooste seyde, and swoor, 'By Goddes bones,
> Me were levere than a barel ale
> My wyf at hoom had herd this legende ones!
> This is a gentil tale for the nones,
> As to my purpos, wiste ye my wille;
> But thyng that wol nat be, lat it be stille.' (1212^{a-g})

Manly and Rickert call this 'probably a fragment of a link written by Chaucer but discarded, though not adequately cancelled when the standard Clerk-Merchant link was composed . . . Its status seems, therefore, to be the same as that of the Man of Law's Endlink—a bit of Chaucerian work but rejected because of a change of plan.' Plainly puzzled, however, they add: 'Strangely enough, it is preserved almost solely in manuscripts containing the latest work' (III, 266). I do not seek to solve a minor mystery with a major one, but the suggestion that Hoccleve provided some or all of these links is surely worth considering. They ring variations on two of his favourite themes: the eager deference of youth to age, and the less successful stock battle of the sexes, more monotonously handled than anywhere else in Chaucer's work.

I am aware that I have entered deep waters, and will go no further. I must stress again that in this last section I have been dealing in possibilities, and have proposed nothing definite. I have merely set down questions that the literary history of the Squire's Tale has led me to ask. I am persuaded, however, that they are real questions about real possibilities. I am concerned that Chaucer criticism is not fully reflecting the implications of modern textual scholarship and slightly older source study, and I am surprised by the confidence with which some modern criticism has approached explication of the Tale in moral or psychological, 'dramatic' terms. It strikes me as premature: in the best tradition of the Emperor's new clothes, a parade of omniscience in ignorance of facts.

Burrow is right to say that modern critical preconceptions do not equip us to appreciate the Squire's Tale. This is the Tale's importance. It challenges critical preoccupations of Chaucer studies since the 1950s. It points to the inadequacy of selective rhetorical study, to the need for a tactful study of tone and for a critical vocabulary with which to conduct it. The Tale's fragmentary nature underlines the dangers of close reading: in order to understand what is there we must try to grasp what is not. Most of all, it shows the inescapable relevance of textual study; and how the historical study of criticism itself, back to the first editors, is a thoroughly worthwhile critical discipline. It raises all the questions that need asking. The Squire's Tale would make the ideal set text for a modern introduction to Chaucer studies.

AFTERWORD

Some Post-Chaucerian Narrators

This is a genuine afterword, for the main argument of this book is complete. Yet it seems useful to offer one more way of bringing Chaucer's narrators into focus, by showing examples of what they are not. The interest of these examples is that they are all drawn from a tradition that took Chaucer as its fountainhead, whose poets none the less sound nothing like him. The purpose of this brief sketch is not to show that great poets are inimitable, though they generally are, nor to demonstrate that their effect on their successors is a dead hand, though it generally is. It is to show how rare Chaucer's achievement was, for it occurred in circumstances that seldom recur: when what in hindsight turns out to be a tradition is a running argument with authority/(auctoritee), and when that authority's claim to univocal speech is subverted by play with multiple contexts and the textual processes of writing. As soon as the argument is won, it becomes a new authority—this time a written one, to be memorialised in writing. To accept that authority is immediately to change its terms; to subscribe to it as a tradition is progressively to lose contact with what gave rise to it. There is a parallel in modern critical debates.

The Fifteenth Century

The only resource for a historical account of narratorial *persona* and voice in the fifteenth century would be close reading. Such an account would be extensive, considering many writers and works barely to be mentioned here. Lydgate would occupy a prominent position: his rather dry and literal reworking of the Chaucerian histories in *The Fall of Princes* is influential as late as Sackville's 'Induction' to the *Mirror for Magistrates* or Cavendish's *Metrical Visions*. The main interest of such a study would lie in the carefully cultivated dullness of Lydgate's voice which, for example, makes disappointingly little out of his *persona*'s discussion with Petrarch and Boccaccio in the Prologue to Book VIII of the *Fall*.[1] Late in the period Hawes would also demand attention, if only to illuminate a use of *persona* so casual that he recounts his own death and epitaph in two poems.[2] Hoccleve would rate enthusiastic mention for his much underrated originality, the introduction of a wholly new tone, 'the first unambiguously personal voice in English poetry.'[3] But it does not require an extensive account to demonstrate the influence of Chaucer. However un-Chaucerian the consequences, Chaucer's precedent is formative. One thinks of Lydgate in the Prologue to the *Siege of Thebes* paying elaborate homage to Chaucer and at the same time annexing the entire *Canterbury Tales* as pro-logomenon to Lydgate's leaden epic.[4]

Chaucer is conceived as a resource not primarily of new and volatile subject-matter but of style, as the master rhetorician, and consummate gilder of lilies. The reverence for Chaucer is in every sense pious. In the tribute to Chaucer at the end of the *Regement of Princes*, Hoccleve passes from the Chaucer 'peynture' to the defence of religious images. He carefully, and characteristically, does not draw the implication, turning the sequence instead into a prayer for Chaucer's soul: 'Passe ouer þat. Now blessid trinite, / Vpon my maystres soule mercy haue' (5010–11). But the implication is present all the same: as well as being the flower of rhetoricians and 'Thys landes verray tresour and rychesse' (2081), Chaucer has become the patron saint of English poetry.[5] There are two immediate consequences of such universal regard. Firstly, this image of Chaucer—couched in terms of style as much as, or more than, of content—leads to a concentration on high style. I have argued that the narratorial voice of Chaucer's high style is remarkably consistent and stable, responding to the level of the style and subject as the poem's exponent. There is somewhat unwelcome support for this view in fifteenth-century practice: narratorial *persona* is hardly ever intrusive in the narration itself, however strong it may be in prologues. Secondly, and not altogether inconsistently, while reading Chaucer's high style in this way his fifteenth-century successors also appreciated, from contexts like the dream poems and the General Prologue of the *Canterbury Tales*, the presence of a characteristically Chaucerian *persona*. Such contexts furnish, as it were, a Chaucer iconography, and inhibit lesser mortals. Most of Chaucer's successors are encouraged by them to make an occasional performance as if *in propria persona*, but they make little sustained effort to rival the complex and comic quality of the Chaucer *persona*. Much later, Skelton is exceptional. In the first few decades after Chaucer's death only Hoccleve employs a full-scale poetic *persona*, and even this is shaped by Hoccleve's modesty beside his master:

> My dere mayster—God ys soule quyte—
> And fadir, Chaucer, fayn wolde han me taght,
> But I was dul and learned lyte or naght. (*Regement*, 2077–9)

This example, and the fact that Hoccleve's use of *persona* turns into a kind of wry autobiography, highlights three further constraints on Chaucer's successors. The first is the effect of laicisation, seen in the very topic of the *Regement*, the princely virtues. In such a mirror of princely greatness, the layman as commoner seeks his example:

> It is a great auantage
> A man before him to haue a mirour
> Therin to see the path vnto honour. (*Dialogue*, 607–9)

There is not too much room here for instability of tone. The second constraint is the increased social status of the lay poet, the very fact of writing for, or with a speculative eye to, a great patron:[6]

> Allas, the stuf of sad intelligence
> Me faillyth to speke in so hye presence.
>
> (*Regement*, 2071–2)

Humility is appropriate on social as well as literary grounds. There is no reason why a narratorial *persona* should not be comic, but it cannot really afford, in lengthy narration for a noble patron, to appear eccentric. Credibility matters. Nor can the poet confidently tease a single great patron in the way Chaucer's poems challenge the responses of real and imaginary audiences. A *persona* will work perfectly well in a short lyric or complaint, but even here poets will make an effort to be unambiguous. The third is the increased status of writing itself: the context in the fifteenth century is increasingly one in which the poet has to publish his work in manuscript rather than in performance.[7] Hoccleve's poetry takes specific account of this. The famous tribute to Chaucer at the end of the *Regement* incorporates the equally famous portrait ('I haue heere hys lykenesse / Don make,' 4995–6) in MS Harley 4866; and the 'Balade to Master John Carpenter' apparently used the visual space of the margins to list Hoccleve's creditors ('Tho men whos names I aboue expresse', 8). This is not poetry designed to accommodate dramatic recitation, and its image of the reader has gone blank: now it is the reader, not the writer, who is anonymous. It would be easy enough in such cases to lose the sense of interplay between reader and writer that quickens a Chaucerian narrator.

Dream poetry is a special case, for the dreamer-poet link is inescapable, and the fifteenth century continues to exploit it. The terms of its operation, however, are those already described in previous chapters: it cannot be said that the fifteenth century provides much that is new in the handling of a dreamer *persona*, and there is no cause here to re-examine ground already ably investigated by others, notably Spearing.[8] Moreover, the more the poetic surface of fifteenth-century dream poetry became rhetorically ornate and encrusted, the less does its tone range beyond the confines of dignity, and the less integral does a perceived disparity between poet and dreamer become. In the *Golden Targe*, which anthologises so many of the techniques of fifteenth-century poetry, Dunbar's dreamer exists mainly as a pair of eyes, and the one stanza in which he plays an active part, falling in love and lamenting his blindness to reason, is both conventional and (as the appearance of a *persona*) casually handled:

> Than was I woundit to the deth wele nere,
> And yoldyn as a wofull prisonnere
>   To lady Beautee in a moment space;
> Me thoucht scho semyt lustiar of chere
> Efter that Resoun tynt had his eyne clere
>   Than of before, and lufliare of face:
>   Quhy was thou blindit, Resoun? quhi, allace!
> And gert ane hell my paradise appere,
>   And mercy seme quhare that I fand no grace.[3]   (208–16)

The stress in the rest of this poem falls on the self-conscious display of rhetoric in the tradition of Chaucer, Gower and Lydgate that is glorified in the final three stanzas with their overt allusions to the *Troilus* epilogue. As dream poetry tends to the high style, it becomes exposed to other factors in the fifteenth century inhibiting the use of narratorial *persona* in high style poetry generally. For the most part, dream poetry in the fifteenth century goes its own way, with less marked an influence on other poetic productions than in the fourteenth. At best, the dream becomes useful as a frame or prologue device enabling the poet to appear in a stronger *persona* than in the course of a work itself. Many of the best examples are Scots: certain of Gavin Douglas's Prologues to the books of the *Eneados*,[10] and the Prologue to one of Henryson's *Fables*.

In many respects, Henryson's *Fables* are a good illustration of fifteenth-century practice in Scotland and England, in poems where a narratorial *persona* plays some part. In the Prologue to the whole poem, Henryson defends 'feinȝeit fabils of ald poetre' as, like the kernel of truth in the nut of fiction, 'full of frute'. He puts himself forward as translator, 'in mother toung, of Latyng', rather in the Chaucerian mode of *Troilus*, though the genre is very different, and like Chaucer, Lydgate and many others, submits his work to the 'correctioun' of his audience, 'my maisteris', with a standard humility-*topos*:

> In hamelie language and in termes rude
> Me neidis wryte, for quhy of eloquence
> Nor rethorike, I neuer vnderstude.   (Prologue, 36–8)[11]

Under the authority of Aesop, Henryson's job as translator is to point the moral, and what *persona* exists is there to fulfil that role. It involves direct address to 'freindis' (364), 'worthie folk' (586), 'gude folk' (789), and so on—address, that is, to a rather general-sounding audience, vaguely delineated. It also involves articulating a few transitions and lending a steering hand in the transition from narrative to moral:

> This taill is myngit with moralitie,
> As I sall schaw sumquhat, or that I ceis   (2203–4);

> Bot of the inward sentence and intent
> Of this fabill, as myne author dois write,
> I sall reheirs in rude and hamelie dite.   (117–19)

There is some legerdemain in this narratorial control: such as Henryson's refusal to name the noble patron he claims and, above all, the somewhat Chaucerian readiness to supply his own *moralitas* at the expense of Aesop's. But there is no developed *persona* here, and the work ends with no narratorial appearance beyond a short adieu. The voice, where it appears, is that of the sober poet-exponent. In these respects, it is typical of the narratorial voice—in high and middle style—of fifteenth-century poetry.

The exception is the dream prologue of the seventh fable, 'the Lion and the Mouse', in which the narrator-poet, dreaming under a hawthorn in June, meets Aesop and reverences him with an almost comic respect:

'O maister Esope, poet lawriate,
God wait ӡe ar full deir welcum to me.
Ar ӡe not he that all thir fabillis wrate,
Quhilk in effect, suppois thay fenӡeit be,
Ar full off prudence and moralitie?'
'Fair sone,' said he, 'I am the samin man.'
God wait gif that my hert wes merie than.   (1377–83)

The narrator then asks Aesop to tell 'ane prettie fabill / Concludand with ane
gude moralitie' (1386–7). Rather in the spirit of Chaucer's treatment of
Africanus, Henryson has Aesop at first refuse. He doubts the adequacy of
'fenӡeit' fables to meet the spiritual corruption, the 'canker blak' (1396), of the
times:

'For quhat is it worth to tell ane fenӡeit taill,
Quhen haly preiching may na thing auaill?'   (1389–90)

But a renewed request has him relent: '"I graunt", quod he, and thus begouth
ane taill' (1404). The prologue is thus a real prologue, but it is also a brilliant
centrepiece for the *Fables*. The dream allows one carefully limited context for
the appearance of a narratorial *persona*, and it serves only to confirm the poet's
claim throughout: fables may be suspiciously entertaining, but they none the
less have moral applications. Aesop may feel that fifteenth-century Scotland is
evil enough to deserve nothing but penitential sermons, but even so upright a
man as the poet dreams him to be is prepared in the end to countenance the
moral potential of the genre chosen by Henryson for his poem. The *persona* is
not notably comic and takes part in a set piece of limited duration. His function
is to reinforce the existing basis of the poem. He is there to act as foil to a
fictionalised Aesop, and so to underline the real Aesop's authority. This is a
poem which elegantly reasserts authority, and defends fiction—with veiled
political implications—for its moral content.[12]

However, when Henryson confronts Chaucer directly in the *Testament of
Cresseid*, he turns in a strikingly different and uncharacteristic performance.
For the Dunfermline moralist, Criseyde has escaped too lightly in Chaucer's
poem. Henryson wishes to correct this; he wishes this to be done in an
improbably brief compass of time, for he wants Troilus to be an unwitting
witness of her humiliation; and, to do him justice, he also wants to save
her soul. The resulting poem must, I think, be accounted antifeminist.
Henryson's closing address to his (probably fictional) audience begins
prematurely during Cresseid's epitaph:

'Lo, fair ladyis, Cresseid of Troy the toun,
Sumtyme countit the flour of womanheid,
Vnder this stane, lait lipper, lyis deid.'

Now, worthie wemen, in this ballet schort,
Maid for ӡour worschip and instructioun,
Of cheritie, I monische and exhort,
Ming not ӡour lufe with fals deceptioun:
Beir in ӡour mynd this sore conclusioun

> Of fair Cresseid, as I have said befoir.
> Sen scho is deid, I speik of hir no moir.   (607–16)

The mock-preaching tone of this peroration is reminiscent not so much of Chaucer as of Jean de Meun; but it outdoes Jean, and in its not altogether playful venom it also outdoes Filostrato. The tone is in fact very different from Chaucer's, just as the pity the narrator expresses for Cresseid when she has exchanged 'in filth all thy feminitie' (80–4) is defiantly different from Chaucer's 'routhe'. Immediately Henryson proceeds to echo Chaucer's 'I wolde excuse hir yit, for routhe' (V, 1050), and in this context—after he has just spoken of her 'Sa giglotlike takand thy foull plesance' (83)—the echo is parodic:

> ʒit neuertheles, quhat euer men deme or say
> In scornefull langage of thy brukkilnes,
> I sall excuse als for furth as I may
> Thy womanheid . . .   (85–8)

Given this moral critique, there is no way that Henryson can avoid meeting Chaucer's poem head-on. He therefore introduces his poem with a pseudo-Chaucerian narratorial *persona*, and this is a brilliant pastiche. The narrator identifies himself at once as the man who 'began to wryte / This tragedie' (3–4); the scene is set as if for a dream-poem in the cold middle of Lent; the narrator is highly characterised as 'ane man of age' (29), no longer kindled by love 'as in ʒoutheid' (30), and—in a comic objective correlative—mending the fire in his chamber, before settling down to read Chaucer's *Troilus*. His is not to be the narratorial voice throughout, and he is a closed *persona*. Henryson follows Chaucer almost insouciantly by citing a non-existent and anonymous book as his source: 'ane vther quire I tuik' (61). In the following stanza he concedes that he does not know whether his own narration 'Be authoreist, or fenʒeit of the new / Be sum poeit' (66–7). In one way, Henryson here follows Chaucer in abdicating responsibility for the truth of his story; in another, he goes beyond Chaucer in claiming for his 'source' no greater authority than that of a dream. In this he has little choice, for Henryson well knows that the authority to be repudiated is Chaucer himself, for all his 'gudelie termis' and 'ioly veirs' (59). The key line is that beginning the stanza: 'Quha wait gif all that Chaucer wrait was trew?' It is a Chaucerian performance into which nearly every tone and attribute of the Chaucerian *persona* has been incongruously compressed; it enables Henryson at once to defer to Chaucer and, by drawing attention to Chaucer's highlighting of his fiction, to snare him. If Chaucer's poem is no better than a dream, Henryson himself can write anything he likes. His poem simultaneously grows out of *Troilus* and by using it as a stepping-stone places it at a disadvantage. Henryson's use of Chaucer here is that of a gamekeeper turned poacher. It is the single most complex use of a Chaucerian narratorial *persona* in fifteenth-century poetry, even though it occupies only 100 lines in all, 90 at the start and 10 at the end of Henryson's poem of 616 lines. Its narratorial challenge to Chaucer's authority makes it uncharacteristic of fifteenth-century practice, and it is the challenge to authority that gives it life.

The failure of most fifteenth-century poetry to present much of a narratorial challenge is open to broader explanations. The historical impact of Lollardy would be one. Hoccleve's 'Advice to Oldcastle,' for example, contains a spirited defence of auricular confession and the supreme authority of the priesthood: 'Auctoritee of preest excedith alle / Eerthely powers' (291–2). But Oldcastle, as Hoccleve points out, was a layman, and arguments over such matters are not for knights. Hoccleve advises: 'Clymbe no more in holy writ so hie' (193). He also recommends a reading programme for the educated knight: those Biblical books in which war, not theology, preponderates, and otherwise romances—*Lancelot*, the *Siege of Troy* and the *Siege of Thebes*. Hoccleve prescribes and Lydgate dispenses. The formula is prudential and pious, but not intellectually probing. This also means that the 'Chaucer tradition' had almost too easy a victory. The other important type of fourteenth-century narratorial voice becomes highly suspect: the voice of 'public poetry,' speaking without fear or favour to the whole of society from the King downwards. The often complex narratorial *personae* produced by such works—the consummate example is Langland's Will—are also avoided, as open to misunderstanding and misprision.[13] This is a double misfortune, as it is hard not to feel that the existence of the (sometimes strident) public voice was a key factor in Chaucer's English invention of a recreative alternative.

One poet, at the end of the fifteenth century and the first quarter of the sixteenth, revives and combines both these fourteenth-century types of narratorial voice: Skelton. In the sophistication of his narratorial voices Skelton is unmatched by English predecessors except Chaucer and Langland; in the sheer range of his *personae* he surpasses even Chaucer.[14] The medieval tradition reaches its vernacular culmination in Skelton's work, in the exuberance of its comedy and in the scope of its moral concerns as in the handling of *persona*. He is the last great English medieval poet. On the poetic level, he was the last English poet, and arguably the first, to have profited fully from Chaucer's example; the Chaucerian tradition, to which Spenser pays elaborate funereal tribute in the *Shepheardes Calender*, lives in Skelton's poetry. On the cultural level, however, the world that gave Skelton his abiding values and what must have seemed to him eternal truths—Catholic, Latin truths—was eroded by the New Learning and swept away by the English Reformation. These historical events have done much, to the present day, to eclipse the literary period in which Skelton wrote and to obscure his reputation. They also helped ensure that what could have been a renaissance of the medieval types of narratorial *persona* did not occur. Gradually, under the influence of new ideologies and new literary forms, the narratorial voices of medieval poetry, reanimated by Skelton, are displaced.

The Sixteenth Century

In England, as John Burrow has written, 'there is no sharp break perceptible between medieval and Renaissance'. Yet there is substantial change: 'it is a sound instinct which has led literary historians to attach special importance to the Italian influence upon Wyatt and Surrey as a sign of the new age'.[15] This cautious judgement would apply to a study of narratorial voice and *persona*. There is some continuity from Chaucer's time to Spenser's. There is also a radical difference shaped by an enormous influx of new forms and conventions from, especially, Italy, and no less significantly by sweeping changes of worldview. These factors further erode the terms in which medieval narrators have been depicted here.

The high style voice of the Chaucerian narrator long endures in conservative poetic contexts like Sackville's 'Induction' to the *Mirror for Magistrates*, and—of more importance—in the *Faerie Queene*. Spenser's decision to write an epic leads him to recall and trace the course of an English poetic tradition. Its source is 'Dan Chaucer, well of English vndefyled' (IV.ii.32–3).[16] The tribute, introduced by a would-be reminiscence of Chaucer after the manner of Lydgate ('Whylome as antique stories tellen vs'), is an indication of a real debt. The attitude taken by Spenser as narrator rests partly on a serious-minded interpretation of the narratorial voice in *Troilus*. He laments his dullness, calling on the epic Muse to correct it ('O helpe thou my weake wit, and sharpen my dull tong', I *Prol.* 2); he defends his work as 'this famous antique history', a 'matter of iust memory', not as a 'painted forgery', 'th'aboundance of an idle braine' (II *Prol.* 1); and he responds to this history with compassion:

> So oft as I this history record
> My hart doth melt with meere compassion.

The compassion is for lovers. The story of Amoret and Florimel causes him such distress

> That I with teares full oft doe pittie it
> And oftentimes doe wish it never had bene writ.   (IV.i.1)

It involves a sympathetic response to love: the Prologue to Book IV defends the poem against blame for its praise of love 'By which fraile youth is oft to folie led / . . . That better were in vertues discipled'. It also arises from an allegiance, natural in the Elizabethan court, to women: by the prospect of Una in distress Spenser is led to

> Feele my heart perst with so great agonie
> When such I see, that all for pittie I could die.   (I.iii.1)

There is a shift in attitude here from the *Troilus* narration, and it reflects differences in the Italianate Elizabethan view of polite love as well as the dominant figure of Elizabeth herself: in Book III Canto ii the narrator links Britomart and the Queen by blaming men for underrating women's ancient martial prowess. But Spenser has a useful precedent in the *Legend of Good Women*, especially in extolling chastity. The modulation of his readers' responses is accomplished as in Chaucer by the poet's addressing an imaginary audience built into the poem. In Book III Canto vi he addresses the 'faire Ladies' of the court, who may have been wondering why Belphoebe lived in the woods so remote from urbane values; in Canto ix he apologises to 'Redouted Knights, and honourable Dames' for writing of 'a wanton Lady'. He is concerned, like Chaucer before him, to defend the behaviour of 'antique age' against the sophisticated expectations of his contemporary audience, and it leads, as in *Troilus*, to passages warning against over-hasty conclusions. This is Spenser's version of 'som enuious':

> Here well I weene, when as these rimes be red
> With misregard, that some rash witted wight,
> Whose looser thoughts will lightly be misled,
> These gentle Ladies will misdeeme too light,
> For thus conuersing with this noble Knight;
> Sith now of dayes such temperance is rare
> And hard to finde . . .   (IV.viii.29)

But he is also, like Chaucer, prepared to twist his narratorial commentary to reveal a view of the power of women and love that is less than wholly flattering:

> Some men, I wote, will deeme in *Artegall*
> Great weaknesse, and report of him much ill,
> For yeelding so himselfe a wretched thrall,
> To th'insolent commaund of womens will;
> That all his former praise doth fowly spill.
> But he the man, that say or doe so dare,
> Be well aduiz'd, that he stand stedfast still:
> For neuer yet was wight so well aware,
> But he at first or last was trapt in womens snare.   (V.vi.1)

The most interesting passage of this type occurs in the first two stanzas of Book VI Canto viii, where women, addressed as 'Ye gentle Ladies', are exhorted not to abuse their 'chiefdome' in love over men. They should not be tyrants but 'soft and tender eeke in mynde', or else they may 'turne the loue of men to hate'. The final three lines are quite Chaucerian, down to the echo of Chaucer's notion of tragedy in *Troilus* and the Monk's Tale (by way of Lydgate):

> Ensample taketh of *Mirabellaes* case,
> Who from the high degree of happy state,
> Fell into wretched woes, which she repented late.

Such passages ensure that the ship of the *Faerie Queene* is steered into harbour (I.xii. cf. VI.xii) by a plausible Chaucerian navigator: plausible, that is, to sixteenth-century readers, for the voyage would have amazed Chaucer.

Much that affects the narratorial voice of the *Faerie Queene* is unavoidably new: the influence of Ariosto and Tasso, the cult of Elizabeth, the sort of 'chiefdome' women are held to exercise in Petrarchan conventions, the expanded world that allows Spenser with splendid solemnity to meet the charge that, because its location is unknown, Faery Land must be fictitious with a reminder that the same once applied to Peru, the Amazon and Virginia. Notwithstanding these, the allusions to Chaucer—together with the elements of dullness and pity, the use of direct address to an imaginary audience of gentlefolk, particularly women—are enough to show some continuity of the Chaucerian high style narratorial voice. It is less volatile than in *Troilus*, and less frequent in its occurrence, but then the range of tone is deliberately contracted. It is conceived, as generally by Chaucer's successors, as the voice of the poet expounding the worth of his poem. Its slightly archaic quality is very useful, enabling Spenser to keep up a pretence that his poem is historical —when what he really feels, having announced that 'Fierce warres and faithful loues shall moralize my songe', is that its allegory makes the epic at least as valid as if it were.

However, Spenser's use in the *Faerie Queene* of the Chaucerian high narratorial voice is slightly archaic and meant to be: fittingly, in a poem which hauls the English poetic tradition up an epic Parnassus. It is not typical of the later sixteenth century, nor of Spenser's other poetry. In the *Shepheardes Calender*, which is equally concerned with the English poetic past, the position is different. The poem's *Envoy* directly imitates the *Troilus* epilogue ('Go litel bok'), and places Chaucer and presumably Langland[17] in the place of Homer, Lucan and Statius:

> Goe lyttle Calender, thou hast a free passeporte,
> Goe but a lowly gate emongste the meaner sort.
> Dare not to match thy pype with Tityrus his style,
> Nor with the Pilgrim that the Ploughman playde a whyle:
> But followe them farre off, and their high steppes adore . . .

But this is self-consciously a work in the 'mean' style, and the use of the medieval heritage on the linguistic level, of archaic diction, is not entirely a compliment: in spite of the deferential tribute in the *Envoy*, the suggestion lingers that old poets will do for rude and vulgar effects (the effects, in fact, to which Sidney objected).[18] The recovery of the medieval past is also invoked in the *ordinatio* of the work itself, a text with gloss,[19] on the level of iconography; and in the exemplary fables told in the May and February eclogues. It does not extend to narratorial *persona*, as a brief reading of the February eclogue will show.

February is the eclogue in which the aged Thenot debates with the young Cuddie. The two ages here represent the double aspect of the year in this month. Cuddie complains of the winter's cold and looks forward (with calendrical correctness) to warmer weather, while Thenot declares that the world must 'wend in his commun course / From good to badd, and from badde to worse'. The theme of the eclogue and its debate is the conflict of youth and age, and so Thenot tells the tale—falsely attributed to Chaucer—of the noble old oak and the upstart young briar in its shadow. The 'bragging brere', conscious of its own beauty and the oak's ugliness, complains to the husbandman in somewhat theological or royalist terms ('O my liege Lord, the God of my life') and, Thenot comments, 'with painted words . . . (As most vsen Ambitious folke)'. So powerful is the briar's eloquence that without giving the oak a chance to reply the husbandman gets his axe and hacks down the oak. Without the shelter of the oak, the briar then dies of frostbite, 'For scorning Eld': at which point, and in mid-line, Thenot is dramatically and, as E. K. says, 'conningly cutte of by Cuddye, as disdayning to here any more'. Cuddie's reaction is scathing: 'Here is a long tale, and little worth' (240).

If this were a medieval poem, we should have no more licence than here to presume that age has an advantage in debate over youth, but the chances would be greater that the exemplary fable would leave us knowing where we were and what we were meant to conclude: Thenot and the oak would be right, and by his scorn Cuddie would have been seen to repeat the briar's error. This context is by no means so simple. Cuddie has the last word, and E.K.'s gloss on the emblems firmly supports him. E. K.'s feeling is that there is no fool like an old fool: 'It is to plaine, to be gainsayd, that old men are muche more enclined to such fond foolines, then younger heades'. There is perhaps no need to regard E.K. as anything but fallible, yet Spenser's handling of the fable certainly does not rule out E.K.'s construction. Two aspects of it have special force. There is a passage in the fable overtly associating the oak with Popish superstition:

> The Axes edge did oft turne againe,
> As halfe vnwilling to cutte the graine:
> Semed, the sencelesse yron dyd feare,
> Or to wrong holy eld did forbeare.
> For it had bene an auncient tree,
> Sacred with many a mysteree,
> And often crost with the priestes crewe,
> And often halowed with holy water dewe.
> But sike fancies weren foolerie,
> And broughten this Oake to this miserye.   (203–12)

E.K. does not neglect to gloss 'the priestes crewe': 'holy water pott, wherewith the popishe priest vsed to sprinckle and hallowe the trees from mischaunce. Such blindnesse was in those times, which the Poete supposeth to haue bene the final decay of this auncient Oake.' In other words, this is a Catholic oak. The narrator of the fable brings this out; but is the narratorial voice here that of the dramatic *persona* Thenot or the poet, hinting at the fable's coming unstuck in the hands of its ostensible teller? Again, the context provides a surfeit of information without unequivocal guidance.

There is, however, a most interesting hint, in E.K.'s gloss on the emblems, of a dramatic or symbolic connection between Thenot and the oak. E.K. notes the 'old opinion . . . that men of feares haue no feare of god at al, or not so much as younger folke. For that being rypened with long experience, and hauing passed many bitter brunts and blastes of vengeaunce, they dread no stormes of Fortune, nor wrathe of Gods, nor daunger of menne.' The imagery of the gloss refers to Thenot's original description of the oak:

> But now the gray mosse marred his rine,
> His bared boughes were beaten with stormes,
> His toppe was bald, and wasted with wormes,
> His honor decayed, his braunches sere.   (111–14)

E.K.'s hints—presented as those of an alternative narrator or author—build up into a plausible, and unmedieval, reading of the eclogue. Cuddie is right to despise age (and a Catholic past), but, just as the briar cannot do without the oak in the winter, so Cuddie cannot do without Thenot at this stage of his—or the year's—growth (it being February). If any such reading is correct, the relation between Thenot and his tale becomes a crucial element in the eclogue, of central thematic and dramatic relevance.

I have tried here not to offer a full interpretation of the eclogue but simply to show that altogether new questions, many of which are political, have entered into the study of narratorial *persona*—this in the very text in which Spenser is trying to sound most 'Chaucerian'. We have to assume, unless an excellent case can be made to the contrary, that Piers and Thenot are closed *personae*. In addition, there are complications of religious controversy, of genre (for pastoral is well-suited to dramatic monologues of quite a closed kind), and of calendrical significance: I am thinking here of the *December* eclogue, in which Colin explains the four seasons of his life, and of the envoy's claim to have made 'a Calender for euery yeare'. There are also numerological complications,[20] and complications in the glosses and in their and the poem's use of Renaissance mythography. All of these have some impact on the handling of narratorial *personae*. There are also the poem's allegorical aspects and possible political signification,[21] evident in E.K.'s disingenuous claim in the *November* eclogue that the personage of Dido—who, critics agree, is a version of Elizabeth—is 'secrete, and to me altogether vnknowne, al be of him selfe I often required the same'. When in this work we try to identify the voice of the poet, we are directed by E.K. to the *persona* of Colin Clout, who is 'the Authour selfe'. To readers coming to Spenser from medieval poetry it is hard to see on what conceivable level this can be so, unless it be that of autobiography so selective and conventional in its fictionalisation—like in sonnet sequences—as to create a formidably closed *persona*.

In this sort of narratorial world, who is saying what matters at least as much as what is being said. The focus of such piecemeal closed *personae* is not always dramatic: they are caught up in all the many other processes—generic, structural and stylistic—of the works in which they occur. Where the narratorial *persona* is a single individual throughout—like Astrophil or, in prose, for prose can no longer be left out of the account, Jack Wilton in Nashe's *The Unfortunate Traveller*—it is at least as much a means of combining disparate content and a welter of styles as it is a dramatic revelation. The difference between such narrators and the medieval types discussed in the body of this book is not that between dramatic and non-dramatic. It is rather that it is rarely a function of the later narrators to mediate between the work and its audience. This task is more often assumed, if at all, by genre and conventions. The emphasis falls not on what the narrator and the audience hold in common but on the *persona*'s claim to be unique or distinctive.

One sonnet from *Astrophil and Stella*, Sonnet 74, can serve to close this argument by illustrating the drastic difference in narratorial *persona* between the late fourteenth and the late sixteenth centuries. It is anything but a representative sonnet. It is the only sonnet in Sidney's collection that might conceivably be mistaken, in its first two quatrains, for a late medieval production:

> I never dranke of *Aganippe* well,
> Nor ever did in shade of *Tempe* sit:
> And Muses scorne with vulgar braines to dwell,
> Poore Layman I, for sacred rites unfit.
>   Some do I heare of Poets' furie tell,
> But (God wot) wot not what they meane by it:
> And this I sweare by blackest brooke of hell,
> I am no pick-purse of another's wit.
>   How falles it then, that with so smooth an ease
> My thoughts I speake, and what I speake doth flow
> In verse, and that my verse best wits doth please?
> Guesse we the cause: 'What is it thus?' Fie no:

> 'Or so?' Muche lesse: 'How then?' Sure thus it is:
> My lips are sweet, inspired with *Stella*'s kisse.[22]

The first quatrain is an example, albeit a learned one, of an inability-*topos*, of the kind frequently found in Chaucer and still more Lydgate; the second quatrain does refer to 'Poets' furie', which is not a note of Middle English poetry, but hastily disclaims knowledge of it in one of the plainest of (rhetorically) plain lines. The sentiment expressed in line 8—'I am no pick-purse of another's wit'—would just qualify as an extreme note of Middle English poetry, like a reworking of Chaucer's 'I wot myself how best I stonde'. The last six lines are thoroughly unlike anything in Middle English. The poet casually congratulates himself for the facility of his expression, and the quality of his 'verse' as judged by 'best wits'. We may find such a self-congratulation, though not so nonchalantly or urbanely uttered, in Skelton. What we will not find is the conceitful reason provided by Sidney/Astrophil in the last line of the sonnet: 'My lips are sweet, inspired with *Stella*'s kisse'. The coterie, or audience, with which Astrophil has allied himself in lines 12 and 13 ('Guesse we'), and whose conjectures are dramatically overheard, is pushed aside in the glorification of the personal experience in line 14.

It is from that private experience that the poet-*persona* claims to derive his authority. Such authority is conventionally remote from medieval English conceptions. Its invocation changes the nature of the authority claimed by the poem, which is certainly not that of fiction. Nor, however, is it truly that of experience. The wit of the last line is that we do not take it straight: we recognise perfectly the polished compliment to Stella's lips. Nor do we take the reference to 'lips' to mean that Sidney is speaking, or wishes us to feel that the poem is presented as a performance. This is a written work, of the sort Orlando pinned to trees.[23] The poem is itself a self-sufficient defence of poetry; English poetry at last aligns itself with French and Italian precursors. The poem's voice is that of poetic virtuosity and confidence in a wholly secular context. Its narrator writes as a poet not mystically, as a *vates*, nor incidentally, as the exponent of a particular poem, but essentially—as one distanced from his audience by the privilege of poetic eloquence. The narratorial voice is completely unlike anything in Middle English poetry. Its appearance, and Spenser's proclivity for closed *personae*, signal altogether different processes of literary production. They also help build the foundations of modern misreadings of Chaucer, which we must now undo.

The act of undoing would be timely. In the preface to this book I asked whether the question of narrators has any relevance for modern criticism. The evidence now leads to a reply: it is particularly relevant. A writer's use of narrators, and readers' and critics' responses to it, show how and what we think of reading as a relationship—between text and context, writer and reader, 'literature' and 'society'; it also raises a question of authority in literary and interpretative practice. These terms are close enough both to the narratorial voices of some modern fiction, which conventional criticism handles less than confidently, and to the main terms of modern critical controversy. One might say that the dramatic principle in Chaucer criticism belongs now to the end of a critical tradition that accepted as a given the English literary tradition that has here been traced back to Chaucer's first readers. Its exponents have shown their respect for that tradition, albeit with a loss of historical perspective, by referring back to Chaucer the critical method fashioned for a much later part of their canon, the traditional novel. Their excessive reliance on the dramatic fallacy and their universal detection of irony are actually indices of the decadence of the critical tradition, which has fed on the literary one: the critical tradition turns in upon itself, self-reflexive and sometimes self-consuming, like one of its closed *personae*. New critical methods for approaching Chaucer's narrators come from the same quarters as fierce onslaughts on both the old critical tradition and the literary tradition, on the canon and on 'literature' itself as a privileged discourse.

From a medievalist's viewpoint, the main danger is simply that we will replace one canon based on nineteenth-century novels with another. This afterword shows only too well what happens to those who win an argument, and a number of alternative canons already stands by. The paradox is that a successful revolt against one 'literature' can only be mounted in the name of another. To reject the shaping influence of a dominant literary tradition is by no means to repudiate literature itself, still less to deny that it is any different from other discourse. Narratorial voice, in fact, works unremittingly to make discourse both literary and different. Yet if we wish to see what literariness really looks like when it is not encompassed and supported by a dominant literary tradition, we cannot afford to remain in the relatively recent past. If we are serious, we should turn back to medieval poetry: in English studies, to the second half of the fourteenth century. English literary tradition begins there with the emergence of a standard dialect—Chaucer's; and there we will find poetry more or less innocent of a national tradition yet asserting itself so strongly as literature that despite itself it overshadows the future. If at the midnight of modern English studies we retrace the long road of the English tradition, we will meet Chaucer at its original crossroads; and then, perhaps, we can all choose another tale.

Notes

A Modern Preface

1. Umberto Eco, *The Name of the Rose*, trans. William Weaver (London, 1983), p. 5.
2. The terms are those of Wayne C. Booth, *A Rhetoric of Irony* (Chicago, 1974).
3. Robert C. Elliott, *The Literary Persona* (Chicago, 1982), pp. xi–xii.
4. See Barbara Hardy, *Tellers and Listeners* (London, 1976); Peter J. Rabinowitz, 'Assertion and Assumption: Fictional Patterns and the External World', *PMLA* 96 (1981), 408–19, and 'Truth in Fiction: A Reexamination of Audiences', *Critical Inquiry* 4 (1977), 121–42; and Richard Poirier, *The Performing Self* (New York, 1971) for a non-literary argument. Another approach to the range between person and *persona* is the analysis of Free Indirect Discourse. See Ann Banfield, 'The formal coherence of represented speech and thought', *Poetics and Theory of Literature* 3 (1978), 289–314; 'Reflective and non-reflective consciousness in the language of fiction', *Poetics Today* 2 (1981), 61–76; see also Seymour Chatman, *Story and Discourse* (Ithaca, N.Y., 1978); Dorrit Cohn, *Transparent Minds* (Princeton, 1978); and Boris Uspensky, *A Poetics of Composition* (Berkeley, 1973).
5. Maurice Blanchot, 'The Narrative Voice', in *The Gaze of Orpheus and other literary essays*, with preface by Geoffrey Hartman, trans. Lydia Davis, ed. with afterword by P. Adams Sitney (New York, 1981), p. 135.
6. *Roland Barthes by Roland Barthes*, trans. Richard Howard (London, 1975), epigraph.
7. Jonathan Culler, *Structuralist Poetics* (London, 1975), p. 196, quoting from Barthes, *S/Z* (Paris, 1970), p. 157.
8. Blanchot, 'The Narrative Voice', p. 136.
9. M. M. Bakhtin, *The Dialogic Imagination: Four Essays*, ed. Michael Holquist (Austin, Texas, 1983). For further discussion of Bakhtin, see Chapter One below.
10. *Rhetorica ad Herennium*, ed. F. Marx (1894; reprinted Hildlesheim, 1966), IV.liii.66. See Phillip C. Rollinson, *Classical Theories of Allegory and Christian Culture* (London, 1981), p. 160 and generally for a convenient glossary of terms.
11. Paul de Man, *Blindness and Insight: Essays in the Rhetoric of Contemporary Criticism* (New York, 1971), pp. 63–4.
12. Jonathan Culler, *The Pursuit of Signs* (London, 1981), p. 153, from the essay 'Apostrophe', pp. 135–54.
13. de Man, *Blindness and Insight*, p. 64.
14. Blanchot, 'The Narrative Voice', p. 137.
15. Tzvetan Todorov, *The Poetics of Prose*, trans. Richard Howard (Oxford, 1977),

pp. 66–79 (quotation from p. 70); see also p. 27, for the 'I' of the narrator as the 'I' of discourse. The source of this and similar observations on earlier literature in modern criticism is probably the seminal article by Leo Spitzer, 'Note on the Poetic and Empirical "I" in Medieval Authors', *Traditio* 4 (1946), 414–22. I too must acknowledge a great debt to this essay in what follows.

Chapter 1: Apocryphal Voices

1. M. M. Bakhtin, *The Dialogic Imagination: Four Essays*, ed. Michael Holquist, trans. Caryl Emerson and Michael Holquist (Austin, Texas, 1981), p. 293. Bakhtin's comment on medieval literature deserves quotation (p. 69):

> The role of the other's word was enormous at that time: there were quotations that were openly and reverently emphasised as such, or that were half-hidden, completely hidden, half-conscious, unconscious, correct, intentionally distorted, unintentionally distorted, deliberately reinterpreted and so forth. The boundary lines between someone else's speech and one's own speech were flexible, ambiguous, often deliberately distorted and confused. Certain types of texts were constructed like mosaics out of the texts of others.

2. These quotations are from Holquist's introduction to *The Dialogic Imagination*, pp. xx–xxi. For further discussion of Bakhtin, see T. Todorov, *The Dialogical Principle* (Minneapolis, 1983).

3. This and all subsequent Chaucer references are to *The Works of Geoffrey Chaucer*, ed. F. N. Robinson, 2nd edition (London, 1957), IV (E), 1266.

4. Wayne C. Booth, *A Rhetoric of Irony* (Chicago, 1974).

5. Franklin's Prologue, V (F) 721–2. I owe this observation to my colleague Stephen Knight.

6. Bernard F. Huppé, 'The Unlikely Narrator: the Narrative Strategy of the *Troilus*', *Signs and Symbols in Chaucer's Poetry*, ed. John P. Hermann and John J. Burke, tr. (Birmingham, Alabama, 1981), pp. 179–94.

7. E. T. Donaldson, *Speaking of Chaucer* (London, 1970), pp. 68–9. This is a collection of essays from the 1950s, which established a dominant critical orthodoxy about narratorial *persona*. This received one significant early challenge from Bertrand H. Bronson, *In Search of Chaucer* (1960; reprinted Toronto, 1963). Bronson was then a lonely dissenter, but his objections were never fully answered.

8. 'Skelton's Use of *Persona*', *Essays in Criticism* 30 (1980), 9–28.

9. Dieter Mehl, 'The Audience of Chaucer's *Troilus and Criseyde*', in *Chaucer and Middle English Studies in Honour of Rossell Hope Robbins*, ed. Beryl Rowland (London, 1974), pp. 173–89.

10. C. David Benson, 'Their Telling Difference: Chaucer the Pilgrim and His Two Contrasting Tales', *Chaucer Review* 18 (1983), 61–76. See also references to *Troilus* criticism in Chapter Four, n. 1 below. The signs of rebellion against Chaucerian *persona*-criticism are related to a re-examination of character and audience in ancient and medieval literature generally. See Warren Ginsberg, *The Cast of Character: The Representation of Personality in Ancient and Medieval Literature* (Toronto, 1983), though Ginsberg maintains the notion of a narrator-figure with an integral thematic role; and, most important, a recent issue of *New Literary History* 16 (1984), no. 1, *Oral and Written Traditions in the Middle Ages*, including Walter J. Ong, 'Orality, Literacy and Medieval Textualization', pp. 1–12; Brian Stock, 'Medieval Literacy, Linguistic Theory and Social Organization', pp. 13–30; Jill Mann, 'Proverbial Wisdom in the *Ysengrimus*', pp. 93–110: see also n. 14 below.

11. That is why, as the argument of this book develops, I shall distinguish more sharply between narratorial *persona* and narratorial voice. The distinction becomes especially relevant in the consideration of Chaucer's later poetry. I am influenced in this by Spitzer (Preface, n. 15 above), and the argument for the 'community-like' nature of the medieval poetic text in Paul Zumthor, 'The Text and the Voice', in *New Literary*

History 16 (1984), 67–92. Another useful study is Hubert Heinen, 'Ulrich von Lichtenstein: *homo illiteratus* or Poet/Performer?', *JEGP* 83 (1984), 159–72. Compare Uwe Porksen, *Der Erzahler im mittelhochdeutschen Epos* (Berlin, 1971), and Robert Lee Bradley, *Narratorial and Audience Roles in Wolfram's 'Parzival'* (Darmstadt, 1981), which are studies of an older type influenced by Wayne C. Booth, *The Rhetoric of Fiction* (Chicago, 1961).

12. *English Lyrics of the XIIIth Century*, ed. Carleton Brown (Oxford, 1932), no. 12.

13. Rosemary Woolf, *English Religious Lyric in the Middle Ages* (Oxford, 1968), p. 86.

14. See J. A. Burrow, *Ricardian Poetry* (London, 1971), p. 13, and *Medieval Writers and their Work: Middle English Literature and its Background 1100–1500* (Oxford, 1982), pp. 25–8; an important article is that by Ruth Crosby, 'Chaucer and the Custom of Oral Delivery', *Speculum* 13 (1938), 413–32.

15. See E. Faral, ed., *Les Arts Poetiques du XIIe et du XIIIe Siècle* (Paris, 1924); J. J. Murphy, *Medieval Rhetoric* (Berkeley, 1977).

16. Woolf, p. 5: 'There is . . . a distinction between naturally anonymous and accidentally anonymous poetry, and most medieval lyrics can be called genuinely anonymous, for they were written by self-effacing poets, who did not intrude peculiarities of style and thought between the subject-matter and the audience.'

17. *Religious Lyrics of the XIVth Century*, ed. Carleton Brown, 2nd ed., rev. G. V. Smithers (Oxford, 1957), no. 9: this is the first stanza of 'A Winter Song' from MS Harley 2253.

18. *ibid.*, nos 51, 52, 53, 54; see Woolf, p. 315, p. 104.

19. Brown, *XIII Century*, no. 7.

20. This is the sort of poem considered by Professor Burrow in his essay 'Poems without Contexts', *Essays in Criticism* 29 (1979), 6–32.

21. Derek Pearsall, 'The Troilus Frontispiece and Chaucer's Audience', *Yearbook of English Studies* 7 (1977), 68–74; Margaret Galway, 'The *Troilus* Frontispiece', *MLR* 44 (1949), 161–77; *Troilus and Criseyde*, a facsimile of Corpus Christi College Cambridge MS 61, with Introductions by M. B. Parkes and Elizabeth Salter (Cambridge, 1978), especially pp. 15–23. See also Edmund Reiss, 'Chaucer and His Audience', *Chaucer Review* 14 (1980), 390–402. For the court itself, see R. F. Green, *Poets and Prince pleasers* (Toronto, 1980) and *English Court Culture in the Later Middle Ages*, ed. V. J. Scattergood and J. W. Sherborne (London, 1983).

22. Anne Middleton, 'The Idea of Public Poetry in the Reign of Richard II', *Speculum* 53 (1978), 94–114; p. 95. Middleton's argument is that in late Middle English 'public poetry' (not Chaucer's), 'impassioned direct address' sets up 'a common voice' to serve 'the common good' and express social and ethical ideas'. The realised presence of the poetic speaker in this literature becomes a stylistic means of expressing that purpose, and it produced a new kind of experientially based didactic poetry, tonally vivid and often structurally unstable. What is not unstable is the relation of speaker to audience: . . . it is poetry defined by a constant relation of speaker to audience within an ideally conceived worldly community, a relation which has become the poetic subject' (*ibid*).

23. Such over-determination is more a product, in later periods, of low or avowedly non-literary culture: the obvious example is *Pilgrim's Progress*. The medieval situation is different: over-determination is a quality of Latin works of exegesis and instruction, and of vernacular works most indebted to them, whereas serious poetry in a vernacular of lower status seeks for received truth an experiential proof. The two types of poetry and poetic voice described here both do this, but serve rather different kinds of truth.

24. Cited in *OED*, apocrypha B, sb. (1597). It is worth adding that sense A is adjectival, and only two uses are cited:

1387 Trevisa, *Higden* V.105: 'The writynge is Apocripha whanne þe auctor þerof is unknowe.'

1460 Capgrave, *Chron.* 7: '"The Penauns of Adam" be clepid Apocriphum, whech es to sey, whanne the mater es in doute, or ellis whan men knowe not who mad the book.'

These are less pejorative than most of the modern definitions, though Capgrave raises the question 'of doubtful authenticity'. They refer us to the idea of anonymity discussed above.

25. Burrow, *Medieval Writers*, p. 38.

26 A. I. Doyle and M. B. Parkes, 'The production of copies of the *Canterbury Tales* and the *Confessio Amantis* in the early fifteenth century', *Medieval Scribes, Manuscripts and Libraries: Essays Presented to N. R. Ker*, ed. M. B. Parkes and Andrew G. Watson (London, 1978), pp. 163–210; John H. Fisher, 'Chancery and the Emergence of Standard Written English in the Fifteenth Century', *Speculum* 52 (1977), 870–99.

Chapter 2: The Pardoner: Morality and Its Context

1. *The Works of Geoffrey Chaucer*, ed. F. N. Robinson, 2nd edn (London, 1957); all subsequent references are to this edition.

2. G. G. Sedgewick, 'The Progress of Chaucer's Pardoner, 1880–1940', *Modern Language Quarterly* 50 (1940), 431–58: reprinted in *Chaucer Criticism*, ed. R. Schoeck and J. Taylor (Notre Dame, 1960), I 190–220; pp. 210–11.

3. Stephan A. Khinoy, 'Inside Chaucer's Pardoner?', *Chaucer Review*, 6 (1971), 255–67; p. 256.

4. Kittredge's essay is reprinted in his *Chaucer and His Poetry* (Cambridge, Mass., 1915); see especially pp. 215–7. For a review of criticism since Sedgewick, see John Halverson, 'Chaucer's Pardoner and the Progress of Criticism', *Chaucer Review* 4 (1970), 184–202, and Paull F. Baum, *Chaucer: A Critical Appreciation* (Durham, 1958), pp. 44–59.

5. David V. Harrington, 'Narrative Speed in The Pardoner's Tale', *Chaucer Review* 3 (1968), 50–9; pp. 51–2.

6. See, respectively, R. M. Lumiansky, 'A Conjecture Concerning Chaucer's Pardoner', *Tulane Studies in English* I (1949), 1–29 (p. 3), and Charles Mitchell, 'The Moral Superiority of Chaucer's Pardoner', *College English* 27 (1965), 437–44 (p. 441).

7. R. F. Miller, 'Chaucer's Pardoner, The Scriptural Eunuch, and the Pardoner's Tale', *Speculum* 30 (1955), 180–99; reprinted in Schoeck and Taylor, I 221–44.

8. Lee W. Patterson, 'Chaucerian Confession: Penitential Literature and the Pardoner', *Medievalia et Humanistica* NS 7 (1976), 153–74; p. 166. For another kind of sophisticated effort to argue the unity of Prologue and Tale, see Martin Stevens and Kathleen Fahey, 'Substance, Accident and Transformations: A Reading of the Pardoner's Tale', *Chaucer Review* 17 (1982), 142–58.

9. Particularly those by Khinoy and Harrington; on the inter-connection of the sins, A. L. Kellogg, 'An Augustinian Interpretation of Chaucer's Pardoner', *Speculum* 26 (1951), 465–81; and on the uncompromised power of the Tale itself, the telling and original (but overstated) article by Felicity Currie, 'Chaucer's Pardoner Again', *Leeds Studies in English* 4 (1970), 11–22.

10. Donald R. Howard, *The Idea of the Canterbury Tales* (Berkeley, 1976), pp. 333–76.

11. For complete references, see Susan Gallick, 'A Look at Chaucer and his Preachers', *Speculum* 50 (1975), 456–76 and Nancy H. Owen, 'The Pardoner's Introduction, Prologue, and Tale: Sermon and *Fabliau*', *JEGP* 66 (1967), 541–9. For an approach by rhetoric rather than structure see Charles E. Shain, 'Pulpit Rhetoric in Three Canterbury Tales', *Modern Language Notes* 70 (1955), 235–45.

12. *Canterbury Tales* B^2 2081; and see the essay by Laura Hibbard Loomis in *Sources and Analogues of Chaucer's Canterbury Tales*, ed. W. F. Bryan and G. Dempster (New Jersey, 1941), pp. 486–559.

13. *Canterbury Tales* D 1647–8; *Sources and Analogues*, pp. 269–74, 415–38.

14. Iris Origo, *The World of San Bernardino* (London, 1963), p. 131.

15. D. W. Robertson, Jr, *A Preface to Chaucer* (Princeton, 1962), pp. 332–5.

16. Shain, 'Pulpit Rhetoric', p. 238.

17. N. R. Haveley, ed., *The Friar's, Summoner's and Pardoner's Tales from The Canterbury Tales* (London, 1975), p. 156; Haveley points out that some scribes still make the mistake that Chaucer feared.

18. J. Swart, 'Chaucer's Pardoner', *Neophilologus* 36 (1952), 45–50; p. 47.

19. Judges, xiii:2–xvi:30; Numbers, vi, 2–4.

20. Beryl Rowland, 'Animal Imagery and the Pardoner's Abnormality', *Neophilologus* 48 (1964), 56–60; the word 'feminoid' is Howard's, *The Idea of the Canterbury Tales*, p. 344.

21. B. H. Bronson, *In Search of Chaucer* (Toronto, 1960), pp. 79–87.

22. See Philippa Tristram, *Figures of Life and Death in Medieval English Literature* (London, 1976), *passim*, and pp. 70–1 on the Pardoner's Tale; also Eric W. Stockton, 'The Deadliest Sin in *The Pardoner's Tale*', *Tennessee Studies in Literature* 6 (1961), 47–59.

23. See B^1 1166, B^2 3087, 3096, E 1212^b, and the closely related *for cokkes bones*, H 9, I 29.

24. C. H. Miller and R. B. Bosse, 'Chaucer's Pardoner and the Mass', *Chaucer Review* 6 (1971), 171–84; p. 181. See also W. B. Toole, 'Chaucer's Christian Irony: the Relationship of Character and Action in the *Pardoner's Tale*', *Chaucer Review* 3 (1968), 37–43.

25. Christopher Dean, 'Salvation, Damnation and the Role of the Old Man in Chaucer's *Pardoner's Tale*', *Chaucer Review* 3 (1968), 44–9; p. 47.

26. Elizabeth R. Hatcher, 'Life Without Death: the Old Man in Chaucer's *Pardoner's Tale*', *Chaucer Review* 9 (1974), 246–52.

27. Miller, 'Chaucer's Pardoner, the Scriptural Eunuch . . .', *Speculum* 30, p. 196.

28. For summaries of the diverse interpretations, see Dean, pp. 44–5, Hatcher, pp. 250–1, and Alfred David, 'Criticism and the Old Man in Chaucer's *Pardoner's Tale*', *College English* 27 (1965), 39–44.

29. J. M. Steadman, 'Old Age and *Contemptus Mundi* in The Pardoner's Tale', *Medium Ævum* 33 (1964), 121–30.

30. Robert E. Todd, 'The Magna Mater Archetype in *The Pardoner's Tale*', *Literature and Psychology* 15 (1965), 32–40.

31. John Speirs, 'The Pardoner's Prologue and Tale', in *The Age of Chaucer*, ed. Boris Ford (Harmondsworth, 1962), p. 116.

32. Paul E. Beichner, C. S. C., 'Chaucer's Pardoner as Entertainer', *Medieval Studies* 25 (1963), 160–72; pp. 169–70.

33. W. C. Curry, 'The Secret of Chaucer's Pardoner', *JEGP* 18 (1919), 593–606, and in his *Chaucer and the Medieval Sciences* (New York, 1926), pp. 54–70; Jill Mann, *Chaucer and Medieval Estates Satire* (Cambridge, 1973), pp. 145–6; Beryl Rowland, 'Animal Imagery and the Pardoner's Abnormality', p. 58; and see Edward C. Schweitzer, Jr, 'Chaucer's Pardoner and the Hare', *English Language Notes* 4 (1967), 247–50, and Monica E. McAlpine, 'The Pardoner's Homosexuality and How It Matters', *PMLA* 95 (1980), 8–22. I do not share McAlpine's sense of the Pardoner's main aim: 'The goal of the final scene, as of all the Pardoner's maneuvers, is a kiss'. (p. 17).

34. *The Idea of the Canterbury Tales*, pp. 343–5.

35. See Muriel Bowden, *A Reader's Guide to Geoffrey Chaucer* (New York, 1964), pp. 280–6.

36. Beichner, 'Chaucer's Pardoner as Entertainer' and James L. Calderwood, 'Parody in The Pardoner's Tale', *English Studies* 45 (1964), 302–9.

37. See Howard's penetrating discussion of the Pardoner as a grotesque, *The Idea of Canterbury Tales*, pp. 339–57, and Wolfgang Keyser, *The Grotesque in Art and Literature*, trans. Ulrich Weisstein (New York, 1966).

38. 'The Moral Superiority of Chaucer's Pardoner', p. 437.

39. See *Sources and Analogues*, pp. 409–11; and D. S. Fansler, *Chaucer and The Roman de la Rose* (New York, 1914), pp. 162–6.

40. 'Inside Chaucer's Pardoner?', pp. 266–7.

41. The evidence is set out by Aage Brusendorff, *The Chaucer Tradition* (London, 1927), pp. 296–425.

42. Ronald Sutherland, *The Romaunt of the Rose and Le Roman de la Rose* (Oxford, 1967), pp. ix–xxxv.

43. See especially lines 6661–70; 6715–57; cf. especially Pardoner's Prologue 439–51.

44. Francis Bacon, 'Of Truth', *Essays* (1625).

45. See Rodney Delasanta, 'Penance and Poetry in the *Canterbury Tales*', *PMLA* 93 (1978), 240–7, and Charles A. Owen, *Pilgrimage and Storytelling in the Canterbury Tales: the Dialectic of 'Ernest' and 'Game'*, (Norman, 1977).

This chapter first appeared as an essay in *Sydney Studies in English*, in an issue devoted to *Studies in Chaucer* (1981).

Chapter 3: Chaucer's Development of Persona

1. R. F. Green, *Poets and Princepleasers* (Toronto, 1980).

2. All quotation from Chaucer in this chapter is, as usual, taken from Robinson's edition. I have also consulted *The Parlement of Foulys*, ed. D. S. Brewer (London, 1960), particularly for the excellent commentary. I do not try to cite relevant modern criticism here: my greatest debt is to E. T. Donaldson's brief essay in *Chaucer's Poetry: An Anthology for Modern Readers* (New York, 1958), pp. 955–6 and to J. A. W. Bennett, *The Parlement of Foules: An Interpretation* (Oxford, 1957). Green's Chapter 4, 'The Court of Cupid' (n. 1 above) presents valuable evidence about 'the game of love' and an interesting argument about poets' reaction against love in the name of earthly fame (see Green, p. 200). On Chaucer's attitude to love generally it is worth attempting a comparison with the Boccaccio of the *Decameron* as presented by Aldo D. Scaglione, *Nature and Love in the Middle Ages* (Berkeley, 1963). Scaglione comments on 'the absence of the sense of sin in the *Decameron*' (p. 83), and argues that 'sex, sensuality, carnal pleasures, traditionally downgraded as *luxuria, incontinentia, concupiscentia*, become acknowledged with militant sympathy for their value as irreplaceable goods' (p. 2). Yet 'in spite of all appearances, the real accent is not on sense and sex. Boccaccio's message is naturalistic, not erotic' (p. 100)—and of course it was followed by a change of heart. An interesting recent essay is Victoria Rothschild, 'The Parliament of Fowls: Chaucer's Mirror up to Nature?' *RES* 35 (1984), 164–84.

3. The cosmology, and its unexpected, paradoxical effect of reducing one's sense of the earth's—and therefore one's own—importance, is that memorably expounded by C. S. Lewis in *The Discarded Image* (Cambridge, 1967) and in a précis form in 'Imagination and Thought in the Middle Ages', *Studies in Medieval and Renaissance Literature*, ed. Walter Hooper (Cambridge, 1966), pp. 41–63.

4. All quotation from *The Romaunt of the Rose* in this chapter comes from *The Romaunt of the Rose and Le Roman de la Rose: A Parallel-Text Edition*, ed. Ronald Sutherland (Oxford, 1968).

5. *The Parlement of Foulys*, ed. Brewer, p. 110.

6. For the gloss, emphasizing concupiscible appetite, see N. R. Havely, *Chaucer's Boccaccio* (Cambridge, 1980), pp. 130–3. See also Piero Boitani, *Chaucer and Boccaccio*, Medium Ævum monographs NS 8 (Oxford, 1977), p. 6.

7. Donaldson, *Anthology*, p. 956.

8. R. S. Thomas, from his *Collected Poems* (London, 1970); compare his *Poetry for Supper* (London, 1967), the title poem: 'What was it Chaucer / Said once about the long toil / That goes like blood to the poem's making?'

9. See Charles O. McDonald, 'An Interpretation of Chaucer's *Parlement of Foules*', *Speculum* 30 (1955), 444–57, for the most extreme version of this tendency; and Brewer's edition, pp. 37–8, for a more conservative, and guarded, reading in the satiric mode.

10. Italo Calvino, *If On A Winter's Night A Traveller* (London, 1981), p. 156.

11. This is the conception of irony rigorously argued by Wayne C. Booth, *A Rhetoric of Irony* (Chicago, 1974). For another possible and legitimate (etymological) way of defining irony, see J. A. Burrow, *Ricardian Poetry* (London, 1971), pp. 39–42, 46, where it is associated with humility-topoi. While I accept that the term can be used in this way, I have preferred to consider the sort of instance Burrow cites as an aspect of narratorial voice. The alternative definition is relatively loose where in its other use the term is relatively precise, and critics have not infrequently sheltered behind it while actually claiming ironies of the second (precise) type. The association of *allegoria* and *ironia* is a commonplace from ancient times to the Renaissance. See, for example, Quintilian, *Institutio Oratoria* 9.2.46.

12. Jill Mann, 'Chaucer and the Medieval Latin Poets', Part B, in *Geoffrey Chaucer*, ed. Derek Brewer (London, 1974), p. 182. This essay is discussed below.

13. This is a common view of Chaucer's dreamers. See, for example, James Winny, *Chaucer's Dream Poems* (London, 1973); Wolfgang Clemen, *Chaucer's Early Poetry* (London, 1963); Constance B. Hieatt, *The Realism of Dream Vision* (The Hague, 1967).

14. This is not to underrate the claims of Derek S. Brewer in 'The Relation of Chaucer to the English and European Traditions', in *Chaucer and Chaucerians*, ed. Brewer (London, 1966), pp. 1–38: but they have little relevance to *persona*.

15. *Ricardian Poetry*, pp. 12–23.

16. Maurice Blanchot, 'The narratorial voice or the impersonal "He"', *The Sirens' Song*, ed. Gabriel Josipovici (London, 1982), pp. 213–21: quotation from p. 214.

17. The invaluable and convenient collection of French material in translation is that of B. A. Windeatt, *Chaucer's Dream Poetry: Sources and Analogues* (Cambridge, 1982). I make use of Windeatt's translations here.

18. Oton de Grandson, *Sa vie et ses poésies*, ed. A. Piaget (Lausanne, 1941); Windeatt, p. 124. See also H. Braddy, *Chaucer and the French Poet Graunson* (Baton Rouge, 1947).

19. James Wimsatt, 'Chaucer and French Poetry', in *Geoffrey Chaucer*, ed. Brewer (see n. 12), pp. 109–36: pp. 121–2. For Machaut's self-consciousness, see K. Brownlee, 'The Poetic Oeuvre of Guillaume de Machaut: the Identity of Discourse and the Discourse of Identity', *Machaut's World: Science and Art in the Fourteenth Century*, ed. M. P. Cosman and B. Chandler (New York, 1978), pp. 219–33, and S. J. M. Williams, 'Machaut's Self-Awareness as Author and Producer', *ibid.*, pp. 189–97.

20. For an account of Chaucer's presentation, see Robert O. Payne, 'Making His Own Myth: The Prologue to Chaucer's *Legend of Good Women*', *Chaucer Review* 9 (1975), 197–211; and for the still pervasive influence of Jean de Meun, see Sherron Knopp, 'Chaucer and Jean de Meun as Self-Conscious Narrators: The Prologue to the *Legend of Good Women* and the *Roman de la Rose* 10307–680', *Comitatus* (1973), 25–39.

21. Windeatt, *Chaucer's Dream Poetry*, pp. ix–x.

22. This is true of Wimsatt in *Chaucer and the French Love Poets: the Literary Background of the Book of the Duchess* (Chapel Hill, 1968) and of J. B. Friedman, 'The Dreamer, the Whelp, and Consolation in the *Book of the Duchess*', *Chaucer Review* 3 (1969), 145–62. The most influential formulation of this view is that of John Lawlor, 'The Pattern of Consolation in *The Book of the Duchess*', *Speculum* 31 (1956), 626–48. See also M. H. Means, *The Consolatio Genre in Medieval English Literature* (Gainesville, 1972).

23. P. M. Kean, *Chaucer and the Making of English Poetry* (London, 1972), 160. This sort of view, along with many other aspects of agreed interpretation, is rejected by B. F. Huppé and D. W. Robertson, Jr, *Fruyt and Chaf* (Princeton, 1963). For other readings of the poem, see also Martin Stevens, 'Narrative Focus in *The Book of the Duchess*: A

Critical Revaluation', *Annuale Mediaevale* 7 (1966), 16–32; G. R. Wilson, Jr, 'The Anatomy of Compassion: Chaucer's *Book of the Duchess*', *Texas Studies in Language and Literature* 14 (1972), 381–8; Bertrand H. Bronson, '*The Book of the Duchess* Re-opened', *PMLA* 67 (1952), 863–81; and, on the *persona*, J. B. Severs, 'Chaucer's Self-Portrait in the *Book of the Duchess*', *Philological Quarterly* 43 (1964), 27–39. A recent view of the Black Knight is that by Ruth Morse, 'Understanding the Man in Black', *Chaucer Review* 15 (1981), 204–15.

24. The relevant description occurs in *Metamorphoses* X 86–147. The remaining tales of Book X are supposedly sung by Orpheus in the wild, and his death does not occur until Book XI 66ff., only two hundred lines before the Ceyx and Alcyone story. I am not aware that this strong analogue has been previously noted. On the medieval Orpheus, see J. B. Friedman, *Orpheus in the Middle Ages* (Cambridge, Mass., 1970).

25. See Havely (n. 6 above), p. 11. On Dante generally, see Howard Schless, 'Chaucer and Dante', in *Critical Approaches to Medieval Literature*, ed. Dorothy Bethurum (New York, 1960), and Piero Boitani, 'The *Monk's Tale*: Dante and Boccaccio', *Medium Ævum* 45 (1976), 50–69. There is a general discussion of 'The Italian Influence on Chaucer' by Paul Ruggiers in *A Companion to Chaucer Studies*, ed. Beryl Rowland, revised edition (London, 1979), pp. 160–84. More detailed recent studies are *Chaucer and the Trecento*, ed. Piero Boitani (Cambridge, 1983) and David Wallace, *Chaucer and the Early Writings of Boccaccio* (Cambridge, 1985).

26. This is the view of Elizabeth Salter, *The Knight's Tale and The Clerk's Tale* (London, 1962), and shared in great measure by A. C. Spearing, *Criticism and Medieval Poetry*, 2nd ed. (London, 1972), pp. 76–106. The process can clearly be seen in J. B. Severs, *The Literary Relationships of Chaucer's Clerk's Tale* (1942; rpt. Hamden, Conn., 1972). See also Anne Middleton, 'The Clerk and His Tale: Some Literary Contexts', *Studies in the Age of Chaucer* 2 (1980), 121–50.

27. Howard Schless, 'Transformations: Chaucer's Use of Italian', *Geoffrey Chaucer* (n. 12 above), pp. 185–223: p. 208.

28. Vittore Branca, *Boccaccio Medievale*, 3rd ed. (Firenze, 1970), pp. 191–249.

29. The translation is Havely's. I am much indebted to his book for its useful apparatus. See also C. S. Lewis, 'What Chaucer Really Did to *Il Filostrato*', *Essays & Studies* 17 (1932), 56–75; Ian C. Walker, 'Chaucer and *Il Filostrato*', *English Studies* 49 (1968), 318–26; Robert P. ap Roberts, 'Love in The *Filostrato*', *Chaucer Review* 7 (1972), 1–26.

30. Schless (n. 27 above), p. 208.

31. For the glosses, see Havely's translation and Boitani, *Chaucer and Boccaccio*, pp. 113–16, 6–7 and 13: quotation from p. 13.

32. *Decameron*, ed. Vittore Branca, vol. IV of Branca's *Tutte le Opere di Giovanni Boccaccio* (Milan, 1976): quotation from pp. 3 and 962. The translation is that of J. M. Rigg, 2 vols. (London, n.d.). See also Donald McGrady, 'Chaucer and the *Decameron* Reconsidered', *Chaucer Review* 12 (1977), 1–26; Francis L. Utley, 'Boccaccio, Chaucer and the International Popular Tale', *Western Folklore* 33 (1974), 181–201.

33. Peter Dronke, 'Chaucer and the Medieval Latin Poets', Part A, in *Geoffrey Chaucer* (n. 12 above), pp. 154–72: see especially pp. 161–4.

34. Mann, 'Chaucer and the Medieval Latin Poets' (n. 12 above): p. 176. The following quotations from p. 179, pp. 178–9, p. 181 respectively.

35. This is extended in Mann's excellent essay, 'The *Speculum Stultorum* and the Nun's Priest's Tale', *Chaucer Review* 9 (1975), 262–82.

36. The notion of the self-reflexivity of texts is associated with the criticism of Stanley E. Fish. See his *Self-Consuming Artifacts: the Experience of Seventeenth Century Literature* (Berkeley, 1972). It works better for some periods than others; it is not a generally useful approach to medieval poetry (any more than it would be to *Paradise Lost*). But compare Hugh Kenner, 'Art in a Closed Field', *Virginia Quarterly Review* 3 (1962), 597–613.

37. John M. Fyler, *Chaucer and Ovid* (New Haven & London, 1979), p. 23. See also Richard L. Hoffmann, *Ovid and the Canterbury Tales* (Philadelphia, 1967).

38. Bruce Harbert, 'Chaucer and the Latin Classics', in *Geoffrey Chaucer* (n. 12 above), pp. 137–53: see esp. p. 145.

39. R. W. Frank, Jr, *Chaucer and the Legend of Good Women* (Cambridge, Mass., 1972).

40. Judson Boyce Allen and Theresa Ann Moritz, *A Distinction of Stories* (Columbus, Ohio, 1981). On this interesting book, see Derek Pearsall's provocative review in *Studies in the Age of Chaucer* 4 (1982), 3–32, esp. p. 137: 'they are saying that Chaucer used a method of reading as a method of writing'. See also A. J. Minnis, 'A Note on Chaucer and the *Ovide Moralisé*', *Medium Ævum* 48 (1979), 254–7, and his recent book *Chaucer and Pagan Antiquity* (Cambridge, 1983).

41. See Chapter 2 above, pp. 29–31. On the *Roman* generally, I am influenced by the account of A. C. Spearing, *Medieval Dream Poetry* (Cambridge, 1976), esp. pp. 8–9, 33, 39–40, and 70. I have also consulted with profit Rosemond Tuve, *Allegorical Imagery* (Princeton, 1962); H. R. Jauss, *Genèse de la poésie allegorique française au moyen age* (Heidelberg, 1962); J. V. Fleming, *The Roman de la Rose: A Study in Allegory and Iconography* (Princeton, 1969); D. Poirion, *Le Roman de la Rose* (Paris, 1974); and L. Friedman, 'Jean de Meun, antifeminism and bourgeois realism', *Modern Philology* 57 (1959), 13–23. The English text is that edited by Sutherland (n. 4 above). For the French I have used the edition of Daniel Poirion, *Le Roman de la Rose* (Paris, 1974). Modern English translations are those of Charles Dahlberg (Princeton, 1971). See also the stylistic analysis of Caroline D. Eckhart, 'The Art of Translation in *The Romaunt of the Rose*', *Studies in the Age of Chaucer* 6 (1984), 41–64.

42. *Medieval Dream Poetry*, p. 33. The gulf between poet and narrator is the main ground of the famous argument about the *Roman* constructed by D. W. Robertson, Jr in *A Preface to Chaucer* (Princeton, 1963). My differences from Robertson's argument lie in his reconstruction of the 'irony' he finds in the *Roman* to serve a rather dogmatic purpose.

43. Northrop Frye, *The Anatomy of Criticism* (Princeton, 1957), p. 40.

44. Jill Mann, 'Chaucerian Themes and Style in the *Franklin's Tale*', *Medieval Literature: Part One: Chaucer and the Alliterative Tradition*, New Pelican Guide to English Literature, ed. Boris Ford (Harmondsworth, 1982), pp. 133–53, esp. p. 142.

45. Piero Boitani, *English Medieval Narrative in the Thirteenth and Fourteenth Centuries* (Cambridge, 1982), trans. Joan Krakover Hall, p. 166.

Chapter 4: Voices of Performance: Chaucer's Use of Narrators in Troilus and The Canterbury Tales

1. The study arises from my essay 'Irony and Sympathy in *Troilus and Criseyde*: A Reconsideration', *Leeds Studies in English* 14 (1983), 94–115. For further references, see this essay. See also Ann Chalmers Watts, 'Chaucerian Selves—especially Two Serious Ones', *Chaucer Review* 4 (1970), 229–41, and Thomas Bestul, 'Chaucer's *Troilus and Criseyde*: The Passionate Epic and its Narrator', *Chaucer Review* 14 (1980), 366–78. An interesting reading of 'The Narrator's Frame for *Troilus*' is that by Charles Dahlberg in *Chaucer Review* 15 (1981), 85–100, building on his earlier study of the *Roman de la Rose*, 'First Person and Personification in the *Roman de la Rose*: Amant and Dangier', *Mediaevalia* 3 (1977), 37–58. Dahlberg's reading claims as 'ironic' what I would claim as unstable tone (including irony as one device). The impact of Donaldson (see Chapter One) is already apparent by 1958, the year of Robert M. Jordan's essay, 'The Narrator in Chaucer's *Troilus*', *ELH* 25, 237–57. There is a common emphasis thereafter on the difference between Chaucer the poet's and the narrator's 'point-of-view'. This persists as late as 1981: see Richard D. Osberg, '"Between the Motion and the Act": Intentions and Ends in Chaucer's *Troilus*', *ELH* 48 (1981), 257–70, a perceptive essay that is committed to the view of the narrator as a consistent character

with a single purpose. By 1983 Richard Waswo, 'The Narrator of *Troilus and Criseyde*', *ELH* 50 (1983), 1–25, still insists on the centrality of the narrator: 'My excuse for worrying once again what one critic has called the "Chaucerian persona puzzle" is that with respect to *Troilus* this persona has not been generally regarded as puzzling enough . . . Precisely *because* of his contradictory self-portraiture, Chaucer's ironies are what make his texts so centrally problematic' (p. 1). By p. 12, however, Waswo defends his calling the narrator 'Chaucer'; and here the critical wheel is close to coming full circle.

2. R. F. Green, *Poets and Princepleasers* (Toronto, 1980), p. 160.

3. Italo Calvino, speaking of the example of R. L. Stevenson, in his introduction to *Our Ancestors* (London, 1980), p. viii.

4. Piero Boitani, *English Medieval Narrative in the Thirteenth and Fourteenth Centuries* (Cambridge, 1982), p. 134.

5. I make no attempt here to list books and essays of Chaucer criticism; a bibliography of ironic readings would be a separate book in its own right. For further references, see Vance Ramsay, 'Modes of Irony in the *Canterbury Tales*', *A Companion to Chaucer Studies*, revised edition, ed. Beryl Rowland (Cambridge, 1979), pp. 352–79, and Edmund Reiss, 'Chaucer and Medieval Irony', *Studies in the Age of Chaucer* 1 (1979), 67–82. This sort of irony is all-embracing, far removed from the modest claims of Germaine Dempster, *Dramatic Irony in Chaucer* (1932; rpt. New York, 1959). Yet what one critic has called 'The Golden Ambiguity of the *Canterbury Tales*' (*Erasmus Review*, 1, i, (1971), 1–9) has had a long innings. See Earle Birney, 'Is Chaucer's Irony a Modern Discovery?', *JEGP* 41 (1942), 303–19. The problem arises when an appreciation of possible ironies is linked with a dramatic interest in narratorial *persona*. This combination has dominated Chaucer criticism since the 1950s, characterising major criticism as different as Donaldson's and Robertson's. The original formulation, however, was that of R. M. Lumiansky, *Of Sundry Folk: The Dramatic Principle in the Canterbury Tales* (Austin, Texas, 1955); see later works such as Paul Ruggiers, *The Art of the Canterbury Tales* (Madison, 1965), Trevor Whittock, *A Reading of the Canterbury Tales* (Cambridge, 1968), and Robert Burlin, *Chaucerian Fiction* (Princeton, 1977). A good recent critique is H. Marshall Leicester, Jr, 'The Art of Impersonation: A General Prologue to the *Canterbury Tales*', *PMLA* 95 (1980), 213–24. What was, in its day, an exciting advance in Chaucer criticism has to my mind become its own parody, with (real) dissertation titles like 'Tales from Chaucer as Projections of their Tellers' Needs'. It has led, perhaps, to an over-rigid distinction between Chaucer and the immediate narrator of a Canterbury Tale, as in the admirable subtleties of the following: Charles Muscatine, 'The *Canterbury Tales*: Style of the Work and Style of the Man', *Chaucer and Chaucerians*, ed. D. S. Brewer (London, 1966), pp. 88–113; Edward C. Wagenknecht, *The Personality of Chaucer* (Norman, 1968); Donald R. Howard, 'Chaucer the Man', *PMLA* 80 (1965), 337–43; Morton Donner, 'Chaucer and his Narrators: the Poet's Place in his Poems', *Western Humanities Review* 27 (1973), 189–95. Three closely related strands in criticism have seemed in various degrees incompatible with this emphasis on ironic *persona*: ludic; rhetorical; and audience-related. See Stephen Manning, 'Rhetoric, Game, Morality and Geoffrey Chaucer', *Studies in the Age of Chaucer* 1 (1979), 105–118, Charles A. Owen, Jr, *Pilgrimage and Storytelling in the Canterbury Tales* (Norman, 1977), and Gabriel Josipovici, 'Fiction and Game in the *Canterbury Tales*', *Critical Quarterly* 7 (1965), 185–97; Paul Strohm, 'Chaucer's Audience', *Literature and History* 5 (1977), 26–41; Dieter Mehl, 'The Audience of Chaucer's *Troilus and Criseyde* (see Chapter One, n. 9) and Edmund Reiss, 'Chaucer and his Audience', *Chaucer Review* 14 (1980), 390–402, building on older studies like those of Crosby (Chapter One, n. 14 above), B. H. Bronson, 'Chaucer's Art in Relation to his Audience', *Five Studies in Literature* (Berkeley, 1940) and Mary Griffin, *Studies in Chaucer and his Audience* (Quebec, 1956); Robert O. Payne, *The Key of Remembrance* (New Haven, 1963) and 'Chaucer's Realization of Himself as Rhetor', *Medieval Eloquence*, ed. J. J. Murphy (Berkeley, 1978), pp. 270–87; and John Nist, 'Chaucer's Apostrophic Mode in *The Canterbury Tales*', *Tennessee Studies in Literature* 15 (1970),

85–98. Renewed interest in criticism of these kinds, and a more detailed approach to historical criticism, promise departures from the orthodox interest in ironic *persona*. Strong impatience has already been shown by J. B. Allen and T. A. Moritz, *A Distinction of Stories* (Columbus, Ohio, 1981), pp. 11–17, who attack with great effect the view that the Tales are a series of dramatic utterances by individuated *personae*. See also Leicester's article (above), and Diekstra's article, n. 14 below.

6. The proposal is that Chaucer exposes (and criticises) the common taste of his contemporaries for sensational, bloody and emotionally coloured hagiography. This idea is tenable, though I prefer to think of the Tale as Chaucer's experiment in this genre—without any great imaginative preconceptions. When the notion that Chaucer exposes the weaknesses of the genre, and the sensibility to which it appeals, is joined to a critical portrait of the narrator who has no such reservations, serious critical difficulties arise. To my mind, they are insoluble and unnecessary. See R. A. Pratt, 'Chaucer and *Les Cronicles* of Nicholas Trevet', in *Studies in Language, Literature, and Culture of the Middle Ages and Later*, ed. E. B. Atwood and A. A. Hill (Austin, 1969), and Douglas Wurtele, '"Proprietas" in Chaucer's *Man of Law's Tale*', *Neuphilologus* 60 (1976), 577–93. See also Edward A. Block, 'Originality, Controlling Purpose, and Craftsmanship in Chaucer's *Man of Law's Tale*', *PMLA* 68 (1953), 572–616; Marie P. Hamilton, 'The Dramatic Suitability of *The Man of Law's Tale*', *Studies in Language and Literature in Honour of Margaret Schlauch*, ed. M. Brahmer and others (Warsaw, 1966), pp. 153–63; R. E. Lewis, 'Chaucer's Artistic Use of Pope Innocent III's *De Miseria Humane Conditionis* in the Man of Law's Prologue and Tale', *PMLA* 81 (1966), 485–92, and his 'Glosses to the *Man of Law's Tale* from Pope Innocent III's *De Miseria Humane Conditionis*', *Studies in Philology* 64 (1967), 1–16; Alfred David, 'The Man of Law vs Chaucer: A Case in Poetics', *PMLA* 82 (1967), 217–25. Compare the case of the Prioress: Carolyn P. Collette, 'Sense and Sensibility in the *Prioress's Tale*', *Chaucer Review* 15 (1981), 138–50. I wrote this brief discussion of the Man of Law's Tale without the benefit of V. A. Kolve's fine study in Chapter 7 of *Chaucer and the Imagery of Narrative* (London, 1984), a magisterial reinstatement of the Tale's seriousness and far removed from any appeal to 'dramatic' reading.

7. The association of two different types of critical interpretation, as with the Man of Law's Tale, causes extraordinary complexities of reading in the Knight's Tale. See, for a clear example, T. K. Meier, 'Chaucer's Knight as "Persona": Narration as Control', *English Miscellany* 20 (1969), 11–21. Terry Jones, *Chaucer's Knight* (London, 1980), has many a more cautious precursor. Boitani in *Chaucer and Boccaccio* (Oxford, 1977), pp. 165–76, unnecessarily takes the oral dimension in Chaucer's version (pointed out in Spearing's edition, Cambridge 1966, pp. 43–7) as the signature of a *persona* in the narration. This is a crucial step, and I can see no reason for taking it.

8. John H. Fisher, ed., *The Complete Poetry and Prose of Geoffrey Chaucer* (New York, 1977), p. 234.

9. See Stephen Knight, 'Rhetoric and Poetry in the *Franklin's Tale*', *Chaucer Review* 4 (1970), 14–30; Joseph Milosh, 'Chaucer's Too-Well Told *Franklin's Tale*: A Problem of Characterization', *Wisconsin Studies in Literature* 5 (1970), 1–11; D. W. Robertson, Jr, 'Chaucer's Franklin and his Tale', *Costerus* NS 1 (1974), 1–26; J. B. Severs, 'Appropriateness of Character to Plot in the *Franklin's Tale*', in *Studies . . . in Honour of Margaret Schlauch* (n. 6 above), pp. 385–96; Robert Burlin, 'The Art of Chaucer's Franklin', *Neophilologus* 51 (1967), 55–73; Gertrude M. White, 'The Franklin's Tale: Chaucer or the Critics', *PMLA* 89 (1974), 454–62.

10. Donald R. Howard, *Writers and Pilgrims: Medieval Pilgrimage Narratives and their Posterity* (Berkeley, 1980), p. 100. On the General Prologue, I am indebted to Donaldson's famous and provocative essay 'Chaucer the Pilgrim', *PMLA* 69 (1954), 928–36, reprinted in *Speaking of Chaucer*, and to Jill Mann, *Chaucer and Medieval Estates Satire* (Cambridge, 1973).

11. In *English Medieval Narrative* (n. 4 above).

12. In *Chaucer's Poetry*, pp. 940–4; see also 'Patristic Exegesis: the Opposition', in

Speaking of Chaucer, pp. 146–50. A more recent study is Susan Gallick, 'Styles of Usage in the *Nun's Priest's Tale*', *Chaucer Review* 11 (1977), 232–47.

13. This is very well put by H. L. Rogers, 'The Merchant's Tale and the Franklin's Tale', *Studies in Chaucer*, ed. G. A. Wilkes and A. P. Riemer (Sydney, 1981), pp. 1–29. For the sort of criticism to which Rogers and I would object, see Jay Schleusener, 'The Conduct of the *Merchant's Tale*', *Chaucer Review* 14 (1980), 237–50.

14. For an excellent recent article on this tale, see F. K. M. Diekstra, 'Chaucer's Digressive Mode and the Moral of the *Manciple's Tale*', *Neuphilologus* 67 (1983), 131–48. See p. 147: 'It has often struck me that the elaborate characterisations that critics have produced of the narrators are remakable mainly as indirect attempts to describe the variety of Chaucer's stylistic inventory. Moreover, they describe stylistic means which Chaucer applies in other contexts, both for other narrators and for his narrative voice.' My only reservation has to do with the final phrase; but this means here, I think, the narrative voice specifically ascribed to 'Chaucer' in a particular work.

Chapter 5: The Literary History of the Squire's Tale

1. D. W. Robertson, *A Preface to Chaucer* (Princeton, 1963), nowhere mentions the Tale; E. T. Donaldson omits it from *Chaucer's Poetry: an Anthology for the Modern Reader* (New York, 1958), describing it as 'the fragment of a very respectable aristocratic romance, which few readers will wish longer'. (p. 923). The echo of Dr Johnson on *Paradise Lost* is suggestive in the light of what I shall argue below about English epic.

2. Stanley J. Kahrl, 'Chaucer's Squire's Tale and the Decline of Chivalry', *Chaucer Review* 7 (1973), 194–209; p. 209.

3. Robert S. Haller, 'Chaucer's Squire's Tale and the Uses of Rhetoric', *Modern Philology* 62 (1964–5), 285–95; p. 285.

4. Derek A. Pearsall, 'The Squire as Story-Teller', *University of Toronto Quarterly* 34 (1964), 82–92, reprinted in *Sonderdruck aus Geoffrey Chaucer* (Darmstadt, 1983), pp. 287–99, p. 298.

5. John P. McCall, 'The Squire in Wonderland', *Chaucer Review* 1 (1966), 103–9; p. 108.

6. Pearsall, p. 288, p. 294.

7. Joyce E. Peterson, 'The Finished Fragment: a Reassessment of The Squire's Tale', *Chaucer Review* 5 (1970), 62–74; p. 67.

8. For severe exegesis, see John V. Fleming, 'Chaucer's Squire, the *Roman de la Rose*, and the Romaunt', *Notes and Queries* 14, (1967), 48–9, and especially Chauncey Wood, 'The Significance of Jousting and Dancing as Attributes of Chaucer's Squire', *English Studies* 52 (1971), 116–18.

9. McCall, p. 109.

10. J. B. Severs, 'The Tales of Romance', in *A Companion to Chaucer Studies*, ed. Beryl Rowland (London, 1968), p. 23, censuring Pearsall and Haller.

11. J. A. Burrow, *Medieval Writers and their Work* (Oxford, 1982) p. 129. A fuller recent attempt to see the Squire's Tale in a more favourable (and less ironic) light is that of Jennifer R. Goodman, 'Chaucer's Squire's Tale and the Rise of Chivalry', *Studies in the Age of Chaucer* 5 (1983), 127–36. Goodman's response to the Tale—in its suggestion that it is 'a composite romance' (p. 135)—is similar to my own. Goodman devotes space to a valuable discussion of similarities between Chaucer's tale and other English romance, such as *Valentine and Orson* and *Generides*; I have followed the French leads provided by an older tradition of source study. Goodman expresses the view that the Squire's Tale is 'left unfinished by design' (p. 135); my own suggestions are perhaps more radical. The degree of concurrence none the less augurs a new chapter in the literary history of the Tale.

12. J. M. Manly and Edith Rickert, eds., *The Text of the Canterbury Tales*, 8 volumes (Chicago, 1940), description of the manuscripts in Volume I. It is likely that '*in terminis*'

relates to clause-endings—and so, by extension, rhetorical ornaments—rather than to structural endings of the parts of the Tale. See Paul Strohm, 'Jean of Angoulême: a Fifteenth-Century Reader of Chaucer,' *Neuphilologische Mitteilungen* 72 (1971), 69–76.

13. Spenser's *Faerie Queene*, ed. J. C. Smith (Oxford, 1909, reprinted 1978), Book IV, Canto ii, stanzas 32–4. The ambiguity of the 'labours lost' is that they may simply have remained unwritten, treasure the world never received; but Spenser does allude to 'workes of heavenly wits' as being 'quite devoured, and brought to nought by little bits'. Generally, see Morton W. Bloomfield, 'Chaucer's Squire's Tale and the Renaissance', *Poetica* 12 (1981), 28–35.

14. *John Lane's Continuation of Chaucer's 'Squire's Tale'*, ed. F. J. Furnivall, Chaucer Society, Second Series 23 (London, 1887), Part I: Lane's Advertisement.

15. Quoted by Skeat in *The Complete Works of Geoffrey Chaucer* (Oxford 1894–97), III 464. For the quotations from Warton below, see respectively Thomas Warton, ed., *Poems upon several Occasions by John Milton* (London, 1785), p. 82, and *The History of English Poetry* (London, 1804), p. 273. See also Caroline Spurgeon, *Five Hundred Years of Chaucer Criticism and Allusion 1357–1900*, I (Cambridge, 1925), li–lii, and p. 479.

16. *Fables: Consisting of Selected Parts from Dante, Berni, Chaucer and Ariosto, Imitated in English Heroic Verse* (London, 1804): II: *Cambuscan, an heroic poem in six books, founded upon and comprizing a free imitation of Chaucer's fragment on that subject* (London, 1805), p.vii; quoted in Karl Heinz Göller, 'Chaucer's "Squire's Tale": "The Knotte of the Tale",' in *Chaucer und seine Zeit: Symposion für Walter F. Schirmer*, ed. Arno Esch, *Buchreihe der Anglia Zeitschrift für Englische Philologie* 14 (Tubingen, 1968), pp. 163–88; p. 165. I have not discussed Wharton's or other eighteenth and nineteenth century 'imitations' of the *Squire's Tale* here: they tell us little compared to earlier continuations.

17. Leigh Hunt, *Imagination and Fancy* (1844), p. 16, quoted by Burrow, p. 129, and elsewhere.

18. Skeat's monumental Chaucer appeared in 1894–7. Its reception was not uncritical: Manly's essay on 'Marco Polo and the Squire's Tale', PMLA 11 (1896), 349–62, was a response to Manly's disappointment at Skeat's failure to revise 'the opinion of Chaucer's indebtedness to Marco Polo expressed by him several years ago' (p. 349).

19. Kahrl, p. 195, quoting H. S. V. Jones, 'The Squire's Tale', in *Sources and Analogues of Chaucer's Canterbury Tales*, ed. W. F. Bryan and Germaine Dempster (Chicago, 1941), pp. 357–76; p. 357.

20. Jones, *Sources and Analogues*, p. 357.

21. Manly's essay is that noted in n.18.

22. H. S. V. Jones, 'Some Observations upon the Squire's Tale', *PMLA* 20 (1905), 346–59; 'The *Cléomadès*, the *Méliacin*, and the Arabian Tale of the "Enchanted Horse"', *JEGP* 6 (1906–7), 221–43; and 'The *Cléomadès* and Related Folk-Tales,' *PMLA* 23 (1908), 557–98; J. L. Lowes, 'The Dry Sea and the Carrenare', *Modern Philology* 3 (1905), 1–46, and 'The Squire's Tale and the Land of Prester John', *Washington University Studies* 1 (1913), 3–18.

23. Lowes, 'The Squire's Tale,' pp. 15–16.

24. Haldeen Braddy, 'The Oriental Origin of Chaucer's Canacee-Falcon Episode', *MLR* 31 (1936), 11–19; 'The Genre of Chaucer's Squire's Tale', *JEGP* 41 (1942), 279–90.

25. Albert C. Friend, 'The Tale of the Captive Bird and the Traveler: Nequam, Berechiah, and Chaucer's Squire's Tale', *Medievalia et Humanistica* I (1970), 57–65.

26. Lowes, 'The Dry Sea', p. 46.

27. W. A. Clouston, *On the Magical Elements in Chaucer's Squire's Tale, with Analogues*, in Part II of *John Lane's Continuation*, Chaucer Society Second Series 26 (London, 1889).

28. Jones, 'Some observations', pp. 348–9.

29. On p. 359 of 'Some Observations', Jones appears to favour direct translation by Chaucer of a version of *Cléomadès* more like the Squire's Tale than any extant version, but rapidly abandoned this view in face of objections from H. B. Hinckley, 'Chaucer and the *Cléomadès*', *MLN* 24 (1909), 95. For the horse, see also the English parallels adduced by Goodman (n. 11 above), though these are probably direct imitations of Chaucer.

30. *Sources and Analogues*, p. 364.

31. Gardiner Stillwell, 'Chaucer in Tartary', *Review of English Studies* 24 (1948), 177–88; p. 187. All quotation from the Squire's Tale is from *The Works of Geoffrey Chaucer*, ed. F. N. Robinson, second edition (London, 1957).

32. Pearsall, p. 294; ct. Kahrl, p. 203: 'this snobbery is laced with a good dose of anti-intellectualism'.

33. Peterson, 'The Finished Fragment', p. 63.

34. Pearsall's essay opens with a defence of the 'dramatic principle' against criticism by R. M. Jordan, 'The Non-Dramatic Disunity of the *Merchant's Tale*', *PMLA* 78 (1963), 293–9; see Pearsall, p. 288, n.4, and n.3 for studies by which Pearsall's method is prompted, with their heavy stress on 'structural irony'.

35. The seminal works were Donaldson's essay 'Chaucer the Pilgrim', *PMLA* 69 (1954), 928–36, and his later essays on the 'narrator-persona' in *Troilus*, all reprinted in his *Speaking of Chaucer* (London, 1970); Robertson's *Preface*; and R. M. Lumiansky's *Of Sundry Folk: the Dramatic Principle in the Canterbury Tales* (Austin, 1955), all of which developed the concept of *persona* in new and interesting ways. Robertson brilliantly combined dramatic and exegetical criticism.

36. Marie Neville, 'The function of the Squire's Tale in the Canterbury scheme', *JEGP* 50 (1951), 167–79. Neville's essay serves as a reminder that stress on a 'dramatic principle' grew partly out of Kittredge's sense that certain tales—like Friar and Summoner—were interruptions of the 'Marriage Group': that is, a *dramatic* interruption into a *thematic* continuum; but Kittredge, though dramatic, was unironic.

37. Pearsall, p. 296.

38. Haller, 'The Uses of Rhetoric' (n.3 above), p. 293.

39. *ibid.*, p. 286: the purpose is to examine the Squire's 'rhetorical ability . . . to see to what extent it reflects credit on him'.

40. So Stillwell, p. 181 ('he balks at the first hoop'), Haller, p. 291, see Göller's essay (n.16 above).

41. This note from the Northumberland manuscript (Manly and Rickert, IV 484), is disingenuous, since the copyist stopped before the end of the fragment; but there are several such bemused notes cited in Manly and Rickert. Ellesmere leaves the rest of the page blank, as if hoping for further copy.

42. Manly and Rickert, *loc. cit.* Their joke seems half in earnest: for those who do not subscribe to a 'dramatic interruption', the mid-sentence break has been strong subliminal support for a late date.

43. Pearsall, p. 297, citing Robinson, p. 721, note to line 667. See also Peterson's extraordinary argument from 'the action of the tale itself. If that action is complete within the tale as it stands, it is unlikely that the prospectus given by the Squire at the end of part two is really a preview of things to come' (p. 67).

44. This suggestion is made by John H. Fisher, ed., *The Complete Poetry and Prose of Geoffrey Chaucer* (New York, 1977), p. 186; but Fisher does not take it seriously enough to resist noting later that the 'summary listing of an unmanageable number of possible plots, like the unmanageable number of talismans at the beginning . . . , is evidence of lack of control of his material on the part either of the Squire or the poet himself' (p. 197, note to 1.656 ff.).

45. *Faerie Queene*, Book IV, Canto iii: they are restored and reconciled by the magic drink Nepenthe brought by Cambina.

46. Peterson, p. 74; but the feeling is widespread, and sustained—see Pearsall, p. 299 citing Raymond Preston, *Chaucer* (London, 1952), p. 273; McCall, p. 108—by an

unfortunate and jocular tendency to compare the Squire's Tale with 'the first performance of a fairly good student in Freshman Composition.'

47. Manly and Rickert, IV 484.

48. It is strange that Spenser here chose a name, Cambina, similar to, and confusible
with, Camballo: almost as if he senses, and tries to resolve, scribal corruption in the
double occurrence of the latter in the *Squire's Tale*'s closing prospectus.

49. See *John Lane's Continuation*, Part I, p. 199 (XI, 145ff.):

But ô, how mote a weaklinge poet*es* penn
describe, delineate, limn, in sound poem
(in th' presence of the Classis Laureat*e*),
the glories of this king*e* and Queene in state?
the bounteous riches of theire courtlie traine;
the maiestie w*hich* did all those sustaine;
the knowne magnificence of their expense;
the grand allowances w*hich* issue thence;
the yoncker iollities of each brave knight;
the shininge bewties of each *l*addie bright;
the goodlie comportance, the sweete demeanoure;
their constant loves, vnder the roial streamer;
the virtuous prowesse of all them w*hich* bide,
and tooke their lodginges vp on th' kinges owne side;
The vanities of thother knightes and ladies;
the fickell pompe of dilld vp-whifflinge babies . . .

50. *ibid.*, p. xii (Furnivall's introduction).

51. Lowes, 'The Squire's Tale' (n.22 above), p. 17.

52. All citation and quotation of Ariosto is from *Orlando Furioso*, ed. Lanfranco
Caretti (La Letteratura Italiana: Storia e Testi volume 19), (Milan, n.d.), and translation is that of Guido Waldman, *Ariosto: Orlando Furioso* (London, 1974).

53. C. P. Brand, *Ludovico Ariosto: A preface to the 'Orlando Furioso'* (Edinburgh,
1974), p. 47: Brand speaks here of 'The Literary Tradition' of the *chansons de gestes* in
France and Italy.

54. Brand's treatment of Boiardo, pp. 54–5, is suggestive: 'Boiardo is led into all
sorts of irrelevancies, repetitions, omissions, ambiguities and the like by his lack of
planning: and the result is often tedious or disquieting: characters get lost, stories are
not finished, incidents are repeated.' See *Orlando Innamorato*, ed. A. Scaglione, 2 vols.
(Turin, 1966).

55. This is Robinson's note, 'Canon and Chronology of Chaucer's Writings' (p.
xxix), for the period 1372–80.

56. *John Lane's Continuation*, Part I, p. xii.

57. *The Canterbury Tales by Geoffrey Chaucer, edited from the Hengwrt Manuscript*
(London, 1980); 'The Relationship between the Hengwrt and Ellesmere Manuscripts
of the *Canterbury Tales*', *Essays and Studies* NS 32 (1979), 1–18.

58. The best succinct discussion is in Fisher's edition, p. 101, note on 11, 1179. All
the manuscripts advertise the next speaker as either 'Squyer', 'Sumnour' or 'Shipman'.
Fisher boldly substitutes 'Wif of Bath', in defiance of the manuscripts but in keeping
with modern editorial arrangement. In Hengwrt, the link is missing, though a space is
left; the next tale, as in Blake's edition, is The Squire's Tale. This order, plus link,
prevails 'in far the larger number of the MSS' (Manly & Rickert, IV 479), though Manly
and Rickert argue strongly that 'there is no reason to think that this was ever Chaucer's
intention.' The question is not only how recoverable 'Chaucer's intention' may be, but
also how fixed it ever was.

59. A. I. Doyle and M. B. Parkes, 'The Production of Copies of the *Canterbury
Tales* and the *Confessio Amantis* in the Early Fifteenth Century', in *Medieval
Scribes, Manuscripts and Libraries: Essays Presented to N. R. Ker* (London, 1978),
pp. 163–212.

60. Manly and Rickert, II 495–6; for editorial arrangements and early shifts of place, see II 475–6.

61. Doyle and Parkes, p. 198: 'How well he knew Chaucer or Gower personally, despite his claims, remains doubtful, although he could have had contact with their literary executors.' The view echoes the caution of Jerome Mitchell, 'Hoccleve's Tribute to Chaucer', *Chaucer und seine Zeit* (n. 16 above), pp. 275–83, and *Thomas Hoccleve: A Study in Early Fifteenth Century English Poetic* (Urbana, 1968), pp. 1–19 ('The Autobiographical Element'). The caution is justifiable, given the lack of confirmation for Hoccleve's claims from historical records, but there is no cause for undue scepticism, since both Chaucer and Hoccleve occupied Civil Service positions in London in the 1390s, albeit of widely different ranks, and, as Doyle and Parkes acknowledge, 'Hoccleve was a man of letters whose own writings make manifest an interest in this contemporary vernacular literature.' Furnivall pointed out that 'Hoccleve was daily at work in Westminster Palace,' and that Chaucer's last house was in the Abbey grounds: 'Surely the pupil must have often visited his Master before the latter's death.' *Hoccleve's Works*, volume I: *The Minor Poems in the Phillipps MS 8151 (Cheltenham) and the Durham MS III.9*, ed. F. J. Furnivall, EETS ES 61 (1892), p. xxxi. Mitchell's counter, *Hoccleve*, p. 118 ('If Hoccleve had really known Chaucer and studied under him, surely he would have had more to tell us'), seems unduly cautious.

62. Quoted by Furnivall from The Prologue to the *Regement of Princes* (2077–9), text from BL Harley MS 4866, in *Minor Poems*, ETTS ES 61, p. xxxii. Quotation elsewhere is from the revision of *Minor Poems*, ed. Furnivall and Gollancz, EETS ES 61 (1892) and 73 (1925, for 1897), by Jerome Mitchell and A. I. Doyle (1970); for the *Regement*, from Furnivall's edition, EETS ES 72 (1897).

63. The phrase, 'Chaucer's work-shop', is used casually by Jones, 'Some Observations', p. 359.

64. E. P. Hammond, *English Verse Between Chaucer and Surrey* (Durham, N.C., 1927), pp. 55–63, see also H. S. Bennett, *Chaucer and the Fifteenth Century* (Oxford, 1947), pp. 285–6.

65. The lexical information on Chaucer is drawn from J. S. P. Tatlock and A. G. Kennedy, *Concordance to the Complete Works of Chaucer and to the Romaunt of the Rose* (1927; Gloucester, Mass. 1963).

Afterword: Some Post-Chaucerian Narrators

1. John Lydgate, *The Fall of Princes*, ed., H. Bergen, 4 vols., EETS ES 121–4 (1924–7). See also Derek Pearsall, *John Lydgate* (London 1974).

2. *The Pastime of Pleasure* and the *Example of Virtue*. See also Stephen Hawes, *The Minor Poems*, ed. F. Gluck and A. B. Morgan, EETS OS 271 (1974): 'The Conuercyon of swerers' (especially lines 1–63) and 'A Ioyful Medytacyon' are productions in the voice of Lydgate as historian.

3. *Selections from Hoccleve*, ed. M. C. Seymour (Oxford 1981), p. xxv; see also p. xi and J. A. Burrow, *Medieval Writers and their Work*, pp. 41–2. Hoccleve quotation here is from Seymour's edition. I have also consulted *The Minor Poems*, ed. F. J. Furnivall, EETS ES 61 (1892), and I. Gollancz, EETS ES 73 (1925 for 1897), 2 vols., rpt. as 1, rev. J. Mitchell and A. I. Doyle (1970); and *The Regement of Princes*, ed. F. J. Furnivall, EETS ES 72 (1897).

4. The Prologue is included in E. P. Hammond's anthology, *English Verse between Chaucer and Surrey* (1927: rpt. New York, 1965); see also part 1 of *The Siege of Thebes*, ed. A. Erdmann, EETS ES 108 (1911).

5. On the fifteenth century generally, see *English Verse between Chaucer and Surrey*, ed. E. P. Hammond, still the best anthology; Derek Pearsall, *John Lydgate* and 'The English Chaucerians', *Chaucer and Chaucerians*, ed. D. S. Brewer (London 1966), pp. 201–39; H. S. Bennett, *Chaucer and the Fifteenth Century* (Oxford, 1947); Denton Fox, 'Chaucer's Influence in Fifteenth Century Poetry', *Companion to Chaucer Studies*, ed.

Beryl Rowland (Toronto, 1968), pp. 385–402; and, on language, N. F. Blake, 'The Fifteenth Century Reconsidered', *Neuphilologische Mitteilungen* 71 (1970), 146–57.

6. The difference between Hoccleve and Lydgate, if one compares Pearsall's account of Lydgate with Jerome Mitchell, *Thomas Hoccleve* (Urbana, Ill., 1968), is that Lydgate's invocation of patron generally reflects a commission while Hoccleve's reflects a resigned speculation.

7. On this, see Burrow's remarks in *Medieval Writers and Their Work*, pp. 53–4.

8. A. C. Spearing, *Medieval Dream Poetry* (Cambridge, 1976).

9. *The Poems of William Dunbar*, ed. James Kinsley (Oxford, 1979).

10. See *The Complete Works of Gavin Douglas*, ed. J. Small, 4 vols. (Edinburgh, 1874) and *Selections from Gavin Douglas*, ed. D. F. C. Coldwell (Oxford, 1964). For a complete discussion, see Priscilla Bawcutt, *Gavin Douglas: A Critical Study* (Edinburgh, 1976), pp. 164–91: Bawcutt points out that Henryson's prologue to 'The Lion and the Mouse', discussed below, is the closest influence on Douglas's Prologue to his Book XIII.

11. *The Poems of Robert Henryson*, ed. Denton Fox (Oxford, 1981): all quotation from this edition. For the best recent discussion, see Douglas Gray, *Robert Henryson* (Leiden, 1979). On the *Testament*, below, I take a less sympathetic view of Henryson's attitude to Cresseid than Spearing, *Criticism and Medieval Poetry*, pp. 157–92. For another view, see Peter Godman, 'Henryson's Masterpiece', *RES* 35 (1984), 291–300.

12. For the political implications, see Ian Simpson Ross, *William Dunbar* (Leiden, 1981), pp. 240–4.

13. See Anne Middleton's challenging essay, 'The Public and Audience of *Piers Plowman*', *Middle English Alliterative Poetry and its Literary Background*, ed. David Lawton (Cambridge, 1982), pp. 101–23, and Paul Strohm, 'Chaucer's Fifteenth Century Audience and the Narrowing of the "Chaucer Tradition",' *Studies in the Age of Chaucer* 4 (1982), 3–32.

14. David Lawton, 'Skelton's Use of Persona,' *Essays in Criticism* 30 (1980), 9–28.

15. Burrow, *Medieval Writers and Their Work*, p. 11: see also pp. 119–27.

16. Quotation from the *Faerie Queene* follows the edition of J. C. Smith (Oxford, 1909, rpt. 1978), 2 vols. I do not argue here that Spenser's narrative voice is wholly shaped by Chaucer (and, I suppose, Lydgate), but that Italian epic influences from Ariosto and Tasso, for which see Robert M. Durling, *The Figure of the Poet in Renaissance Epic* (Cambridge, Mass., 1965), are greatly modified by native precedents. Spenser does not sound like Chaucer; he tries to forge the sound of Chaucer. It is interesting that Spenser criticism reproduces many of the *causes célèbres* of Chaucer studies; ironic and psychological readings of the narratorial voice vie with non-ironic ones. My greatest debt here is to Paul Alpers, 'Narration in the *Faerie Queene*', '*ELH* 44 (1977), 19–39, and *The Poetry of 'The Faerie Queene'* (Princeton, 1967), esp. pp. 26–9. I have also consulted Donald M. Rosenberg, *Oaken Reeds and Trumpets: Pastoral and Epic in Virgil, Spenser and Milton* (London, 1981); Louis A. Marre, *Ironic Historian: The Narrator of Books III and IV of the Faerie Queene* (Salzburg, 1979); Judith Anderson, *The Growth of a Personal Voice* (New Haven, 1976) [see pp. 21–49 for the narrator's 'evolving role', p. 184 for an 'ironic mask' and pp. 219–20 for psychological reading]; Jerome S. Dees, 'The Narrator of the *Faerie Queene*: Patterns of Response', *Texas Studies in Language and Literature* 12 (1971), 537–68; and Kathleen Williams, 'Vision and Rhetoric: the Poet's Voice in the *Faerie Queene*', *ELH* 36 (1969), 131–44.

17. This is how I read line 4 of the quotation in the text below: and in this I see eye-to-eye with Anderson, *Growth of a Personal Voice*, p. 206. It must be added, *pace* Anderson, that Spenser shows no familiarity with *Piers Plowman* whatever, as indeed the line quoted implies. It seems to conflate poet, dreamer and Piers in a manner typical of Protestant propagandist use of 'Piers' in the sixteenth century.

18. In *A Defence of Poetry*, ed. K. Duncan-Jones and J. van Dorsten, *Miscellaneous Prose of Sir Philip Sidney* (Oxford, 1973), p. 112: 'The same framing of his style to an

old rustic language I dare not allow, since neither Theocritus in Greek, Virgil in Latin, nor Sannazzaro in Italian did affect it.'

19. The closest analogy is Boccaccio's *Teseida*. I do not commit myself to an opinion that 'E.K.' is the author himself, but certainly, like Boccaccio as glossator, he puts himself forward as a strong alternative narratorial voice. On the *Shepheardes Calender* generally see Helen Cooper, *Pastoral* (Cambridge, 1977), pp. 152–61 ['February', 156–8; 'May', 158–60]; Patrick Cullen, *Spenser, Marvell and Renaissance Pastoral* (Cambridge, Mass., 1970); Richard Mallette, *Spenser, Milton and Renaissance Pastoral* (Lewisburg, 1981); Michael McCanles, 'The *Shepheardes Calender* as Document and Monument', *Studies in English Literature* 22 (1982), 5–19; Harold Stein, *Studies in Spenser's Complaints* (New York, 1934). On 'February', see Roland B. Bond, 'Supplantation in the Elizabethan Court: the Theme of Spenser's February Eclogue', *Spenser Studies* 2 (1981), 55–65, for a political reading, and Louis A. Montrose, 'Interpreting Spenser's February Eclogue: Some Contexts and Implications', *ibid.*, pp. 67–74. On 'May', see Anthea Hume, 'Spenser, Puritanism and the May Eclogue', *RES* NS 20 (1969), 155–67; Edgar F. Daniels, 'Spenser's *The Shepheardes Calender*', *Explicator* 4 (Summer, 1979), 19; W. P. Williams, 'The Fable in Spenser's May Eclogue', *American Notes and Queries: Supplement*, volume I, ed. J. L. Cutler and L. S. Thompson (Troy, N.Y., 1978), pp. 39–42. The text is quoted from *Spenser: Poetical Works*, ed. J. C. Smith and E. de Selincourt, Oxford Standard Authors (London, 1912, rpt. 1969).

20. For these, see the essay by Maren-Sofie Røstvig, '*The Shepheardes Calender*: A Structural Analysis', *Renaissance and Modern Studies* 13 (1969), 49–75, and an earlier reading of 'Spenser's "Twelve Aeglogues Proportionable to the Twelve Monethes"', by Mary Parmenter, *ELH* 3 (1936), 190–217.

21. The most unrestrained reading of these remains Paul E. McLane, *Spenser's Shepheardes Calender: A Study in Elizabethan Allegory* (Notre Dame, 1961).

22. *The Poems of Sir Philip Sidney*, ed. William A. Ringler, Jr (Oxford, 1962), pp. 203–4. Ringler's note (p. 480) mentions the conventional nature of the first four lines and refers to parallels in 'Persius, Du Bellay, Ronsard, and others'. The closest parallels, however, are to be found in Lydgate.

23. This is a major change from the Chaucerian voice, and has much to do with factors discussed by E. Eisenstein, *The Printing Press as an Agent of Change* (Cambridge, 1979). It is also, with rare exceptions, a permanent change. The modern English novel grows out of letters (Richardson), or journals (Defoe). The voice may be colloquial, but it is authenticated by a *written* record.

Index